A good biography is a portrait. A great biography is an introduction to a living breathing person, someone who becomes truly knowable in its paragraphs and pages.

A great biography is a rescue mission. It kicks in the door of one-dimensional history and liberates its subject from stereotypes and marble busts. Kevin Belmonte has done all this and more in *The Sacred Flame*. What he did for Wilberforce he has now done for Hannah More.

MICHAEL CARD,
Author and songwriter,
composer of "El Shaddai" and "Immanuel"

There cannot be enough written about the delightful, inspiring, and faithful life of Hannah More. And there cannot be a writer more able than Kevin Belmonte to narrate this life in a manner equally delightful, inspiring, and faithful. This is a work that every lover of good biography, interesting history, and steadfast saints will relish reading.

KAREN SWALLOW PRIOR
Author of *Fierce Convictions:*
The Extraordinary Life of Hannah More – Poet, Reformer, Abolitionist

Kevin Belmonte tells the story of one of the most remarkable women of a generation. By weaving together Hannah More's writings, historical documents, and letters from her contemporaries, he helps us recognize and admire her reputation and influence.

TREVIN WAX,
Columnist for The Gospel Coalition,
author of *The Thrill of Orthodoxy*

T0262470

Lively. Thoughtful. Substantial. Intelligent. Daring. These words have been used to describe Hannah More; they might happily serve to describe this wonderful book.

Belmonte's experience with the fine art of biography serves him well. Hannah More deserves our best attention, and I can think of no better guide.

DIANA PAVLAC GLYER,
Professor in the Honors College at Azusa Pacific University, author of *The Company They Keep: C.S. Lewis and J.R.R. Tolkien as Writers in Community*

In *The Sacred Flame*, author and historian Kevin Belmonte gives us a life of Hannah More rich with fact, and woven with meaning: a kind of stained glass to view finely detailed context, and with each glance, a more nuanced understanding of Hannah More's life.

LANCIA E. SMITH,
Founder and Executive Director
Cultivating and The Cultivating Project

The
Sacred
Flame

Hannah More, by John Opie, R.A. (1786), oil on canvas
from the Girton College collection, Cambridge University

The
Sacred
Flame

A BIOGRAPHY OF HANNAH MORE

KEVIN BELMONTE

Copyright © Christian Focus Publications 2024

Paperback ISBN: 978-1-5271-1160-8
Ebook ISBN: 978-1-5271-1236-0

10 9 8 7 6 5 4 3 2 1

First published in 2024
by
Christian Focus Publications Ltd,
Geanies House, Fearn, Ross-shire,
IV20 1TW, Great Britain

www.christianfocus.com

Designed and typeset by Pete Barnsley (CreativeHoot.com)

Cover artwork: Hannah More, John Opie, 1786, oil on canvas, 73x59cm used with permission from the Mistress and Fellows, Girton College, Cambridge.

Printed by Bell & Bain, Glasgow

Perspectives on a Life

I continued to read about Hannah More. The account of her work in the Clevedon, Blagdon and Wrington neighbourhood...throws a lot of interesting light...[1]

— C.S. Lewis (1926)

During an outbreak of typhus fever in 1822, More sent 'almost the daily dole' through the apothecary who attended her and her neighbours...

effectively quarantined, she pinned 'a little bag' of money to her curtain, and the apothecary acted as the go-between.[2]

— Patricia Demers (1996)

In financial terms, she was the most successful British author of the romantic period...[3]

— William St. Clair (2004)

---

1   Walter Hooper, ed., *All My Road Before Me: The Diary of C.S. Lewis* (New York: 1991), 396.

2   P.A. Demers, *The World of Hannah More* (Lexington: 1996), 11.

3   William St. Clair, *The Reading Nation in the Romantic Period* (Cambridge: 2004), 162. On page 621, More is called "one of the most prolific and commercially most successful authors of the romantic period."

*[She was] a fascinating woman: able, witty, in many
ways remarkable...* [4]

— *The New York Herald Tribune*
via *The Atlantic Monthly* (1947)

*I composed for myself a most towering and lofty entrance-
scene, when I came in glory at the head of my troops. I could
not help plagiarising Miss Hannah More's first line:*

"On Jordan's banks, proud Ammon's banners wave." [5]

— Harriet Beecher Stowe (1870)

*[Hannah More was] the woman who, for many years, educated
at her own expense a thousand children annually. [Her]
munificent charities were not maintained by any inherited
wealth or rank, but by the product of her own talents...* [6]

— Clara Lucas Balfour (1869)

*Hannah More will be Hannah More to the end of time; but
how she came to be one of the chief women of her day, and that
a very great day—great in its product of philosophers, poets,
painters, and musicians—can only be understood by reference
to the life she lived...* [7]

— Lucy Bethia Walford (1888)

---

4   from *The New York Herald Tribune's* review of *Hannah More and Her Circle*, by M.A. Hopkins, an
     advertisement in *The Atlantic Monthly*, March 1947.

5   H.B. Stowe, *Oldtown Folks* (London: 1870), 381.

6   C.L. Balfour, *Working Women of this Century*, 3rd edition (London: 1869), 41.

7   L.B. Walford, *Four Biographies from 'Blackwood'* (Edinburgh: 1888), 167. Here, a note states:
     "Appeared in *Blackwood's Magazine*, 1887."

Dedication

...to the memory of Hannah More,
walking the Mendip Hills, and Barley Wood, in summer—
with gratitude for these words, apropos to her life, and the
views from that home...

...the canvass of nature is covered—
the Great Artist has laid on His colours... [8]

When kindness, love, and concord, may be ours,
The gift of ministring to others' ease... [9]

For to the end, I keep as I began... [10]

---

8   Hannah More, *Coelebs in Search of a Wife,* volume two, 4th edition, (London: 1809), 112.

9   *Poems by Hannah More* (London: 1816), 183; lines 306-307 of "Sensibility."

10 a poem for Sir Thomas Dyke Acland, dated Dec. 22, 1821, in William Roberts, *Memoirs of...Hannah More,* v. 2 (New York: 1835), 351.

Contents

So many characters before us

Amazed, we see the hand divine
Each thought direct, inspire each line...
Still shall the sacred fire survive,
Warm all who read, touch all who live.[1]

— **HANNAH MORE**
from *The British Review* (September 1821)

Amid the bitter cold that gripped north-eastern America in January 1835, with below zero readings from the campus of Harvard to the Potomac River in Virginia, the citizens of Boston's Cornhill section kept home fires burning, and few thought to venture outside.

Yet some did in Cornhill, Boston's literary centre, with reasons why.

---

1   *The British Review and London Critical Journal,* Sept. 1821, (London: 1821), 104.

This fine thoroughfare, set out by Uriah Cotting in 1816, 'from Court Street to its terminus with Washington Street at Adams Square,'[2] was home to the city's most prestigious booksellers. On its cobblestone walks, surrounded by handsome brick buildings of the early Federal style, tradesmen and teamsters had to brave the cold to make deliveries.

So they did: for the well-to-do patrons of bookshops, like Brattle Street Book Store, wished to stay current and fully apprised of literary news from London, and elsewhere in Europe. New arrivals, from these ports of call, were always much in demand.

But one periodical from the city itself commanded the attention of Boston's literati. It was *The North American Review*, at that time under the editorship of A.H. Everett, the noted diplomat, politician, and man of letters. His brother Edward, two years younger, would later give a famous speech prior to Abraham Lincoln's *Gettysburg Address*.

A man of intellect and brilliance, Everett had graduated from Harvard 'at sixteen with the highest honors.'[3] With his connections, and literary acumen, he secured contributions from writers like Daniel Webster, George Bancroft, and Henry Wadsworth Longfellow. In cultural standing *The North American Review*, it was asserted, 'had no occasion to ask quarter from its English rivals,' the *Quarterly* or the *Edinburgh Review*.[4]

So it was that for the January 1835 number of *The North American Review*, Everett had published William Bourne

---

2   R.W. Owen, "Cornhill." In *Forgotten New England*, an online regional magazine. This article is archived and published at the following web portal: https://forgottennewengland.com/2012/06/04/cornhill-once-bostons-literary-center-today-replaced-by-government-center/

3   R.W. Griswold, *The Prose Writers of America: A Survey of…Intellectual History…*, (Philadelphia: 1852), 284.

4   J.H. Ward, "The North American Review," in *The North American Review* (New York: 1915), 128.

Oliver Peabody's long, insightful article about Hannah More,[5] and her 'Life and Correspondence.' And if patrons of Brattle Street Book Store bought this issue of *The North American Review*, they came upon a fascinating discussion.

For this copious, nineteen-page article told a literary story all its own...

Peabody opened with an informative, arresting premise— meant to capture readers' attention. The life of Hannah More, he stated—

covers a large space in literary history, reaching back from the present times to those of Garrick, Johnson, and Burke; she was thrown into acquaintance and intimacy with a great variety of characters, and all who were capable of appreciating character seem to have felt great respect for her excellent heart, and her active and practical mind...

She secured the respect and attachment of such a variety of eminent persons, that we are actually confounded at the wide reach of associations which her life brings before us in a single view.[6]

This was telling; but here, a cautionary word was called for. Peabody did not shy away from stating it decisively. William Roberts, the author of Hannah More's *Memoirs,* was 'not, by any means,' the writer who 'should have been chosen for the office.'[7]

Indeed, he showed a 'want of grace and skill in writing' that was disqualifying. Such a book called for 'taste and

---

5   "The Life and Correspondence of Hannah More," in the January 1835 issue of *The North American Review* (Boston: 1835), 151-170. See also page 142 of *The Index for The North American Review,* vols 1-125 (Cambridge: 1878), confirming Peabody's authorship of this review.

6   *North American Review,* January 1835, 151.

7   *North American Review,* January 1835, 151.

discrimination' to 'produce his materials to the best advantage.' But Roberts' text, incessantly 'grave and inanimate,'[8] was far from that kind of book.

Peabody greatly regretted this, given the wealth of materials to be used—

There is Horace Walpole on one page, with his lordly foppery, writing to his 'dear St. Hannah;' on the other, we see the melancholy majesty of Johnson. Here is Garrick, 'whose death eclipsed the gaiety of nations;' there is Burke with his wonderful powers, resembling that pavilion in the fairy tale, which could cover the territory of a nation, or be contracted to the dimensions of a sentry-box, at pleasure.

But it would take too much time even to run over the list of memorable names, which are thus connected with [Hannah More].

We know of nothing, except the Waverley *novels, which brings so many various characters before us; and we cannot help thinking that a writer, thoroughly versed in literary history, might have made a work from these materials, which would have taken as fast hold of the public mind as* Boswell's Johnson.[9]

Building on this unique, if unexpected premise, Peabody proceeded to describe the kind of book he sincerely wished *had* crossed his desk—

Say what we will of [Boswell's] coxcombry, nothing is more certain, than that his work is the model for a biography, since it tells what the reader wants to know.

---

8   *North American Review,* January 1835, 151 & 152.

9   *North American Review,* January 1835, 151-152.

This is the great point, on which success in this kind of writing depends,--to tell what the intelligent reader wants to know. In the case of Johnson, [one] wants to know his conversation, his familiar remarks...

In writing the Life of Hannah *More...Boswell, had he undertaken it, would have liked nothing better than sketching an illustrious group of distinguished characters, himself also among them. In his hands, all would have been life and bustle...*[10]

Roberts' failure notwithstanding, portraits do exist of the kind Peabody wished to see: one in prose, while another is a painting of Hannah More by the artist John Opie, a member of the Royal Academy.

* * *

As to the prose portrait, in the June 1866 issue of *The Art Journal of London*, S.C. Hall, F.S.A., recounted the story of a visit to Barley Wood, the home of Hannah More.

It took place in January 1825, when she was nearly eighty. Yet Hall's recollections cast images far from the common road, as to someone then considered an elderly invalid.

Indeed, the person who met Hall's gaze was not at all what he expected. And given this, his thoughts afterward were both vivid and arresting. As he remembered—

---

10 *North American Review,* January 1835, 152. See also W.H. Prescott's review of Lockhart's *Life of Sir Walter Scott* in *The North American Review,* April 1838, 433: "in passing from the letters of Scott, with which the work is besprinkled, to the text of the biographer, we find none of those chilling transitions...in more bungling productions; as, for example, in that recent one, *in which the unfortunate Hannah More is done to death by...Roberts.*"

Her form was small and slight, her features wrinkled with age; but the burden of eighty years had not impaired her gracious smile, nor lessened the fire of her eyes, the clearest, the brightest, and the most searching I have ever seen.

They were singularly dark—positively black they seemed as they looked forth, among carefully-trained tresses of her own white hair; and absolutely sparkled while she spoke of those of whom she was [the] link between the present and the long past.

Her manner, on entering the room, while conversing, and at our departure, [was] sprightly; she tripped about from console to console, from window to window, to show us some gift that bore a [famous] name...some cherished reminder of other days—almost of another world, certainly of another age...

She was clad, I well remember, in a dress of rich pea-green silk. It was an odd whim...yet [withal, it] was in harmony with the youth of her step, and her unceasing vivacity, as she laughed and chatted, chatted and laughed; her voice strong and clear [and] her animation as full of life and vigour as it might have been in her spring-time.[11]

Not quite forty years before S.C. Hall visited Hannah More, in 1786, artist John Opie painted her likeness, and created 'the most flattering of her portraits.'[12] Opie had made his London debut in 1781, and became famous as 'the Cornish Wonder.' His style was one of 'strong realism, and striking contrasts of light and dark.' He was widely recognized 'as a painter of historical and literary subjects, especially for *Boydell's Shakespeare*

---

11 S.C. Hall, "Memories of the Authors of the Age: Hannah More," in *The Art Journal of London,* 1 June 1866 (London: 1866), 186.

12 Anne Stott, *Hannah More: The First Victorian* (Oxford: 2003), 200.

Gallery,'[13] which was sited 'in Pall Mall, one of London's most sophisticated neighbourhoods.'[14]

Hannah More, by John Opie, R.A. (1786),
from the Girton College collection, Cambridge University

The Opie portrait of Hannah More is now kept in a hallowed hall of British academia: Girton College, Cambridge University.

---

13 see The National Portrait Gallery biographical sketch, "John Opie (1761-1807)," at: https://www.npg.org.uk/collections/search/person/mp03371/john-opie

14 see the academic article chronicling this facet of British eighteenth-century history, "Marketing Shakespeare: the Boydell Gallery, 1789–1805, & Beyond," at: https://folgerpedia.folger.edu/ Marketing_Shakespeare:_the_Boydell_Gallery,_1789–1805,_%26_Beyond

To stand before it is to see why it won praise as soon as it was completed; and to understand also why one of Hannah More's most famous friends, Horace Walpole no less, promptly ordered a copy to be made after seeing it.[15]

The play of light, especially, sets Opie's portrait apart: it falls softly and perceptively—to suggest and unriddle a story the painting has to tell.

Here, subtleties persist, the first in the gaze of Hannah More's dark brown eyes. Opie rightly discerned how they captured who she was: keenly intelligent, kind, and vivacious— in keeping with the 'playful woman'[16] that Marianne Thornton (novelist E.M. Forster's aunt) so fondly remembered. Then too, there is much of thoughtfulness and depth in More's likeness. These two traits were the 'lucid streams'[17] of her poems, plays, and essays.

All this is a credit to John Opie's gifts, and his fine discernment as a painter.

Last of all, there's a quality in this painting that beckons to the world Hannah More looked upon, *and the world that she hoped to see.* The touch of a smile is there also, revealing a warmth of heart that many found—in a person they wished to know better.[18]

William Wilberforce was one of them, writing gratefully of Hannah More's kindness in 1786, arranging an introduction to Charles Wesley that he remembered all his life with deep gratitude.[19] He cherished Hannah More, and her constant gift

---

15 Stott, *Hannah More*, 200.

16 E.M. Forster, *Marianne Thornton* (London: Edward Arnold, 1956), 140. Edward Arnold Publishers no longer exists as a publishing firm.

17 line 469 from John Hunter, ed., John Milton, *The First Book of Paradise Lost* (London: 1861), 44. Milton was, with Shakespeare, one of the poets Hannah More admired most.

18 Stott, *Hannah More*, 64: "above all perhaps, [through] the warmth of her affections, she had become valued and accepted by literary London."

19 Robert and Samuel Wilberforce, *The Life of William Wilberforce* volume one (London: 1838), 248.

of fostering friendships among those she knew—who had yet to meet one another. Over time, he became the younger brother she never had. As both delighted in Shakespeare, they took to citing passages with great spirit from the Bard in their many letters, often from *Henry IV*.[20] An opening from one of Wilberforce's letters was typical: "What! Did I not know thy old ward, Hal?"[21]

1786 was a watershed year for More in another way; for it was then her much-admired poem, *The Bas Bleu,* was published. One among its admirers was King George III, who 'liked it so much that he wanted a copy of his own,' and More 'sat up one night to write it out for him.'[22] When the poem was first composed, in 1782, it circulated for some time among her friends in manuscript. Samuel Johnson was one of them, and after he finished reading it, 'the great Cham' said 'there was no name in poetry that might not be glad to own it.'[23]

Not long after, in a letter to Hester Thrale, Johnson stated: 'Miss More has written a poem called *Bas Bleu,* which in my opinion is a very great performance.'[24] This was the more singular, as Johnson had said to More herself, 'I give you the opinion of a man who does not rate his judgement very low in these things.'[25]

Fast forward to 2003. In the pages of a distinguished Oxford University Press study, More's multifarious legacy, too little known today, was captured this way—

---

20 Stott, *Hannah More*, 273. "In 1965, the Rare Book, Manuscript, and Special Collections Library at Duke University acquired from Winifred A. Myers an album of approximately 130 autograph letters from [Hannah] More to William Wilberforce, dated 1790-1830."

21 Wilberforce, *Life of Wilberforce,* volume 3, 399.

22 Stott, *Hannah More*, 64.

23 M.G. Jones, *Hannah More* (Cambridge: 1952), 47-48; "the great Cham" was a sobriquet for Dr. Johnson in Boswell's *Life of Samuel Johnson* (London: 1910), 215.

24 Jones, *Hannah More*, 48.

25 Jones, *Hannah More*, 48.

'In the history of her age, she was one of its prime movers, leaving her imprint on the theatre, the bluestocking circle, the political debates sparked by the French Revolution, elementary education, the anti-slavery movement, the growth of Evangelical religion, foreign missions, and female philanthropy.'[26]

* * *

I first learned about Hannah More through my study of William Wilberforce, during research for a master's thesis in the early 1990s. Their friendship, and philanthropic work, chiefly in the spheres of abolition and education of the poor, left a lasting impression. Lives were changed for the better, in many places, because of this.

I saw too that Hannah More had written deeply eloquent lines, like these—

Let us implore the aid of holy hope and fervent faith, to show that religion is not a beautiful theory, but a soul-sustaining truth.[27]

And of faith also, she described what it meant 'to communicate the sacred flame.'[28]

Here, I began to see why Wilberforce set such store by More's letters and writings. They lent richness and meaning to his journey of faith, as they did for many others.

---

26 Stott, *Hannah More*, 333.

27 Hannah More, *Practical Piety*, volume two, 4th ed., (London: 1811), 246.

28 Hannah More, *An Essay on the…Writings of Saint Paul*, volume one, 4th ed., (London: 1815), 275.

Her own journey, I found, was often trying, as she experienced chronic pain for much of her life, saying in her later years: 'and as for pain, I never was absolutely free from it for ten minutes since I was ten years old.'[29] There were deep wells of fortitude in her character.

* * *

Ten years following my thesis, during a trip to York Minster, I met an elderly woman who'd been part of a 'women's benefit club' Hannah More had established.

In those few moments, something special unfolded.

Stepping into a hotel elevator, I said hello to this thoughtful lady and her friend. My American accent caught her attention, and she asked what I was doing in England.

It was then she noticed I had a newly-published biography of Hannah More in my hand. 'Hannah More,' she exclaimed, 'I was once a member of one of her women's benefit clubs! It closed sometime in the 1950s, but I remember it very fondly.'

This unlikely meeting, and point of connection, was a gift I've thought about often. Somehow the life of a twenty-first century American had touched, however tangentially, strands of a story that had been unfolding in England since the early 1800s.

Not long after this, I was able to visit Hannah More's homes, Cowslip Green and Barley Wood. I will always remember time inside Barley Wood, seeing beautifully carved woodwork all around, and wondering what it must have been like to see her

---

29 S.C. Wilks, "Reminiscences of Mrs. H. More," in *The Christian Observer*, March 1835 (London: 1835), 168n. That laudanum was a palliative used by the More sisters at need (during illness or injury causing excessive pain) is confirmed in Stott, *Hannah More*, 308, and 301: "She took it herself, under prescription." From this "purely medicinal" use she may, like William Wilberforce, have suffered opium poisoning over time, which weakened her eyesight.

room full of books—handsome texts that were like so many friends for Hannah More the reader.

Later, at Syon House, the Duke of Northumberland's home, I was invited as a visiting historian to look through any volumes on the shelves of the Long Gallery I wished to. Seeing a rare 19-volume set of Hannah More's *Collected Works*, I spent time looking through it in a great room she would have happily lost hours in—it was 136 feet long, and full of books.

Here, words recur that biographer Mary Alden Hopkins wrote about Hannah More: 'she leaped at any library that came her way.'[30]

Last, I've stood in the Church of All Saints, Wrington, where More worshipped, and walked the Mendip Hills she knew in Somerset. To see these places is to catch a glimpse of a world from long ago—and while there, recall that it did much to influence our own.

That is no small part of Hannah More's legacy: for its tributaries remain.

Tracing them, there's much to discover. And therein lies a story—but not of someone who was a faultless paragon: for none of us are—then, as now.

Rather, the story concerns someone who, yes, did much good in the world—but someone as well who knew what it was to fail, to suffer, to sorrow and succeed. She knew beautiful places, and fascinating people; but she also knew sombre scenes and moments marred by brokenness. In an era when revolution unfolded in France, and war threatened England's shores, she weathered those storms, and worried over what might happen.

---

30 M.A. Hopkins, *Hannah More and Her Circle* (London: 1947), 71.

Amid those trying times, from 1789 through to 1815, she remembered words spoken by Lord Halifax, and set them on the title page of one of her books: 'may you so raise your Character that you may help to make the next Age a better thing.'[31]

Faith bestowed fortitude and hope as she tried to.

For faith was, as she said, 'a sacred flame,'—alight and renewing.

* * *

To better understand the sacred flame More cherished in her life, her writings are the key: letters, yes,—but also what may be gleaned from a careful reading of her published works. They trace the tenets of her Christian belief, and her thoughts about so many things.

Here, I am grateful for an insight that, at first blush, might seem a world away from anything connected with Hannah More. But really, it isn't.

In her review of modern composer Brian Wilson's instrumental album, *At My Piano,* jazz musician Aimee Nolte's reflections cast a guiding thought for me as I considered how to approach a reading of the thousands of pages that comprise Hannah More's *Collected Works.*

Looking to Wilson's stature, as a composer, Nolte said it required something—

This is…Brian Wilson [I thought,] and he needs all of your attention…

---

31 *Miscellanies by the Late Lord Halifax* (London: 1700), 83; and Hannah More, *Strictures on the Modern System of Female Education* (London: 1799), title page.

So I decided to go on a walk, I went on a long walk in the hills, and I listened to the entire album. It didn't take long for me to feel the depth of this music…

[We] get to hear Brian Wilson in his 79th year, re-tell his stories—the way that he wants us to hear them—the way that he hears them—and at such a sacred place—sitting at his piano…[32]

The gist of this review—about an artist from a different time—and very different from Hannah More, led me to picture something in idea—a glimpse of her, writing in the library at Barley Wood. Because of sickness, and her invalid state in later years, this was the only way she *could* speak to many then. But as I thought about it, I realized this was also the way that she "spoke," through all her works, during the whole of her writing life.

This is to be kept in mind, as More's letters have to be cited carefully. The only source for so many is none other than Roberts' *Memoirs of…Hannah More.* And scholarly guidance is often needed as to what lines from Roberts' much-edited text may be cited safely.

But when it comes to More's published works, a very different scenario arises.

There, we have the words *she chose,* and the final texts *she approved.*

This brings a reminder of what she once told William Wilberforce, with an admirable dash of wit: 'I will be answerable for nobody's faults, but my own.'[33]

---

32 Aimee Nolte's YouTube review of Brian Wilson's *At My Piano* album is posted online at: https://www.youtube.com/watch?v=LW7mb62Ls8w&t=113s

33 Demers, *Hannah More*, 130.

Last, rather than treat all of More's works, including, say, her fiction or didactic works, I have focused on books exploring her Christian belief, especially two companion volumes that were a late-in-life flourishing of her writerly gifts: *Practical Piety* and *Christian Morals*.[34]

These books, to follow Aimee Nolte's wisdom, call for the kind of reflection that rests, metaphorically, in the image of a 'long walk in the hills;' taking time to discover the person these writings reveal her to be, tracing the tenets and signposts of her faith.

To look across the years, and tell of such things, is the task of these pages.

Here also, I recall Hannah More's insight about letters, and what she looked for in them. 'I have a particular notion about correspondence,'[35] she stated. 'What I want in a letter is a picture of my friend's mind, and the common sense of his life.'[36] Citing these words, in 1915, *The Yale Review* said: 'Hannah More never wrote wiser sentences than these.'

And they've much to do with the art of biography.

---

34 Due to space limitations, I do not cover the writing of More's best-selling novel, *Coelebs In Search Of A Wife* (1808). It "went through twelve London editions in its first year, was translated into German and French…and appeared in six American editions in More's lifetime." Here, I commend Dr. Patricia Demers' definitive scholarly edition of the novel (Peterborough: 2007).

35 Roberts, *Memoirs…of Hannah More,* volume two, (New York: 1834), 190.

36 C.B. Tinker, "Walpole and Familiar Correspondence," in *The Yale Review: New Series,* volume four, (New Haven: 1915), 585: See also Jones, *Hannah More,* ix.

CHAPTER ONE

The Hamlet of Fishponds

I frequently recollect some lines of Miss More's, in her "Sir Eldred of the Bower," describing a mixture of hope and anxiety. She says: 'twas such a sober sense of joy, as angels well might keep.[1]

— **ABIGAIL ADAMS** (1784)

Sir,—Being retired, as you now are from the affairs of State, you doubtless have much time which you devote to reading. Permit a friend to recommend the writings of Bishop Porteus, the late Bishop of London. Also Dr. Buchanan's researches in Asia.

And should you wish to look at the productions of any Lady, I think you would find the writings of Miss Hannah More, especially her late work, called Practical Piety, to be well worthy of your perusal...[2]

— A Letter from "Goodwill" to
Thomas Jefferson, June 1, 1812

---

1   C.F. Adams, ed., *Letters of Mrs. Adams,* 4th edition, (Boston: 1848), 163.

2   See Anonymous ("Goodwill") to Thomas Jefferson, 1 June 1812, at: https://founders.archives.gov/documents/Jefferson/03-05-02-0078

If, from the mid 1780s to the early 1800s, Hannah More's fame was such that she was quoted in one presidential family, and recommended to another (Thomas Jefferson's family, as it happens, did own an 1806 edition of More's *Sacred Dramas*),[3] her early life was quite different in character, and far more obscure.

If not the destitute beginnings proverbial in many biographies, her immediate family setting was one, nonetheless, characterized by challenge and achievement. Her life followed a path few would have foreseen, especially those who knew the very modest circumstances of her upbringing. To see a photo of the schoolmaster's cottage where she was born, a building which survives today, is to see a story cast in stone. For Hannah, with her parents and four sisters, lived in close quarters: all seven in the left-wing of this two-storey building.[4]

To win literary fame from such origins, becoming 'the most successful British author of the romantic period,'[5] stands out vividly in a summary for the setting of Hannah More's early life. One scholar's sentence begins the account: 'By the time she was middle-aged,' she 'was mixing with the gentry, the aristocracy, and even royalty.'[6]

But this was not all. Another part of Hannah More's life story stood out. She was one of five sisters born into near poverty, who, 'forced to earn their livings, and succeeding triumphantly in their vocations,' showed 'what it was possible for women to

3   As of March 2022, Advanced Book Exchange listed an 1806 American edition of Hannah More's *Sacred Dramas*, with Martha Jefferson Randolph's signature on the rear end page. Randolph (1772 - 1836) was the daughter of President Thomas Jefferson. This book was listed online at: https://www.abebooks.com/servlet/ SearchResults?an=More&bi=0&bx=off&cm_sp=SearchF-_-Advs-_-Result&ds=30&kn=Martha%20 Randolph&recentlyadded=all&rollup=on&sortby=17&sts=t&tn=Sacred%20 Dramas&xdesc=off&xpod=off

4   see Anne Stott, "Hannah More: the gaps in the early life," a 2 Feb 2014 article at: https://claphamsect. com/2014/02/02/more-information-on-hannah-more/

5   William St. Clair, *The Reading Nation in the Romantic Period* (Cambridge: 2004), 162.

6   Stott, "Hannah More: the gaps in the early life."

achieve in an environment that was at best ambivalent, and at worst hostile to women on their own.[7]

With eloquent insight, More herself once said: 'the intellectual eye seldom runs along the whole train of consequences, which is the only true way of taking our measure of things.'[8] That is a most fitting thought for telling hers, or anyone else's story.

* * *

To capture something of the way readers learned about her in the nineteenth century, it may be said that 'Hannah More was born at the hamlet of Fishponds, in the parish of Stapleton, Gloucestershire, about four miles from Bristol, on the 2nd of February, 1745.'[9]

She was the fourth of five daughters born to Jacob and Mary More, who wed in 1735.[10] Their names, apart from Hannah, were Mary (born in 1738), Elizabeth (born in 1740), and Sarah (born in 1743). Her younger sister, Martha, was born in 1747.[11]

From here, gathering details of life in the More family up to and including Hannah's earliest years is something of a challenge, due to a lack of surviving papers. Government and church records, and documents from neighbouring families help; but the wish for vignettes set down by Hannah cannot be

---

7   Stott, *Hannah More*, 332.

8   Hannah More, *Christian Morals*, volume two, 6th edition, (London: 1813), 297.

9   Henry Thompson, *The Life of Hannah More* (London: 1838), 5.

10   William Evans, "Hannah More's Parents," in *Trans. Bristol & Gloucestershire Archaeological Society* 124 (2006), 120. Scholar Anne Stott says of Hannah More's parents: "There is no trace in the local records of a Jacob More marrying a Mary Grace, previously believed to have been Hannah More's mother. However in the records of St. Werbergh's church there is an entry for the marriage by licence on 2 July 1735 of Jacob More and Mary Linch." See the 2 February 2014 article by Anne Stott, "Hannah More: the gaps in the early life," at: https://claphamsect.com/2014/02/02/more-information-on-hannah-more/

11   S.J. Skedd, "Hannah More," in *The Oxford Dictionary of National Biography*, copyright 2004.

met, or 'some affecting story…associated in the memory,'[12] for no such papers survive today.

Some helpful details about her father exist; but precious few about her mother.

Here is what can be told of both, beginning with her father.

* * *

Though uncertain, it has been said Jacob More was a 'supervisor of excise in Bristol,'[13] or minor local official. But it is known that in Michaelmas 1743, or 29 September of that year, More was 'established in the Mastership of the Free School at Fishponds.'[14]

Further details have come to light in recent years about his tenure at the Fishponds School, and what family life was like in the years Hannah More grew up. Her father added to his modest income 'by land surveying and valuing.' In 1751, Silas Blandford, the land steward for Norborne Berkeley, 'paid him for drawing a map of Kingswood.' In the years to follow, Jacob More kept to work of this kind, while Hannah More had "warm memories" of Silas Blandford, whom she regarded 'as a benevolent guardian of her family.'[15]

Jacob More had need to supplement his income, for his initial salary as schoolmaster was only £16 a year. Though it's not clear if More was indeed a surveyor of excise, a position

12 Hannah More, *Strictures on the Modern System of Female Education,* 8th edition, (London: 1800), 289.

13 Stott says of Hannah More's parents: "It has not been possible to corroborate the statement of More's early biographer Henry Thompson that Jacob More was a supervisor of excise in Bristol as the records for the relevant period have not survived. He may have held a post of which there is no longer a documentary trace, or perhaps a lower post than that of surveyor." See the 2 February 2014 article by Anne Stott, "Hannah More: the gaps in the early life," which has been posted online at: https://claphamsect.com/2014/02/02/more-information-on-hannah-more/

14 Evans, "Hannah More's Parents," 118.

15 Stott, "Hannah More: the gaps in the early life." See also N.D. Smith, *The Literary Manuscripts and Letters of Hannah More* (New York: 2016), 136.

with a salary of £90 a year, he seems to have constantly sought other streams of income. He had to. And perhaps, apart from responsibilities at the Free School, he privately taught 'paying students' in the way a tutor would.[16]

Still other documentary evidence suggests that More, 'like other schoolmasters who knew some geometry and trigonometry, was recognised as having some ability at land surveying and valuing,' tasks consistent with his having been a gauger.[17]

So, as one fluent in Latin, mathematics, with skill reading and writing, Jacob More became versatile, and a man of many trades. But it was a catch-as-catch-can existence. True, he had some stature as a schoolmaster; yet it was a rather humble kind of gentility.

For family income was cobbled together as opportunity allowed.

More's skill in geometry and trigonometry brought work land surveying and valuing. In October 1751, Norborne Berkeley's land steward Silas Blandford paid More for map drawing. Eight years later, More received £5 10s. 6d. towards the cost of prosecuting a man called Miles, which suggests More had competency to prosecute a legal case. In April 1762, Silas Blandford paid More a guinea for measuring enclosure land and common meadow.

From 1733 to 1735, Stoke Gifford estate records show More 'brought up oxen, paid board wages to workmen, and signed an accounts balance.' And in July 1735, More was paid 18 guineas 'in full for wages and all accounts.' So his employment

---

16 Evans, "Hannah More's Parents," 120.
17 Evans, "Hannah More's Parents," 120.

brought aspects of estate management that were, in essence, somewhat 'short of being a full land steward.'[18]

Given the frequent mention of Silas Blandford's name, it's clear he aided the More family on many occasions. Young Hannah remembered him fondly, and his wife Elizabeth.

One can see why. Blandford took a kind, abiding interest in the More children. Since the Blandford children were close in age to the Mores, they were likely friends in their youth. Blandford, Hannah said, was a family friend 'of the most unfeigned simplicity of manners and purity of life imaginable.' Years later, she returned his kindness by caring for him in his final illness. She may also have written the obituary for him which stated: 'he was always the warm friend of virtuous industry in others, and honest and laborious poverty were the objects of his protection.'[19] Hannah also cared for Elizabeth Blandford in her final days, saying near that time: she was 'the oldest friend I have in the world.'[20]

* * *

Here kindness and shared affection lived in a debt of gratitude—not unlike these lines of later verse, written near the close of More's long, eventful life—

For memory still delights to trace
Friends loved so long, so dear.[21]

---

18   Evans, "Hannah More's Parents," 120.

19   Stott, *Hannah More*, 8.

20   Smith, *Literary Manuscripts and Letters of Hannah More*, 136.

21   "Recollections and Anticipations," in *The Christian Observer*, January 1828 (London: 1829), 34.

And kind actions, like the channels of benevolence the Blandfords fostered, would be taken up in years to come, through Hannah's assistance to families in need.

* * *

Still another, all-too-brief glimpse of family life, survives in a 1777 letter about a visit with her father's extended family in Norfolk. 'We arrived at Bungay,' Hannah wrote—

> *a little before nine. In my way thither, Thorpe Hall, where my father was born, was pointed out to me. Our Cousin Cotton's house is about a quarter of a mile out of the town...On Tuesday, we went to dine at Mr. John Cotton's, a romantic farm-house buried in the obscurity of a deep wood. A great number of Cottons were assembled, of all ages, sexes and characters. The old lady of the house... took a good deal of pains to explain to me genealogies, alliances, and intermarriages, not one word of which I can remember.[22]*

This passage suggests that while Hannah More had feelings of nostalgia and interest in places associated with her family roots, she did not care overmuch at this time for detailed accounts of genealogy. But care should be taken about inferring too much from this letter.

Written at age thirty-two, she might simply have been distracted by thoughts of other places she had yet to visit in her country travels, or tired from travel, and not at the moment interested in a long rehearsal of family connections.

---

22 Evans, "Hannah More's Parents," 115.

Her comments don't indicate, in and of themselves, that she cared nothing for family history at all.

Indeed, one quatrain of her verse indicates quite the reverse was true—

> *Yet dwell I oft on scenes long past,*
> *Scenes the fond heart retains;*
> *There tender recollections last*
> *Of mingled joys and pains.*[23]

Of Hannah's immediate family, early sources cast Jacob and Mary More as 'intelligent and sensible,' believing their daughters 'should be so brought up as to be able to make their own living.'[24] And little wonder, given the hard lesson Jacob More had forced upon him: the need to be self-reliant, and to work very diligently when patrons like Silas Blandford offered employment. Such industry led to additional opportunities, and ones greatly needed.

So each of the More daughters grew up as intelligent, very capable young women; and in time, they would open a highly successful and profitable school for young ladies.

With reason, parental pride must have shone.

* * *

The education the More sisters themselves received was crucial in this light.

Customary to the era, as a Church of England family, they were taught the Catechism. Jacob More taught 'stories of classical history, and anecdotes from Plutarch,' in addition to

---

23 "Recollections and Anticipations," 34.

24 Stephen, *Dictionary of National Biography*, 414.

'Latin and mathematics.' As the eldest daughter in the family, Mary More 'was sent to take lessons at a French school at Bristol.'

They read English literature (Hannah's nurse had cared for the poet Dryden in his final illness, and she loved to hear stories of him) and they were taught history. Hannah was also fond of Addison's essays.[25] Beyond fluency in these subjects, instructors at the More sisters' school were retained to teach Italian, Spanish, and Latin.[26]

So it was that, not long before the school opened, an 11 March 1758 announcement ran in one of Bristol's newspapers:

"On Monday, after Easter, will be opened a school for young ladies by Mary More and sisters, where will be carefully taught French, Reading, Writing, Arithmetic, and Needlework." The announcement was repeated the following week, with the additional statement: "A dancing master will properly attend."[27]

In establishing a school with such a cultured milieu, the More sisters showed that they were gifted educational entrepreneurs. As one writer has said: 'The boarding school started under good auspices, and at a propitious time. The middle-class all over England was thriving and Bristol folk were especially successful. Bristol merchants, traders, and sea captains were well-to-do.'[28] Families who held aspirations for their children sought this school out.

Adding to this, biographer Mary Alden Hopkins observed—

---

25 Demers, *Hannah More*, 5: More, it's noted, was "proud of the addition of Addison's *Spectator* to the school's library."

26 Stephen, *Dictionary of National Biography*, 415.

27 Hopkins, *Hannah More*, 15-16.

28 Hopkins, *Hannah More*, 18.

In this prosperous, lively, cultured town, the three eldest More girls opened their academy at Six Trinity Street, College Green, near the Cathedral. The school made money from the start, and four years later the sisters built at Forty-Three Park Street, the first house on that steep thoroughfare.

In thirty-odd years they made enough money to retire in comfort.[29]

The More sisters' prosperity allowed them to move their parents from Fishponds, on retirement, 'and install them in comfort at Stoney Hill, near [their] school.'[30] This is much worth noting, for schools that were launched by two other sets of famous sisters, the Brontës and Wollstonecrafts, failed. This underscores the More sisters' singular achievement.

* * *

How young the More sisters were in all this must be recalled also. When they started their school, Hannah More's elder sisters, Mary, Elizabeth, and Sarah, were 'approximately nineteen, seventeen, and fourteen.' Before long, Hannah and her younger sister Martha joined them, at similar ages.[31] And if location then, as now, was everything, the More sisters chose propitious sites for their school: for it moved address as it prospered.

Starting at 6 Trinity Street, 'near the College Green,' it relocated to 43 Park Street, 'one of the first houses erected when Park Street was laid out.' Both sites, strategically, were

---

29 Hopkins, *Hannah More*, 19-20.

30 Stott, *Hannah More*, 10; and Hopkins, *Hannah More*, 3: "[the More sisters] made a fortune."

31 Hopkins, *Hannah More*, 16.

within walking distance of Bristol Cathedral and the Theatre Royal, built in 1766.[32]

* * *

Hannah More, for her part, had shown great promise early.

The following lines from biographer Sir Leslie Stephen, the scion of a family known for its intellect and attainments, is highly revealing—

Hannah was a delicate and precocious child.

Before she was four, she had learnt to read by listening to her sisters' lessons and could say the catechism so well as to astonish the clergyman of the parish...

When she was eight, she was fond of listening to stories of classical history and anecdotes from Plutarch related by her father. He then began to teach her Latin and mathematics, and was "frightened at his own success," though the entreaties of Hannah and her mother induced him to persevere.

Her eldest sister was sent to take lessons at a French school at Bristol, and communicated her knowledge to Hannah, who further improved herself by talking to some French officers living on parole in the neighbourhood.

She began to [write] essays.

[In 1758,] her eldest sister...set up a boarding-school in Trinity Street, Bristol, in which she was joined by [Hannah and] the other sisters...[33]

---

32 Demers, *Hannah More*, 4-5.
33 Stephen, *Dictionary of National Biography*, 414-415.

In her youth, More's love of literature showed itself, 'not only in perusing with great avidity the books which her father's slender library supplied, but in the composition of poems, essays, and imaginary correspondence.'[34] This showed a keen intelligence on the one hand, and a creative mind on the other.

The following years would bear witness that each of these traits flourished. These lines of verse point to the artistry she cultivated and cherished—

> *I loved indeed the Muse when young,*
> *And faintly touch'd the lyre...*[35]

As Hannah entered her teens, and the wideness of her learning grew, the intent was always to prepare her to be well qualified, "together with her sisters, for the management of a ladies' school upon principles" more accomplished and multi-disciplinary "than those which generally obtained in such establishments at that time."[36]

Thus Jacob and Mary More each played a key role in their daughters' learning.

When it came to Hannah, it was her mother who taught her to read, and her father who took up the baton when Hannah entered a phase of her education that exceeded her mother's training. And it should always be remembered that when Hannah's attainments in Latin and mathematics developed so quickly that her father considered whether he should continue to teach her, Mary More entreated her husband to continue.

---

34 Thompson, *Hannah More*, 6.

35 "Recollections and Anticipations," in *The Christian Observer,* January 1828 (London: 1829), 34.

36 Thompson, *Hannah More*, 6-7.

Mary helped Jacob understand something his love for his gifted, able daughters had already half-persuaded him to see: the prevailing bias against the education of young women beyond a 'certain point,' like the view of contemporary finishing schools, was ill-conceived and wrong. Henry Thompson, an early biographer, states that Jacob More's 'good sense and parental feeling corrected his practice,'[37] and this holds truth in some measure.

But Mary More's role was also, and indisputably, a pivotal one.

Beyond this, and since we know from later sources of Hannah's fondness for knitting, gardening, and landscaping, her mother's instruction and influence may be felt.[38] The image of a family circle, knitting by firelight on winter evenings, comes to mind, along with images of tending a garden early, on warm spring mornings. Favourite flowers brought colour to earthenware vases in the stone cottage, and home garden crops set the family table.

In later years, when Hannah More had a famous home of her own, Barley Wood, she kept the folkways of her youth. Friends recalled that she loved to knit red mittens.[39]

In addition, the early instruction More received from her sisters was crucial, and it must have been extensive and ongoing. At every turn, it seemed, there were members of the family determined to help her flourish.[40]

With hindsight, given the success of the pioneering school the More sisters founded, the gift Jacob and Mary More gave in educating their daughters led not only to the benefit of their

---

37 Thompson, *Hannah More*, 8.

38 Stott, *Hannah More*, 5.

39 E.M. Forster, "Mrs. Hannah More," in *The Nation and the Athenaeum*, 2 Jan 1926 (London: 1926), 493: "once I had a red mitten she knitted." See also N.D. Smith, *The Literary Manuscripts and Letters of Hannah More* (Surrey: 2008), 103, which lists a pair of red mittens HM knitted.

40 Skedd, "Hannah More."

own children, but the families of many students 'committed to their trust.'[41]

It was a flourishing school, but it was also a philanthropic endeavour. The More sisters gave—as they were taught to do—and as they'd been given. They always would.

* * *

With the fine features of the boarding school the More sisters had founded, it is not surprising that they attracted the notice of a wealthy patron in Bristol; and in their case, such a patron emerged in Anne Gwatkin, whose daughter attended their school. Her influence in Bristol was considerable, her financial support instrumental, and both these factors helped the Mores' school to grow in celebrity and enrolment.

So, in 1763, as Henry Thompson has written, and 'to evince her grateful sense of this lady's kindness,'[42] Hannah (now teaching school) wrote and published a 'pastoral drama' she called *The Search After Happiness*.

'This little poem,' as she called it, 'was composed [at] age eighteen.'[43]

It was intended for a local setting, as a creative way to instil culture among students.

Yet this play, quite literally, would set the stage for many things to come.

---

41 Thompson, *Hannah More*, 9-10; the school "became *fashionable;* and schools of similar constitution began to multiply." See also Hopkins, *Hannah More*, 18.

42 Thompson, *Hannah More*, 12.

43 Hannah More, *The Search After Happiness*, 2nd edition, (Bristol: 1773), v.

CHAPTER TWO

Fond Hopes, Crestfallen Days

*Bristol was theatre mad…As long before as 1716, an
anonymous shilling pamphlet on The Consequences of a New
Theatre to the City [was published. Thence to 1766, when] the
King Street Theatre, a building rich in carving, gilding, and
painting, was the pride of Bristol, and was pronounced the
most complete of its size in Europe.*

*Before the theatre was finished, [David] Garrick came to
inspect and praise it…[1]*

— MARY ALDEN HOPKINS (1947)

*Whate'er exalts, refines, and charms—invites
to thought, to virtue warms…[2]*

— THE GENTLEMAN'S MAGAZINE (1774)
The Search After Happiness

---

1   Hopkins, *Hannah More*, 42.
2   *The Gentleman's Magazine*, May 1774 (London: 1774), 232.

Still in her teens, Hannah More had written a play; and though intended solely for performance among the students of the school she and her sisters had established, it won no small amount of local interest. Bristol was a city where the theatre arts flourished. Now one of their own, and she a young woman of eighteen, had crafted a work of 'literary merit.'³

As one biographer phrased it, 'Hannah's talents were known, not only through the commendations of friends, but especially through the celebrity of *The Search After Happiness,* of which many transcripts had got abroad.'⁴

The play's theme was universal, in keeping with a tenet of classical literature: a pursuit of the highest good, or, in Latin, the *summum bonum.* Significantly, yet another point arises: *The Search After Happiness* might have been influenced by Samuel Johnson's slender novel, *Rasselas,* published in 1759.⁵ And good circumstantial evidence would allow for this.

We do know that the More family read the novel with rapt approval, and that they greatly admired the novel's author, as well as its namesake and protagonist, for Sarah (Sally) More wrote of one visit that she and her sister Hannah had with Dr. Johnson in 1774—

> *Miss Reynolds…ordered the coach to take us to Dr. Johnson's very own house; yes,* Abyssinia's *Johnson!* Dictionary *Johnson!* Rambler's, Idler's, *and* Irene's *Johnson!*
>
> *Picture to yourselves the palpitation of our hearts as we approached his mansion. The conversation turned upon a new work of his…the* Tour to the Hebrides…*When our visit was ended, he called for his hat (as it rained)*

---

3   Thompson, *Hannah More,* 12.

4   Thompson, *Hannah More,* 13-14.

5   Thompson, *Hannah More,* 70. Here affinities between *Rasselas* and More's novel *Coelebs in Search of a Wife* are noted, and contrasts between the two.

to attend us down a very long [walkway] to our coach, and not Rasselas himself could have acquitted himself more en cavalier.[6]

THE

SEARCH AFTER HAPPINESS:

A Pastoral Drama.

AND OTHER

POEMS.

BY HANNAH MORE.

A title page detail from More's pastoral drama, *The Search After Happiness* (1816 edition), a play in verse with many affinities to Samuel Johnson's novel *Rasselas*.

Here, a closeness in chronology should be noted. *Rasselas* was written in 1759, and *The Search After Happiness* in 1763.

6   William Roberts, ed., *Memoirs…of Hannah More*, volume one, 3rd edition (1835), 49.

A mere span of four years separates the two, and we know—from Sally More—that the More family avidly read Johnson's essays—many of which were published before 1759. It is entirely plausible, then, that the More family read *Rasselas* when it was first published, and if this was true in Hannah More's case, she would have been fourteen at the time. Many works read in youth leave a lasting impression, and to judge from Sally More's letter of 1774, *Rasselas* was most certainly a prime favourite in the family.

Then too, there is a similarity of plot and theme. Scholar C.H. Ford has noted this, writing: 'Like the youthful travellers of Samuel Johnson's *Rasselas,* [More's heroines] find peace of mind elusive. They seek Urania, an elderly shepherdess in "whose sagacious mind"' and words they discern that the real key to lasting felicity may be found.[7]

So kindred lines are given in *The Search After Happiness,* with a pleasing turn of phrase. They are lines that would not be out of place in *Rasselas,* and lines well-suited to a didactic romance, or work of fiction meant to instruct. Though a first work, and from a young author, *The Search After Happiness* fits clearly within this literary tradition.

In keeping with it, More had written—

In its true light this transient Life regard…
Tho' rough the passage, peaceful is the port…
On holy faith's aspiring pinions rise…[8]

For More, raised in a devout Church of England family, *The Search After Happiness* was resolved in the benisons of Christian belief. One could pursue many delusory paths in

---

7   C.H. Ford, *Hannah More: A Critical Biography* (New York: 1996), 9.

8   Hannah More, *The Search After Happiness,* 2nd edition, (Bristol: 1773), 39.

life, and she spoke of what these might be; but the path that led to the haven of faith was the one that was best. So, as Henry Thompson said, 'religion is the soul of this little drama.'[9]

Among its closing lines were these. They were a kind of prayer, in their way:

> FOUNTAIN of BEING—teach us to devote
> To Thee each purpose, action, word, and thought;
> Thy grace our hope, Thy love our only boast…
> Be this in ev'ry state our wish alone,
> ALMIGHTY, WISE, and GOOD, Thy Will be done.[10]

And here and there, within the play, were lines that many a playwright might admire—lines from the morning of a young artist's inspiration—

> Like beaming Mercy, wipe Affliction's tear.[11]

For More, who had ardently loved reading plays from her early years, the affirmation she found must have been exhilarating. Her first foray as a playwright had won success, and she had seen it staged on the dais of her family's school at Trinity Street.

It was a flourishing time for the More sisters more generally also, as Henry Thompson related in his Memoir—

> Shortly after the composition of this [play], the sisters had prospered sufficiently to enable them to build a house on a more extensive scale…the first [built on] Park Street, Bristol. The order and management of [their school

---

9   Thompson, *Hannah More*, 12.
10 More, *The Search After Happiness*, 39.
11 More, *The Search After Happiness*, 38.

made it] the most celebrated of its kind in the kingdom. It
comprised upwards of sixty pupils; and twice the number
might have been easily entered, had the accommodations
admitted. The Land's End, and the Highlands of Scotland,
contributed at once to its supply.

It is pleasing to record the filial gratitude of the sisters.

They now took a house and garden for their excellent
father at Stony Hill, Bristol, and kept two female servants
to attend on him. Their substance, thus dedicated, was
blessed and increased. The school advanced in reputation,
and patrons multiplied.[12]

For Hannah More, the four years between eighteen and
twenty-two were particularly important. At the outset, she
knew what it was to have people she respected in her home
city of Bristol offer praise and commendation for her play.
She'd seen it staged, and known the kind pleasure of friends
wishing to see it in manuscript.

This was of a piece with her lifelong love of 'the fine arts,
in all their lovely and engaging forms of beauty, [and] the ever
new delights of literature.' For her, and for others, she said, they
'shed sweet, and varied, and exhaustless charms' on leisure
hours, sending us 'back with renewed freshness.'[13]

And when it came to plays themselves, More's lifelong
appreciation of Shakespeare was well-nigh boundless. She
cherished the Bard's 'happy intuition into the human mind,'
with 'an originality which has no parallel.' She often recurred to
scenes and traits of favourite characters, such as 'the beautiful
and touching reflections of Henry IV,' or 'the conflicting

---

12 Thompson, *Hannah More*, 13-14.
13 More, *Christian Morals*, vol. 2, 259-260.

passions' of Lear.[14] One late-in-life letter to Sir William Pepys captured it all—

> *I have forgotten half the poetry of my early reading, but Shakespeare is stamped on my memory and my heart in ineffaceable, indelible characters. He has always had such a power over my feelings, that even in my early youth I durst not read him after supper, as he shook my nerves so, as by his power of excitement to prevent my sleeping.*[15]

The four years after the writing and staging of *The Search After Happiness* were eventful years, and More's rise in Bristol society was well underway.

To recall the summer of 1764 is to find much of the reason why she was fast gaining celebrity in a city famed for its devotion to the theatre. In this summer, the London actor William Powell gave performances at The Jacob's Well Theatre, in the title role of *King Lear,* said to rival those of David Garrick himself. Hannah More and all of Bristol, it seemed, were caught up in this. And as someone with ambitions to write for the theatre, Hannah secured an introduction to Powell, as a local writer of promising verse. This may have been arranged by her cultured friend Anne Gwatkin, who'd inspired *The Search After Happiness.*[16]

When Powell returned to Bristol for the 1765 season, More saw an opportunity. Since Powell was to give a benefit performance of *Hamlet,* she decided to write a Prologue for it.[17]

---

14 Hannah More, *Hints Towards Forming the Character of a Young Princess,* volume two, 2nd edition, (London: 1805), 176, 178, 179, and 182.

15 *The Correspondence of Sir William Weller Pepys,* volume two (London: 1904), 390-391: a 21 October 1824 letter from More.

16 Stott, *Hannah More,* 14.

17 Stott, *Hannah More,* 14.

Running to fifty-six lines, More's verse read, in part—

If, to draw characters most justly bright,
To contrast light with shade, and shade with light;
To trace up passions to their inmost source,
And greatly paint them with uncommon force,
If these, obedient still to nature's laws,
Excite our wonder, and exact applause,
Be these, immortal Shakespeare! ever thine;
To feel, to praise, and to adore them, mine.[18]

One can only imagine the feelings of a twenty-year-old author on hearing these lines read before the performance of an actor as famous as Powell, before a full house on a gala theatre evening. In two years, More had gone from writing her first play, staged in a school performance, to writing the prologue for a marquee event. Bristol was the 'London' of the summer season, home to a company of actors from the great metropolis. More was moving within this circle, winning friends who recognized her talent.

For a schoolteacher not far beyond school-age herself, from such humble beginnings, it must have seemed a radiant time.

One year later, all Bristol had cause for civic pride with the completion of the opulent new Theatre Royal, to replace the close confines of The Jacob's Well Theatre, which had proven far too small to house the large crowds that wished to attend performances.[19]

The new theatre opened on 30 May 1766. One early text described it—

---

18 Hannah More, "A Prologue to Hamlet," from *The Works of Miss Hannah More in Prose and Verse* (Cork: 1778), 228; lines 37-44.

19 Stott, *Hannah More*, 15.

The Theatre-Royal...King-street, is a perfect model of elegance and convenience: the internal part round the pit, is semi-circular, and the whole decorated with carving, gilding, and painting. The late Mr. Garrick, *who surveyed it before it was quite finished, pronounced it to be the most complete in Europe of its dimensions; and wrote a Prologue and Epilogue, which were repeated by* Powell *and* Arthur *when it was opened, May 30, 1766.*

The scenes were painted by the late Mr. French, *and are done in a masterly stile.*

The theatrical performances here are little (if any) inferior to those in London. Here, Amusement, Literature... Improvement, and a School for Elocution, *are united.*[20]

This was the storied setting for a performance of *King Lear* that Hannah More, along with her sisters, and all the students of their school, attended. And this visit was not without moment for the school itself, as it could now boast among its teachers, uniquely, a poet who had contributed meaningfully to the culture of the theatre in Bristol, with her prologue for William Powell's benefit performance of *Hamlet.* So, consequently, a number of the students at the school came from families connected with the theatre.[21]

* * *

In this fine season of verse-writing, play-going, and a flourishing of the Park Street School, More met someone she wished to marry. Why she would have won a fiancé is

---

20 Bristoliensis, *The Bristol Guide,* 3rd edition, (Bristol: 1815), 187.
21 Stott, *Hannah More,* 15.

easy to see. As biographer Mary Alden Hopkins has written, at twenty-two—

> *Hannah had a pleasing personality. She was attractive in appearance, with marvellous dark eyes, a slender graceful figure, and quick pretty ways. Her nature was friendly, affectionate and loyal...though she was a little spoiled by too much praise.*[22]

The gentleman in question was William Turner of Belmont, an estate near Wraxall, some six miles away from Bristol. He was twenty years older than More; and if the difference in their ages raises an eyebrow, there were good reasons why she was drawn to him.

Turner, whom she met and got to know through his two younger cousins, students at the Park Street School, had a number of shared interests with More, all in a setting that would catch a thoughtful young woman's eye. His fine estate, Belmont, was

> *an especially lovely spot on the southern side of a hill, with a neat house against a back-ground of tall elms, small oak, and twisted aged yews. Paths were cut through the ancient woodland and the views over the valley [below] were delightful.*
>
> *[Turner, as] the owner of this charming estate had horses to ride and drive, a good income, a liking for young people, and a respectable housekeeper to act as chaperone [when] the Turner sisters...visited him in the holidays.*

---

22 Hopkins, *Hannah More*, 34.

[They] were accustomed to invite Hannah and Patty, only slightly their seniors, to accompany them.

Hannah and her host had many tastes in common: love of scenery, fondness for planning gardens, and appreciation of poetry. The lovely grounds of Belmont were the first on which Hannah exercised her ingenuity...[23]

And Turner as the 'squire of Belmont,'[24] to use writer M.G. Jones' phrase, presided over this estate in ways that More, as a frequent visitor, found charming. During chaperoned walks over the grounds of this estate, they very likely read poetry together, and we do know that More wrote poetry to capture scenes and moments at Belmont, lines of verse that Turner had painted on handsome wooden signboards, and set on trees around the estate.

These signboards held fine, pastoral verse, that poets of the romantic era twenty years in the future would have appreciated. More's verse, like the poetry of this school, was written in words that drew on phrases with a common touch, or vernacular voice, and celebrated scenes of natural beauty as renewing, and revivifying—

Stop traveller, a moment lose...
Think it not much to steal an hour...
To court this sweet tranquil scene...[25]

~ ~ ~

---

23 Hopkins, *Hannah More*, 32-33.

24 Jones, *Hannah More*, 9.

25 see Smith, *Literary Manuscripts and Letters of Hannah More*, 132. This poem is part of an album belonging to Dora Wordsworth, dated 1828. The poem's text is also displayed on a tree board in the woodland poetry walk created by The National Trust at Tyntesfield.

O you who pass these sylvan glades,
Embower'd in cool refreshing shades…
At length, determin'd to pursue
The object that enchants our view…[26]

All during these visits, Turner was kind and solicitous in ways that More was drawn to. He sought her thoughts, and her advice, for ways to set out the grounds of his estate to create newer, handsome prospects. They began to have a sense of shared purpose in this.

Sometime in 1767, it seemed natural for him to ask this talented, attractive young woman if she might ever consider becoming the lady of Belmont, the lovely place she had become so fond of. That way, they could always take walks together. She said yes.

Inasmuch as no papers from More, describing this time of courtship and betrothal, have survived, how romantic this relationship was in nature cannot be known precisely. Yet, as Mary Alden Hopkins has written perceptively, it is

> *unlikely that [More] pledged her hand to Mr. Turner without giving him her heart, although her love was probably decorous rather than intense. The slight, easy verse which she composed during this period of engagement… indicates…she was moving tranquilly from the [home] of her sisters into the care of a middle-aged man with a good income, a fine estate, and congenial tastes.*[27]

And perhaps all this was more than a little like the idyllic sylvan setting depicted in *The Search After Happiness,* which

26 Thompson, *Hannah More,* 17.
27 Hopkins, *Hannah More,* 34.

could be considered More's poetic re-casting of *Rasselas*. Was Belmont More's version of 'the happy valley,' as described in Johnson's novel?

It might have been. She had only written her pastoral drama four years before, and it may have continued on as her vision of the ideal—one to be sought after. And lines from her poem, *The Bleeding Rock,* could carry a double meaning that expressed this wish—

Where beauteous Belmont rears its modest brow
To view Sabrina's silver waves below,
Liv'd LINDAMIRA...[28]

So a wedding date was set, and plans put in motion for More to become the lady of Belmont she had perhaps hoped to be, for some time, in cherished idea. A church was selected, a minister asked to perform the wedding, and a bridal dress thought about.

More also made arrangements to close her shared financial interest in the Park Street School. She would have had no need of that income, moving forward. Many people, among them many friends in the cultured circles of Bristol, must have warmly congratulated her on this wonderful 'stroke of good fortune,' as a phrase from this time had it.[29]

But then, when all seemed so very promising and welcome, William Turner showed a side of who he was that sent More into a wholly undeserved time of humiliation. For three times over the next several years, close to six years in all, he postponed their wedding.[30]

---

28 *Sir Eldred of the Bower and The Bleeding Rock,* by Miss Hannah More (Dublin: 1776), 27.

29 Many sources use this phrase in the time of HM's early life, see *Memoirs of a Young Lady of Family* (London: 1758), 37.

30 Information given in Stott, *Hannah More,* 18.

She somehow summoned the reserves to forgive these trials, though she was doubtless the subject, each time, to gossip and innuendo in Bristol society. Finally, by spring 1773, and in the aftermath of it all, she apparently suffered a nervous breakdown.[31] She sorrowed over what might have been—slowly, painfully, falling apart around her. It was a personal wound; needlessly inflicted, and witnessed publicly by many others. Some were kind and caring, as with family and close friends—but others were unkind, in rounds of speculation.

After she recovered in some measure from her breakdown, More took a long holiday in Weston-Super-Mare in late summer and early autumn 1773 to further convalesce.[32] Long walks on pathways around this seaside town in North Somerset, with their views of the Bristol Channel, helped somewhat in their way. But when she returned home, many things were still uncertain—not least knowing if she would ever wed.

But, at least, she had the caring support of her sisters, which meant the world.

Meanwhile, through the counsel of family friend James Stonhouse, a clergyman, More wrote to Turner in October 1773, to break off their engagement. Sir Leslie Stephen, writing of this in *The Dictionary of National Biography*, recounted essential facts—

and as Miss More had given up her share in the [Park Street] school in view of the marriage, Turner wished to make compensation. He offered £200 a year, which Miss More declined positively to accept. Stonhouse, however, agreed to become trustee for the fund without

---

31 Skedd, "Hannah More."
32 Stott, *Hannah More*, 19.

the lady's knowledge. She was afterwards induced to take the money.[33]

This is a sparse recital of what unfolded. More was hurt, angry, and her pride deeply offended. But this left many things about her future unresolved. So Rev. Stonhouse, after what may well have been consultation with More's sisters, had sought to intervene.

Yet all this, as one biographer has rightly observed, meant Stonhouse and Turner had gone 'over her head to sort out her life,' another source of hurt, anger, and wounded pride. But Stonhouse, a genuine friend, however much he had forced the issue, countered with the unflinching need to face facts. He told her that 'the malicious world, who had so cruelly slandered her, would not provide for her.'[34]

As this could not be denied, More relented, and accepted the annuity. It was a bitter pill: but in this way, 'she gained both financial security and independence.'[35]

Martha More, the younger sister whom the family called Patty, described this by saying £200 a year was 'not to be sported with, tis a noble provision…this Poet of ours is taken care of and may sit down…and read, no devour, as many books as she pleases.'[36]

So things were thus far resolved at the close of 1773, More's *annus horribilis*. Fortitude, faith, friends, and family were needed as never before.

* * *

---

33 Stephen, *Dictionary of National Biography*, 415.

34 Stott, *Hannah More*, 20.

35 Skedd, "Hannah More."

36 quoted in Stott, *Hannah More*, 20.

About one year later, with the healing perspective that time brings, More wrote verses for James Stonhouse, who'd sent her a gift book of his *Tracts and Meditations*. In these lines, one couplet especially, she described his character and friendship—

> *…actions, more than sermons, teach;*
> *For Stonhouse lives, what others only preach.*[37]

Beyond this, though it staggers the imagination, More found a way in time to resume a kind of friendship with William Turner, even allowing occasional visits. Here, the charity of her Christian faith was much in evidence. Surely everyone would have understood if, once forgiveness was given, she never wished to see him again.

Turner, for his part, is said to have observed 'that Providence had overruled his wish to be her husband in order to preserve her for higher things.'[38]

What More may have thought of this has not been recorded; but the events and tenour of her future life suggest she may well have found a way to see some truth in it, though born of her time of long sorrow. If she did, many who knew her wouldn't have been surprised.

The qualities of who she was went to things beyond any literary gifts she had.

---

37 Thompson, *Hannah More*, 212.
38 Hopkins, *Hannah More*, 37.

CHAPTER THREE

On the Wing in London

Miss Hannah More, a lady sufficiently eminent in the literary world to claim attention for whatever she communicates to the public.[1]

— THE EUROPEAN MAGAZINE and LONDON REVIEW (1782)

...you are the fashion...[2]

— FRANCES BOSCAWEN to Hannah More (1788), quoted in *The Imperial Magazine* (1834)

...a professional yet genteel author...a respectable British 'woman of letters'.[3]

— BRILLIANT WOMEN: 18th-Century Bluestockings (2008)

---

1   *The European Magazine and London Review,* March 1782 (London: 1782), 205.

2   *The Imperial Magazine,* October 1834 (London: 1834), 470.

3   Eger, Elizabeth and Peltz, Lucy, *Brilliant Women: 18th-Century Bluestockings* (New Haven: 2008), 77 & 79.

...in London, where I have spent a long spring for
near thirty years...[4]

— **HANNAH MORE**, to Bishop Richard Beadon (1802)

Within a year of her return from Weston-Super-Mare, another change of scene took place in Hannah More's life. She was now in her late twenties, and had been active for several years in the circles of culture at Bristol, writing verse, prologues, and plays, as well as striving to instil elements of literary culture and education among the students who attended the now increasingly prestigious Park Street School.

In these settings, London was often spoken of: in gatherings of theatre friends who arrived for the summer season at the Theatre Royal, or in the classroom, where London was the storied home of famous writers, and well-known publishers who brought books before the reading public.

It was the centre of things literary, and held keen attraction for More. She had won her way in Bristol, and won a measure of literary celebrity there. But now, with the settlement of her annuity, and the means to live independently as a writer, she could think of going to London to see the city she'd read about all her life. Perhaps she might gain an entrée to literary and cultured circles there, as she had done in Bristol. And with friends in the greater Bristol area who had connections in London, this might well be possible.

Then too, More had continued with her writing, which always brought a renewing sense of purpose. As to why this was, there are sources of insight worth taking a few moments to consider. They reveal things that inspired her to write.

---

4   Thompson, *Hannah More*, 29.

When, for example, More wrote of John Milton and William Cowper, and what she admired in their verse, she spoke of things she loved about the craft of writing, and what could be woven in it. In Milton she found 'loftiness of conception,' and 'the variety of his learning,' were set within 'the structure of his verse.' For her, *Paradise Lost,* and its unrhymed lines of iambic pentameter, were 'the boast of our island, and of human nature.'[5]

It was the finest example of epic poetry; and Milton 'God's own poet.'[6]

When it came to Cowper, things of faith showed supremely also, but in elements that differed from Milton's greatness. Cowper's verse was redolent with 'familiar allusions, and touching incidents' that had a way of coming home to readers. Lyrically, she said that he 'felt the beauties of nature with a lover's heart, beheld them with a poet's eye, and delineated them with a painter's hand.' Last, Cowper 'gratifies the judgment as much as he enchants the imagination...he directs the feelings to virtue, and the heart to heaven.'[7]

Beyond this, More admired the 'acuteness of Dryden,' 'the vigour of Johnson,' and the 'familiar, elegant' lines present in Addison's writings, which prepared 'the mind for more elaborate investigation.' Then too, of Addison's writings about poetry, she said things very revealing about her own understanding of the art, such as this insight: 'the effect produced by poetry on the mind cannot always be philosophically accounted for.'[8] So, if Addison was at times, in writing about poetry, 'too cordial a

---

5   Hannah More, *Hints Towards Forming the Character of a Young Princess,* volume two, 2nd edition (London: 1805), 157.

6   Hannah More, *Sacred Dramas* (London: 1782), 1.

7   More, *Hints,* 158n.

8   More, *Hints,* 158-159.

critic to withhold expressions of delight,' it was 'merely because he could not analyse the causes which produced it.'[9]

In this context, More described 'that species of writing, whose felicities consist in ease and grace,' or 'flights of the lyric muse,' and 'finer touches of dramatic excellence.' For her, these were key elements of literary beauty. In tandem with facets of expression that she most admired in other writers, these were elements she wished to shape her own writing.

To date, with such things in view, and in the practice of her art, she'd known a deep sense of fulfilment, in keeping with her acceptance in the cultured settings of Bristol.

Now, perhaps, the same might prove true in London. She would attempt it.

* * *

Here, once more, James Stonhouse showed himself a stalwart, caring friend. He knew David Garrick, one of the finest Shakespearian actors in the history of the theatre. And since his friend Hannah had a new play, set in Rome, titled *The Inflexible Captive,* Stonhouse offered to send it to Garrick, with a view towards staging it at the Drury Lane Theatre.

In this Augustinian era, and given the wide fame of plays like Addison's *Cato,* More's play, set in Rome like Addison's tragedy, was written with discerning awareness of the current tastes of theatre audiences.[10] It was artistry poised to meet with success.

So around the end of 1773, Stonhouse sent More's play to Garrick in London.

Here, timing is important. It's possible, though not known for certain, that Stonhouse undertook this literary mission, in

9   More, *Hints,* 159.

10   Ford, *Hannah More,* 25: "*The Inflexible Captive* pleased all the various segments of the theatrical public."

part, to help buoy More's spirits in the aftermath of her broken marriage engagement. At the least, the hopes cherished for such an endeavour would have been a welcome distraction (not to say kindness) that would have taken More's mind off her troubles; and this endeavour would have given just the sense of purpose she needed, given her lifelong love for the theatre.

* * *

All the same, this effort to win an entrée in London's literary circles took some little doing, or some "pertinacity,"—a word current in the late 1700s. True to his word, Stonhouse sent More's play on to Garrick. And though he declined the play, she was set on trying to meet the great actor. So a first trip to London was planned.

Garrick's decline notwithstanding, More found favourable signs of encouragement, with her successes to date in Bristol, and the publication in late summer 1773 of *The Search After Happiness*. Brought out in London, by Thomas Cadell, the play obtained a fine commendation[11] in *The Monthly Review*. More was cited as a young and "ingenious author," noteworthy for "the harmony of her verse," "the happiness of her sentiments, her strength of thought, [and] purity of expression."[12] That was something to build on.

So early in 1774, with a several-week stay in view, More, and her sisters Sally and Patty,[13] boarded the stagecoach from Bristol for the 80-mile trek to London.

---

11 "recommended in our review for September, 1773." See *The Monthly Review* (of London), April 1774 (London: 1774), 243.

12 see the September 1773 issue of *The Monthly Review* (London: 1773), 202.

13 a point of conjecture given in Stott, *Hannah More,* 23. Sally was HM's sister Sarah's nickname, while Patty was her sister Martha's nickname.

On arrival, they secured lodgings; but as it was, they'd no time for sightseeing, or anything else. They hadn't been settled there long before More became ill with fever. At the same time, it so happened that Garrick wasn't well. Thus, had she been in good health, More would have been unable to secure the visit and meeting she hoped for.

Crestfallen and ailing, she returned to Bristol. Yet she was undeterred. Once fully recovered, she began to lay more careful plans for a second foray in London. Metaphorically, it was all rather like a benign siege upon the castle of King Lear.[14]

Her publisher, Cadell, agreed to send Garrick a courtesy copy of *The Inflexible Captive*, published in March, while her good friend and sometime patron, Anne Gwatkin, wrote a letter of introduction to her friend, Frances Reynolds. A gifted artist, and the sister of painter Sir Joshua Reynolds, any visit to the Reynolds home could facilitate the setting, or perhaps another letter of introduction, for a meeting with Garrick.

A choice of lodgings was placed strategically also. More, along with Sally and Patty, took rooms at 'Mr. Howson's in Southampton Street,' just across the Strand from Garrick's London home at the Adelphi.[15] There was now every chance of a good meeting.

Meantime, just before her early May trip, More was the subject of a second feature article in the April 1774 issue of *The Monthly Review*. It began with a six-line poem that set her in a Parnassus where she resided among the 'nine muses' of Britain—

> *To Greece no more the tuneful maids belong,*
> *Nor the high honours of immortal song;*

---

14   Stott, *Hannah More*, 23.

15   Stott, *Hannah More*, 23.

To MORE, BROOKS, LENOX, ATKIN, CARTER due,
To GREVILLE, GRIPFITH, WHATELEY, MONTAGU!
Theirs the strong genius, theirs the voice divine;
And favouring Phoebus owns the British Nine.[16]

After this came a guided tour, in literary discussion, 'through the well-drawn scenes'[17] of *The Inflexible Captive*. It culminated with this passage:

She has, indeed, in all instances, supported—in many, improved—upon the sense and spirit of the Italian poet [Metastasio's Attilio Regolo, *from which* The Inflexible Captive *was taken, working from her own translation;] and where she has found it necessary to have recourse to herself, and enlarge the original plan, she has done it with a degree of judgment that could be expected only from every privilege of experience, [and] with a degree of genius which leaves not even Metastasio to look down upon her.*[18]

Then followed the text of Act Three of More's tragedy—a staging in print, as it were—for readers to experience something of her remarkable achievement. It was a moment of singular praise, and attention, for a young artist in her twenties.

More would set out for London with a fair wind prevailing.

* * *

Not long after her May 1774 arrival in London, More had the chance to see Garrick perform as King Lear at the Drury

---

16 *The Monthly Review* (of London), April 1774 (London: 1774), 243.

17 *The Monthly Review*, April 1774, 243.

18 *The Monthly Review*, April 1774, 245.

Lane Theatre. They'd yet to meet; but a letter she wrote to James Stonhouse, after the curtain fell, showed how meaningful this was—

> *How shall I convey to you the remotest, the most glimmering idea of what were my feelings at seeing Garrick in King Lear!*
>
> *…His talents are capacious beyond human credibility. I felt myself annihilated before Him, & every faculty of my soul was swallowed up in attention…I thought I should have been suffocated with grief: it was not like the superficial sorrow one feels at a well-acted play, but the deep, substantial grief of real trouble.*[19]

Reading over this letter, some biographers have stated it was a well-timed piece of flattery, written solely to be sent on to Garrick to win favour and secure the meeting More long wished for. That may be true, in whole or in part; but it might just as well have been the letter of a young 'provincial schoolteacher'[20] who was well and truly star-struck.

In the absence of a letter by More (or Stonhouse after the fact) stating first, 'please send this on to Mr. Garrick,' or second, 'I have sent the letter on that you asked me to send,' one cannot say for certain that flattery-to-leverage-a-meeting was solely More's intent.

It is just as plausible to say she sent her letter to Stonhouse, with whom she frequently corresponded, and charmed by it, he sent it on, without any prompting from More. Coming from a young playwright winning acclaim (as feature articles in *The*

---

19 Kerri Andrews, *Ann Yearsley and Hannah More* (London: 2016), 9-10; and Peter Ackroyd, *Revolution: The History of England, Volume Four* (London: 2016), 323.

20 Andrews, *Ann Yearsley and Hannah More*. 9.

Monthly Observer show), Stonhouse might well have reasoned that seeing More's letter would be a tonic for an aging actor, now frequently subject to illness, and knowing his performing days wouldn't carry on much longer. One satirist had driven this home in lines of doggerel—

> *I'm on the edges of three-score,*
> *'Tis really time to give it o'er.*[21]

Cruel words, compounded by sickness and doubts, brought a trying time.

Under such circumstances, for Garrick to learn of a younger artist's keen appreciation could well have been a very encouraging thing in and of itself: even as it was a charming note that made him wish to meet this young playwright, about whom he'd been hearing so much of late from his friend Stonhouse.

More's letter, on one level, reads like the missive of one who saw an actor she thought would have 'deathless fame,' a phrase ubiquitous in this era, as in Edward Young's *Love of Fame* (1750), Samuel Johnson's *Lives of the English Poets* (1781), or *Danby's Second Book of Catches, Canons, & Glees* (1789), to name but three examples.[22] At the same time, she quite honestly stated that she felt overwhelmed by the portrayal of Lear that she'd seen.

For an artist who had cherished plays all her life to have seen one of the greatest actors of the era was more than a little likely to have this effect. Many a theatre-goer has shed tears at the close of a moving performance, rapt attention to

---

21 Florence Parsons, *Garrick and His Circle* (New York: 1906), 342.

22 Young, *Love of* Fame (London: 1750), 31; Johnson, *Lives of the English Poets* (Dublin: 1781), 310; & Danby's *Second Books of Catches, Canons & Glees* (1789), 41.

what unfolds on the stage leading to a flood of emotion. The flourish of effusive, even florid, language from a provincial twenty-something after a great performance is, seen in this light, quite understandable. A letter that reads, in so many words, 'I've never seen anything like this in my life,' is very much what More seems to have written.

One could say it was solely a calculated letter in its intent, and content. But one could just as easily say it was a letter shaped by keen artistic sympathy on the part of a gifted young playwright, who'd seen a great performance from an actor in the twilight of his career. The pathos of this would have added to the overall impression of More's experience.

There is a greater likelihood for the latter, absent evidence of the former.

* * *

All this notwithstanding, after Garrick saw More's letter, he sent a note to her at her lodgings on Monday, 23 May, saying he would visit the next day.

Opening the letter, the More sisters' rooms at Mr. Howson's must have echoed with jubilant voices over what was in it. But as it turned out, the hoped-for meeting had to wait a bit longer: Garrick wrote round soon after to say his visit would have to wait until Friday, the 27th. However, he would send his carriage along to collect More and her sisters for the quick transit to his residence at no. 5 Adelphi Terrace.

Adelphi Terrace in Garrick's time, from *The Literary History of the Adelphi* (1909)

No detailed account from More's pen captures this day of days; but we may gather an idea of it, to start, from a contemporary description of the Adelphi, dated June 1771—

Durham-yard in the Strand, [it begins,] had long been in a ruinous condition, when Messrs. Adam, architects, purchased the lease of the ground, then belonging to the

Duke of St. Albans, and planned a most elegant range of buildings... called the ADELPHI...

[Its] grand front, towards the river Thames, consist[s] of eleven different houses, built of grey stock bricks, with artificial stone dressings, and curious iron balconies at the windows of the principal floors; the three centre and corner houses being decorated with artificial stone pilasters richly embellished with Grecian ornaments.

One of the centre houses...purchased by Mr. Garrick, is almost completely fitted up in a truly classic style. The ceiling of the front room on the principal floor is painted by [Antonio] Zucci, in the middle of which is represented the Graces attiring Venus, Cupid standing by her. The chimney-piece in this apartment is of white marble, finely sculptured, and is said to have cost three hundred pounds.[23]

Beyond this, a letter from Garrick to James Stonhouse, on 31 May 1774, states that he found his meeting with the More sisters 'most agreeable.'[24] He also went into some little detail, offering his considered opinion of More's gifts as a playwright—

I have seen her last imitation of Metastasio, which I don't think has the merit of Regulus – the foundation and conduct of the fable is too romantic, as I fairly told her, for among many other good qualities, I soon found that I might speak my mind sincerely without offence: her Sisters told me that she writes quick, which is lucky; but then I would advise her to correct slowly – I perceived several marks of haste...

---

23 *The Town and Country Magazine*, volume three, (London: 1771), 305.
24 Stott, *Hannah More*, 27.

Were I worthy to direct her, she should first chuse a happy subject, and well adapted to her genius—then she should take some time carefully to distribute her fable into Acts. Character & circumstances, *alias* Situations; *should be well attended to...*

a Play without them is mere Dialogue....I coud wish to see her outlines, before she writes one verse, and when the road is made a true Dramatic Turn Pike, I woud have her seat herself upon Pegasus, and gallop away as fast as she pleases. If she writes without Plan, I will not insure her success.[25]

This must have been profoundly gratifying for More: the actor she so admired had read her play carefully, and paid her the great compliment of offering a critique that had her best interests as a playwright at heart. Her writing was flawed in places, but it had potential. Should she take care to avoid excessive romance, writerly haste, and select the right subject—taking proper pains to fashion her play—she would follow the best way to let her gifts shine, and to best advantage.

She was only one year beyond the cruel end to any hopes she once had of marriage to William Turner. Showing courage in the wake of her nervous breakdown, and resilience, with encouragement from her sisters and friends like Anne Gwatkin and James Stonhouse, she had picked up the pieces of a broken time, and returned to her first love of the theatre. She had taken steps, and asked for help in getting her work before the finest actor of the age. Her season of hard work, after the

---

25 Yale, Beinecke Rare Book and Manuscript Library, Osborn Collection, MS vault file, Garrick to Sir James Stonhouse, 31 May 1774. Punctuation added.

trial and error of her first trip to London, had ultimately borne fruit—beyond anything she might have imagined.[26]

That was a blessing all its own. Better days beckoned.

* * *

Now, as one biographer has rightly observed, More's 'introduction to the great' was 'sudden and general.'[27] On the day after her meeting with Garrick, Saturday, 28 May, she and Elizabeth Montagu 'were brought together at Mr. Garrick's house,' her first meeting with a member of the celebrated Bluestocking Circle.

Here was a unique, very fulfilling experience—meeting a writer with whom she'd been classed as a peer, in idea, within *The Monthly Review* article of April 1774. Starting now, the 'nine muses' of Britain became friends in reality. The Bluestocking Circle was

> *a tight-knit group of women [that] became a model for rational 'Enlightenment' forms of sociability. The Bluestockings met in the London homes of the fashionable hostesses Elizabeth Montagu, Elizabeth Vesey and Frances Boscawen [beginning in] the 1750s. Together these women, and the eminent men who supported their endeavours, invented a new kind of informal sociability, and nurtured a sense of intellectual community...*
>
> *Guests included the leading literary, political and cultural figures of the day... scholar and classical translator Elizabeth Carter...critic and writer Samuel Johnson, the*

---

26 Stott, *Hannah More*, 27.

27 Roberts, *Memoirs...of Hannah More*, volume one (New York: 1834), 36.

*artists Frances Reynolds and her brother Sir Joshua...
novelist Fanny Burney, and [now,] Hannah More.*

*They got their comical name - 'Bluestockings' - when
another guest, the botanist Benjamin Stillingfleet, was
welcomed at one of Elizabeth Montagu's salons even
though he had arrived absent-mindedly wearing the blue
woollen stockings normally worn by working men, instead
of the more formal white silk.*[28]

Soon after meeting Elizabeth Montagu, More met Edmund
Burke, pre-eminent in yet another famous London circle,
'the Club,' established by Samuel Johnson. Its members also
included Garrick and Sir Joshua Reynolds. A letter written
by Sally More caught the festive spirit of that occasion: 'Since
I wrote last, Hannah has been introduced by Miss Reynolds...
to Edmund Burke, *(the sublime and beautiful Edmund Burke!)*
[and,] from a large party of literary persons, assembled at Sir
Joshua's, she received the most encouraging compliments.'[29]

Meeting Burke, of whom much will be said later, was
special. More had avidly read his books. Now, she met him in
a gathering of new friends who were becoming literary peers.

It was a glittering prospect. One friend, J.S. Harford, said
that when it came to Burke, More *"often dwelt with admiration
on [his] lofty intellect, and brilliant conversational powers."*[30]

It was all rather like the lines of verse she wrote to describe
this time in her life—

28 from the 2008 National Portrait Gallery exhibition article, titled "The Bluestockings Circle:
    Brilliant Women, 18th Century Bluestockings," archived at: https://www.npg.org.uk/whatson/
    exhibitions/2008/brilliant-women/the-bluestockings-circle
29 Roberts, *Memoirs...of Hannah More*, volume one, 3rd edition (1835), 48. Italics added.
30 J.S. Harford, *Recollections of William Wilberforce* (London: 1865), 278.

soft slumbers now, mine eyes forsake
Name but the suppers in th' Apollo,
What classic images will follow![31]

More saw Burke as "a great genius of our own time;" the author of many a "brilliant passage." And one favourite phrase from his pen held a meaning that deepened on reflection, as eloquent as it was memorable. It spoke of "the unbought grace of life."[32] In verse as well, More praised the versatility of Burke's gifts: as a historian, philosopher, and politician—

And Burke, the glory of his age,
His single self a host.[33]

* * *

Over the next six weeks, before she and her sisters returned home to Bristol,[34] More experienced one exhilarating round of meetings after another. Given her family's fondness for his books, meeting Samuel Johnson was highest, perhaps, among the introductions she had after meeting David Garrick. As one 19th century biographer described it—

The desire she had long felt to see Dr. Johnson was
speedily gratified.
    Her first introduction to him took place at the house of
Sir Joshua Reynolds, who prepared her...for the possibility
of his being in one of his moods of sadness and silence.

31 lines 15-16 More's poem, *The Bas Bleu* (1784).

32 Hannah More, *Hints,* volume two, (London: 1805), 107; and see also F.G. Selby, ed., *Edmund Burke, Reflections on the Revolution in France* (London: 1906), 85.

33 *The Christian Observer,* January 1828, (London: 1839), 34.

34 the duration of More's stay in London is confirmed in Stott, *Hannah More,* 28.

She was surprized, [therefore,] at his coming to meet her as she entered the room, with good humour in his countenance, and a macaw of Sir Joshua's in his hand...

Still more, [as he greeted her, he recited] a verse from a Morning Hymn *which she had written at the desire of Sir James Stonhouse [in lines of iambic tetrameter]:*[35]

Soft slumbers now mine eyes forsake, My pow'rs are all renew'd;

May my freed spirit too awake, With heavenly strength endued.[36]

This meeting became famous in literature, and many years later, C.S. Lewis said this about Hannah More, Dr. Johnson, and the colourful macaw—

"Saturday 15 May [1926]...Had only a short stroll in the fields...Spent the rest of the day at home lazily, reading the Life of Hannah More *by William Roberts, Esq. (1838). He is a deliciously pompous and peppery evangelical, but the letters (which make the most part of it) are very interesting. One is glad to see [Dr.] Johnson, with Sir Joshua [Reynolds'] macaw on his wrist."*[37]

From the pen of John Harford, who was rather like a Boswell to Hannah More, we have an account of her first meeting with Dr. Johnson.

---

35 Roberts, *Memoirs...of Hannah More*, volume one, 3rd edition (1835), 48.

36 George Wright, *The Lady's Miscellany* (London: 1793), 179. See also Smith, *Literary Manuscripts and Letters of Hannah More*, 125.

37 Walter Hooper, ed., *All My Road Before Me: The Diary of C.S. Lewis* (New York: 1991), 396.

"Her first interview," Harford wrote, "took place at the house of Sir Joshua Reynolds, in Leicester Square." Then followed Harford's account of what More told him about it—

"I felt," she said, "a little trepidation at entering the apartment where he was, in consequence of something Sir Joshua said to me, just before we did so, about his occasional roughness of manner; but he received me with a kindness which quite removed any such feeling. He was caressing a parrot; and on hearing my name, he took my hand with the utmost cordiality, and addressed me in a few lines of one of my own poems."[38]

More's subsequent meetings with Johnson would often yield memorable moments, such as this vignette, given by Boswell himself in *The Life of Samuel Johnson*—

It was a lively saying of Dr. Johnson to Miss Hannah More, who had expressed a wonder that the poet who had written 'Paradise Lost' should write such poor sonnets.

[To this, Johnson replied]: "Milton, Madam, was a genius that could cut a Colossus from a rock; but could not carve heads upon cherry-stones."[39]

This story points to More's independent mind, and firm convictions about literature, something that may be seen in

---

38 Harford, *Recollections of Wilberforce*, 274.

39 Boswell, *The Life of Samuel Johnson*, 507. NOTE: In January 1835, A.H. Everett says the following of Boswell's often chary estimate of Hannah More: "With respect to Boswell, she gives the same impression with others, that he was a vain, good humored creature, not destitute of talent, but with a singular absurdity of mind. His greatest failing was his convivial propensity; he gave offence to Miss More on one occasion, when he was mightily elevated with wine, and was reproved by her so severely, that he shows some little resentment in his book; not saying anything decidedly against her, but representing her as a great flatterer of Johnson. She was certainly a prime favorite of the giant: and this perhaps was one cause of Boswell's unpleasant feelings." See *The North American Review*, January 1835 (Boston: 1835), 157. Italics added.

another recollection from More herself, from a later edition of Boswell's *Life of Johnson*. It conveys Johnson's penchant for flattery, or flashes of wit in polite company; but also shows that conversations with More about poetry were likely to be lively in character, with a very animated exchange of opinions.

She clearly relished the cut and parry of intellectual, literary debate—

I dined very pleasantly at the Bishop of Chester's [she recalled, Dr. Porteus' home]. Johnson was there; and the Bishop was very desirous to draw him out, as he wished to show him off to some of the company who had never seen him.

He begged me to sit next him at dinner, and to devote myself to making him talk. To this end, I consented to talk more than became me; and our stratagem succeeded.

You would have enjoyed seeing him take me by the hand in the middle of dinner, and repeat, with no small enthusiasm, many passages from the "Fair Penitent,"[40] etc.

I urged him to take a little wine; he replied, "I can't drink a little, child; therefore I never touch it. Abstinence is as easy to me, as temperance would be difficult."

He was very good-humoured...One of the company happened to say a word about poetry; "Hush, hush!" said he [nodding towards me], it is dangerous to say a word of poetry before her; it is talking of the art of war before Hannibal."

He continued his jokes, and lamented that I had not married [Thomas] Chatterton, that posterity might have seen a propagation of poets.[41]

---

40 i.e. Nicholas Rowe's *The Fair Penitent* (1702), a stage adaptation of the tragedy, *The Fatal Dowry*.

41 *Boswell's Life of Samuel Johnson,* volume nine (London: 1835), 325-326.

More knew Dr. Johnson for over ten years, from May 1774 to late December 1784. Four years before Johnson's passing, in 1780, they met and had animated conversation about the Puritans—More defending Richard Baxter especially, when his name came up. At the same time, More wasn't at all above flattery herself, or "peppering," when it came to the light-hearted moments of their visit. As she recalled—

He scolded me heartily, as usual, when I differed from him in opinion; and, as usual, laughed when I flattered him. I was very bold in combating some of his darling prejudices: nay, I ventured to defend one or two of the Puritans, whom I forced him to allow to be good men, and good writers. He said he was not angry with me at all for liking Baxter. He liked him himself; 'but then,' said he, 'Baxter was bred up in the Establishment, and would have died in it, if he could have got the living of Kidderminster. He was a very good man.'[42]

The "peppering" aspect of their friendship was captured best in a letter written by Sally More, near to this time. "On Tuesday evening," she said of one visit in 1775—

we drank tea at Sir Joshua's with Dr Johnson. Hannah is certainly a great favourite. She was placed next him, and they had the entire conversation to themselves. They were both in remarkably high spirits, and it was certainly her lucky night: I never heard her say so many good things. The old genius was as jocular as the young one was pleasant.

You would have imagined we were at some comedy, had you heard our peals of laughter. They certainly tried

---

42 Roberts, *Memoirs…of Hannah More*, 61.

which could "pepper the highest," and it is not clear to me that the lexicographer was really the highest seasoner.[43]

Meanwhile, Johnson's kind greeting and recitation at their first meeting was of a piece with More's increasingly widespread fame at this time.

Her poetry was much in the air of cultured, literary London.

In 1774, the fifth edition of her play *The Search After Happiness* was published, along with a poem rich in allusions to nature, and closely-observed knowledge of country fact.

Titled *Inscription In A Beautiful Retreat Called Fairy Bower,* it discloses a side of More's writing now too-little known: a side that led her to express, some years later, these words of appreciation for the co-author of *Lyrical Ballads*—

"Your young friend Wordsworth surpasses all your other young friends."[44]

Four lines of More's poem clearly anticipate the pastoral ways of the romantic poets, as in "Lines Written In Early Spring;" while a second quatrain points to a literary kinship, some two generations before-time, with poets like John Clare—

Mark where first the daisies blow,
Where the bluest violets grow,
Where the sweetest linnet sings,
Where the earliest cowslip springs.[45]

---

43 Robina Napier, *Johnsoniana: Anecdotes of...Samuel Johnson* (London: 1884), 284-285.

44 Joseph Cottle, *Reminiscences of Samuel Taylor Coleridge,* 2nd edition, (London: 1848), 260: "Hannah More, to whom I...presented the first volume...immediately perceived the merits of the 'Lyrical Ballads.' On my visiting Barley Wood soon after, she said to me, 'Your young friend Wordsworth, surpasses all your other young friends,' when producing the book, she requested me to read several of the poems, which I did." Italics added.

45 Hannah More, "Inscription In A Beautiful Retreat Called Fairy Bower," in *The Search After Happiness: A Pastoral Drama,* 5th ed., (Bristol: 1774), 46. This poem has been included in a prestigious anthology: R. Lonsdale, ed., *Eighteenth Century Women Poets* (Oxford: 1989), 326-327.

~ ~ ~

Come, and mark within what bush
Builds the blackbird, or the thrush,
Great his joy who first espies,
Greater his who spares the prize.[46]

Hannah More in the London years of the 1780s, from *The New Lady's Magazine*

As the summer of 1774 waned, and autumn days unfolded,
More and her sisters became part of a parliamentary election

---

46 Hannah More, "Inscription In A Beautiful Retreat Called Fairy Bower," in *The Search After Happiness,*
5th ed., (Bristol: 1774), 46.

season that Bristol long remembered. The city could send two representatives to the House of Commons, and three prominent figures now vied for that honour: Matthew Brickdale, Henry Cruger, and Edmund Burke. Significantly, "the crisis in America" was the overarching issue of this hotly contested campaign. Burke "took up his headquarters in Park Street, next to the More sisters' school," and Sally More wrote to Anne Gwatkin, "we are very lively at night with the Huzzahs of the Mob."[47]

And all this was taking place less than six months before the first shots, in April 1775, were fired in the War for American Independence.

As for More's thoughts about the conflict to be, we do know. Some years later John Griscom, a noted professor of Chemistry and Natural Philosophy, called for a visit, which he recorded in great detail.

With keen interest, More asked Griscom many questions about the "charitable and religious institutions of our country;" but when the conversation turned to her memories, vis-à-vis the United States, "she acknowledged that she had been much opposed to America during the revolutionary struggle."[48]

As one might suspect, given her friendship with Burke, More was ardent in her support of his candidacy. S.J. Skedd has written that "she contributed to Burke's successful campaign... by ghosting some of his letters to the local press and writing verses singing his praises."[49] In his text, Henry Thompson evokes the vivid atmosphere of this time—

---

47 Stott, *Hannah More*, 28.
48 John Griscom, *A Year in Europe*, volume one, (New York: 1824), 124. See also Robert Hole, *Selected Writings of Hannah More*, (Oxford: 2021), 239: "More was a bitter opponent of the American rebels and her relations with Burke cooled for a while this issue," also page 242: "Burke had been a close friend of More, but the pro-American stance in his *Speech on Conciliation with America* (22 March 1775) alienated her. His *Reflections [on the Revolution with France]*, was, of course, to restore him to favour."
49 Skedd, "Hannah More."

it is seldom that a contested election proves a favourable court of homage for the claims of literature; yet such was now the renown of Hannah, that [one day,] a party of Mr. Cruger's friends suddenly halted beneath the window of the Misses More's house, and were desired by their leader to give "three cheers to Sappho!" and "More, Sappho, and Cruger for ever!" rang to the skies...

[And, when] Edmund Burke was put in nomination, [he], during the election, was frequently the guest of the Misses More. The mind of Hannah could scarcely be insensible to the genius of Burke. Her admiration of him was most ardent.

When his place on the poll rendered his success unquestionable, the sisters sent him one evening a congratulatory tribute in the form of a cockade, in the composition of which the mind and hand of Hannah were conspicuously present.

It was composed of the colours which, in his [famous] treatise, he classes under 'the beautiful and the sublime'; and was enwreathed with myrtle, ivy, laurel, and bay, sprinkled with silver, and decorated with silver tassels.

On the back was the word BURKE, with the following mottoes:

> *He is himself the great sublime he draws.*
> *In action faithful, and in honour clear.*
> *Correct with spirit, elegant with ease.*
> *Justum et tenacem propositi virum.*
> *[Just, and firm of purpose]*[50]

---

50 Thompson, *Hannah More*, 25-26.

Here Hannah and her resourceful sisters hatched a scheme of benign deception. They arranged to have this cockade delivered clandestinely, and insure they were present when Burke opened the package containing it. And so—

The servant was ordered to deliver the box containing the cockade, and to disappear. Burke, not suspecting the contents, opened it in a large company, who were highly delighted with the compliment; and he affirmed it could only come from his Park Street friends [the More sisters]. The cockade graced his [campaign] committee-room until the chairing day, when he wore it in triumph [as he was carried through the streets]...[51]

A sequel no less charming, and gratifying, followed. Burke took steps to make sure that Hannah, and the More sisters, knew how much he appreciated their kindness—

the following day, Burke called on the sisters previous to his departure for town, and expressed himself to Hannah on the cockade "in such terms," says the eldest, [Mary,] in a letter to [Anne] Gwatkin, "that never, no never, were compliments dictated in such a charming manner before." On asking Hannah whether she had any commands to her friend Miss Reynolds (Sir Joshua's sister), she said she would trouble him with a letter.

The letter reached Miss Reynolds by the hands of her brother, and she opened it in the presence of Dr. Johnson; when it was found to contain a complimentary poetical address to Burke. Chary of his commendations

---

51 Thompson, *Hannah More*, 26-27.

as the doctor was, he did not hesitate immediately to say,
"Human language cannot soar higher."[52]

Six weeks in the spring and early summer of 1774, a whirlwind of first meetings, and thereafter a constant round of visits with some of the finest artists, politicians, and writers London could boast. They received Hannah More as one of their own; and in their company, with their commendations, she made a storied entrance on the stage of history.

In less than six months, from the close of 1773, her life had changed completely.

---

52 Thompson, *Hannah More*, 27.

CHAPTER FOUR

Prospects at Every Turn

"Why, Sir, did you not tell me I was in company with a learned lady?"

"With a learned lady, Sir? Why, Sir, that lady is a great genius! Sir, she has published more than you ever will with all your travelling! She is MY DRAMATICK PUPIL, Sir!"[1]

— DAVID GARRICK (1775)

...while the events of youth...are remembered...[2]

— HANNAH MORE (1801)

...by the reflection—that of those persons whose kindness stimulated, and whose partiality rewarded, my early efforts...[3]

— HANNAH MORE (1801)

---

1   Thompson, *Hannah More*, 31.

2   *The Works of Hannah More, in Eight Volumes,* volume six (London: 1801), 148.

3   *The Works of Hannah More, Including Several Pieces Never Before Published,* v. 1, (Philadelphia: 1813), xvi, from the Preface, dated 1801.

As the year 1775 unfolded, More continued to find success at the epicentre of literary London. A new round of bluestocking meetings took place. A very fine description of what they were like appears in *The Cambridge History of English Literature*—

> *A terse description...might serve as a type of most of the bluestocking meetings. This cult of "conversation— the pursuit of ideas," as it has been defined—acted as a subtle leaven to the hard, brilliant materialism of the eighteenth century.*
>
> *Social refinement [coincided with] the bluestocking interest in literature...*[4]

In sum, these gatherings were a popular haven of culture, within the often profligate scenes and settings of London in this era—the famous clubs where excess in drink, gambling, and other kinds of revelry predominated. More described the bluestocking gatherings in a representative account of one evening at her friend William Pepys' home.

Of that evening, she said: *"There was all the pride of London, every wit and every wit-ess... but the spirit of the evening was kept up on the strength of a little lemonade till past eleven, without cards, scandal, or politics."*[5]

More's renewed involvement with these gatherings began in January 1775, when she again visited London. Soon to turn thirty, she had taken lodgings at Henrietta Street, Covent Garden, with her sisters Sally and Patty. Once more, *The Cambridge History of English Literature* caught the spirit

---

4   A.W. Ward and A.R Waller, eds., *The Cambridge History of English Literature*, volume 11 (Cambridge: 1914), 363-364.

5   Roberts, *Memoirs...of Hannah More*, volume 1 (1837) 123. Italics added.

of what these days were like, and More's gift for casting them in prose—

This time, she dined at [Elizabeth] Montagu's, where she met Elizabeth Carter and [Frances] Boscawen, the widow of the admiral. The bluestocking parties were now at their zenith, and the clear-cut thumbnail sketches Hannah gives of the chief dramatis personae *are always vivid and lifelike. Of Mrs. Montagu, she says—*

"She is not only the finest genius, but the finest lady I ever saw...she lives in the highest style of magnificence... her form is delicate, even to fragility...she has the sprightly vivacity of fifteen, with the judgment and experience of a Nestor."[6]

A snapshot glimpse of More's feelings was cast memorably in this passage—

During her first winter among [the bluestocking circle] she was still in her twenties, and her hasty impressionist descriptions of the literary society of London scintillate with the fresh enthusiasm of [one] whose eyes and mind are slightly dazzled by unaccustomed experiences. She was not unworthy to be admitted to the society of those learned ladies and ingenious gentlemen...[7]

A fair idea of More's "impressionist descriptions" may be seen in this passage, from a letter home describing one evening of her London sojourn—

---

6   Ward and Waller, eds., *The Cambridge History of English Literature*, volume 11, 360-361.

7   Ward and Waller, eds., *The Cambridge History of English Literature*, volume 11, 359. The phrase "impressionist descriptions," in relation to More, appears here.

I had yesterday the pleasure of dining in Hill Street, Berkeley Square, at a certain Mrs. Montagu's, a name not totally obscure. The party consisted of herself, Mrs. Carter, Dr. Johnson, Solander, and Matty, Mrs. Boscawen, Miss Reynolds, and Sir Joshua (the idol of every company), some other persons of high rank and less wit, and your humble servant—a party that would not have disgraced the table of Lelius or of Atticus.

I felt myself a worm, the more a worm for the consequence which was given me by mixing me with such a society; but, as I told Mrs. Boscawen, and with great truth, I had an opportunity of making an experiment of my heart, by which I learned that I was not envious, for I certainly did not repine at being the meanest person in company.

Mrs. Montagu received me with the most encouraging kindness; she is not only the finest genius, but the finest lady I ever saw: she lives in the highest style of magnificence; her apartments and table are in the most splendid taste; but what baubles are these when speaking of a Montagu![8]

Then too, ground-breaking book sales had fostered More's success also—

[Even as] Miss More again visited the metropolis [Henry Thompson noted], and mingled with the same distinguished and intellectual society, her "Search after Happiness" had reached a fifth edition in the year previous, and a sixth in this. In the beginning of [1775 also,] an edition was sent from Philadelphia, with two complimentary poems

---

8   Roberts, *Memoirs...of Hannah More,* volume 1 (1837) 39.

*addressed to the author; and the profits of the sale had
netted [the not inconsiderable sum of] £100.*

*She thought, therefore, nor without reason, that she
had established sufficient literary reputation to justify her
in setting a high pecuniary value on her writings.*

*She therefore offered at once to [publisher Thomas]
Cadell two little poems, to form a thin quarto, after the
fashion of the day; requesting to know what he would give
for them, and stating at the same time that she would not
part with them for "a very paltry consideration." Mr. Cadell,
though he had not seen the poems, was so well prepared to
entertain high expectations, that he immediately offered to
give Miss More whatever Goldsmith might have received
for his "Deserted Village."*

*This she was unable to discover; and therefore she laid
her demand at forty guineas, which the popularity of the
volume amply justified.*

*It [held] "Sir Eldred of the Bower," a tale which appears
to have been suggested by the taste for ballad literature,
which Percy's "Relicks of Ancient Poetry" had revived; and
"The Legend of the Bleeding Rock."*[9]

Thompson was quick to also note that "Sir Eldred of the
Bower," was "honoured by the revision, and even more, by the
critical touch, of [Samuel] Johnson," whose pen furnished one
stanza for a subsequent edition of the poem.

These lines of Johnson's collaboration with More read—

> *My scorn has oft the dart repell'd
> Which guileful beauty threw;*

---

9   Thompson, *Hannah More,* 27.

> *But goodness heard, and grace beheld,*
> *Must every heart subdue.*[10]

More had yet to mark one year since her first entrée to literary London, and here, she was collaborating with England's great man of letters. As to the extent of this collaboration, the editors of *The Yale Digital Edition of the Works of Samuel Johnson* say that apart from writing a new stanza for More's poem, Johnson had "suggested some little alterations"[11] in it, in place for the revised edition (1778). When scholar H.W. Liebert compared these first two editions of the poem, he concluded "that Johnson was responsible for all the variants."[12]

Here, the editors of *The Yale Digital Edition of the Works of Samuel Johnson* added: "with this the present editors agree."[13] For Johnson to have rendered this service for More's poem was no little undertaking—"Sir Eldred of the Bower" runs to thirty-five pages' length in the revised 1778 edition. His investment of time attests his high view of More's poetic gifts.

The provincial school-master's daughter had truly arrived on the literary scene. The first lines of her now famous poem began—

> *There was a young, and valiant knight,*
> *Sir Eldred was his name,*
> *And never did a worthier wight*
> *The rank of knighthood claim.*

> *Where gliding Tay, her stream sends forth,*

---

10 Hannah More, Sir Eldred *of the Bower, and The Bleeding Rock: Two Legendary Tales* (London: 1778), 13.

11 Roberts, *Memoirs…of Hannah More*, volume 1 (1837) 46.

12 "'We Fell upon Sir Eldred,'" *New Light on Dr. Johnson*, ed. Hilles, 1959, pp. 233-45.

13 *The Yale Digital Edition of the Works of Samuel Johnson*, "Sir Eldred of the Bower," at: http://www. yalejohnson.com/frontend/sda_viewer?n=108087

To feed the neighbouring wood,
The ancient glory of the North,
Sir Eldred's castle stood.[14]

Yet Sir Eldred, a knightly paragon in most ways, was tragically not immune to sudden storms of passion. "Overcome with sudden jealousy," he stabs a "handsome stranger hugged by his new bride Birtha." The victim, alas, was "Birtha's long-lost brother Edwy." His death set in motion events causing "the deaths from grief of Birtha, and her old father Ardolph."[15]

It was a cycle of tragedy with echoes of Malory's *Morte d'Arthur,* or perhaps plays of Shakespeare, like *Hamlet.* It was also a cautionary tale, set to guard against pride and passion—besetting sins in an age when duels over affairs of honour were still common.

Blinded by both, and after the deaths he'd caused, grief overwhelmed this knight as no foe on the field of battle ever could have. More wrote—

Cold, speechless, senseless, Eldred near
Gaz'd on the deed he had done;
Like the blank statue of Despair
Or Madness grav'd in stone.[16]

Notwithstanding its sombre subject matter as a tragedy, one great happiness came to More through a public reading of her poem.[17] At one gathering, always to be remembered,

---

14 More, *Sir Eldred*, 1-2.

15 Eric Rothstein, *Restoration and Eighteenth-Century Poetry 1660-1780* (Oxford: 2016), 230n.

16 Hannah More, *Sir Eldred of the Bower, and The Bleeding Rock: Two Legendary Tales* (London: 1778), 33.

17 Hopkins, *Hannah More*, 64.

Garrick read it aloud at his home, after "a snug little dinner in the library," where there was "much wit, under the banner of much decorum." More described it all in a letter home—

> *I'll tell you the most ridiculous circumstance in the world.*
> *After dinner, Garrick took up* The Monthly Review *(civil gentlemen, by-the-by, these* Monthly Reviewers*) and read 'Sir Eldred' with all his pathos, and all his graces. I think I never was so ashamed in my life; but he read it so superlatively that I cried like a child.*[18]

This gathering was representative of More's friendship with David and Eva Garrick. After her first meeting with them in 1774, and for weeks at a time during the next five years, she was a guest in their home, or travelled with them, and treated like one of the family. One charming story of a visit survives, affirming the Garricks' affection for More, and their respect for her deeply held faith. On Sundays, to honour the Sabbath, More was in the habit of not attending entertainments of any kind. This sets the context for her letter about one travelling visit, when Garrick, who fondly called her "Nine," or someone with all the gifts of the Muses, honoured her Sunday custom—

> *We reached this place yesterday morning. You will judge of the size of the house, when I tell you there are eleven visitors, and all perfectly well accommodated. The Wilmots live in the greatest magnificence; but what is a much better thing, they live also rationally and sensibly. On Sunday evening, however, I was a little alarmed; they*

---

18 *The North American Review,* January 1835 (Boston: 1835), 157.

were preparing for music...but before I had time to feel uneasy, Garrick turned round and said, "Nine, you are a Sunday woman; retire to your room—I will recall you when the music is over."[19]

And, as for Eva Garrick's fondness for More, circa 1780, she wished for More to come stay with her, as she was still mourning the death of her husband. More readily complied.

Becoming part of a walking party, her time with Mrs. Garrick passed very pleasantly, though in an intrepid sort of way. Ofttimes, the party thought of David Garrick, to whom More had given the nickname "Dragon,"[20] for a friend of noble bearing and gifts—

Hampton is very clean, very green, very beautiful, and very melancholy; but the 'long, dear calm of fixed repose' [as Alexander Pope has it,] suits me mightily, after the hurry of London.

We have been on the wing every day this week; our way is to walk out four or five miles, to some of the prettiest villages, or prospects, and when we are quite tired, we get into the coach, which is waiting for us, with our books, and we come home to dinner as hungry as Dragon himself.[21]

But of all the times she'd known in connection with the Garricks, and their friendship with her, their encouragement of a new work she was writing likely meant the most.

---

19 Roberts, *Memoirs...of Hannah More,* volume one, (London: 1836), 93-94.

20 In literature, dragons are often creatures of noble bearing and wisdom. C.S. Lewis drew on such sources for his creation of the ship, *Dawn Treader,* made to look like a dragon that flew o'er the waves of the sea.

21 R.A. Willmott, ed., *Letters of Eminent Persons* (London: 1839), 252-253. Here, writing of the "long dear calm of fixed repose," More is paraphrasing line 251 of "Eloisa to Abelard," by Alexander Pope, one of her favourite poets, who had written of "long dead calm of fixed repose."

It would bring a pinnacle for her as a playwright. As M.A. Hopkins has said—

Hannah worked during the summer of 1776 on her [new] play, Percy, *[and sent] the acts to the Garricks for criticism. [Eva] Garrick was considered an excellent judge of drama. By [17] December, Hannah had progressed to the point where Garrick wrote her:*
"the 3 [acts] will do, and well do, but the 4th will not stand muster; that must be changed greatly, but how I cannot yet say. Mrs. Garrick, who has been very ill and attended by Dr. Cadogan, has read you too with care—she likes the first 3, but can hardly believe you touched the 4th."[22]

In reply, More wrote: "You will be so good, at your entire leisure, as to put me into a way to recover the right road, from which I have strayed so far in my fourth act; I have blundered from the path, and cannot get back to it."[23] Garrick did so.

Such missives led More to redouble her efforts, crafting and polishing her play. This painstaking labour, with the Garricks' assistance, made all the difference.

Letters like the following helped her stay the challenging course, as work commenced on the fifth and final act of the play. Garrick's counsel would be there when needed—

I hope you will consider your dramatic matter with all your wit and feeling. Let your fifth act be worthy of you, and tear the heart to pieces, or wo betide you! I shall not pass over any scenes, or parts of scenes, that are merely

---

22 *The Letters of David Garrick,* volume three (Cambridge: 1963), 1148.

23 F.L. Clarke, *Golden Friendships: Sketches of the Lives and Characters of Friends* (London: 1884), 102.

written to make up a certain number of lines. Such doings,
Madame Nine, will neither do for you, nor for me.

Most affectionately yours,
Upon the gallop,
D. Garrick[24]

[Postscript:] My wife sends her love.

More finished her play on 2 November 1777, and sent it on
to Garrick.[25] He then went into action, as preparations for
staging *Percy* began. During this time, there was much pleasant
camaraderie. One biographer wrote—

Garrick threw his tremendous energy into the production,
aiding his friend Thomas Harris, the manager, and
writing both prologue and epilogue. Hannah wrote
home in fine spirits that he demanded payment for his
verses because Dryden always got five guineas, but had
generously offered to compromise on a handsome supper
with a bottle of claret. Hannah haggled, holding steak
and porter sufficient payment. While they wrangled,
toast and honey came up from the kitchen, and on that,
they compromised.[26]

So what was More's play about, and its compelling purpose?

Crucially, *The Cambridge History of English Literature*
observes that "*Percy* is a manifesto, and [that it] attempts to
show how the ethics of refined society may be studied through

---

24 Roberts, *Memoirs…of Hannah More,* volume one (1837), 74; see also *The Letters of David Garrick,*
    volume three (1963), 1168.

25 Stott, *Hannah More,* 38.

26 Hopkins, *Hannah More,* 76.

the ensanguined colours of tragedy."[27] Essentially, in the *mise en scène* of a tragedy, drawing on a time of legend, she wished to take the measure of ethics and customs in her own time.

This said, she crafted her play in advantageous ways also. She was "well in touch with the growing taste for romanticism, and was original enough to fill her problem play with the chivalry and architecture of the Middle Age."[28] Specifically—

Percy is based on a twelfth century story of Eudes de Faiel, which [Pierre de] Belloy (the author of Le Siège de Calais*) had already dramatised...*

The action takes place among old-fashioned English heroes and shows how Elwina, betrothed to Percy from her childhood...wed Earl Raby at her father's behest, but cannot return his love...As the Earl's suspicions are being aroused at this coldness, Percy returns with glory from the crusades and hastens to his lady, not knowing that she is married. The spectators watch [as Percy] is gradually trapped by the jealous husband, while the heroine is torn between duty to her marriage vow, and her unconquerable passion for the suitor of her youth. In the end, Elwina goes mad and drinks poison, while Raby slays Percy, and then, learning that his wife was chaste, kills himself...

Percy shows what havoc a virtuous man may work, if he is passion's slave.[29]

This last line from *The Cambridge History of English Literature* strikes a note consonant with the key theme of "Sir Eldred of the Bower": ungoverned pride and passion—the undoing of

---

27 Ward and Waller, eds., *The Cambridge History of English Literature*, volume 11, 273-274.

28 Ward and Waller, eds., *The Cambridge History of English Literature*, volume 11, 273-274.

29 Ward and Waller, eds., *The Cambridge History of English Literature*, volume 11, 273-274.

many in the Georgian Age—in duels, or contests for power in the world of politics—had a counterpart in the pages of history and legend. More knew, from the prevalence of pride, passion, and their fallout in British life, that there was a need to guard against them. As M.A. Hopkins phrased it in her description of the overarching theme of *Percy*—

"The theme of Hannah's play is that revenge is a boomerang."[30]

When it premiered, *Percy* was seen as anything but conventional, staid, or "far-fetched, and the action melodramatic."[31] Quite the contrary, it was "a tremendous success,"[32] and "its combination of emotion, action and theory…considered a revelation."[33]

Beyond wide acclaim in London, the play was staged in Vienna, and More was later elected a member of the Academy of Sciences, Belles Lettres and Arts, Rouen.[34]

More, and her play, were a sensation.

Here, on one level, *Percy* was a straightforward tragedy, skilfully depicted and staged. Yet it also was a call, in circles of cultured society, for Britons to remember the better angels of their nature, and avoid repetitions of the consequences seen in *Percy*. The mindset behind affairs of honour in Georgian England had corrosive tendencies, More ardently believed.

Human nature was constant, regardless of time and place. Against the backdrop of war with America, and contests for empire, many things tied to pride and passion could obscure moral clarity. As for duelling itself, More was only too well

---

30 Hopkins, *Hannah More*, 77.

31 Hopkins, *Hannah More*, 77.

32 Hopkins, *Hannah More*, 77.

33 Ward and Waller, eds., *The Cambridge History of English Literature*, volume 11 (Cambridge: 1914), 274.

34 Ward and Waller, eds., *The Cambridge History of English Literature*, volume 11 (Cambridge: 1914), 274. See also Smith, Nicholas. (2014). New Light on Hannah More's Membership of the Academy of Sciences, Belles Lettres and Arts, Rouen. Notes and Queries. 61. 444-449. 10.1093/notesj/gju106.

aware, as all of England was, that in summer 1772, the actor Richard Brinsley Sheridan and Captain Mathews had fought two duels (the second near Bath, where More later had a home) in an affair of honour over Elizabeth Ann Linley, a beautiful young soprano from Bath.

And More had been a friend of the Sheridan family for nearly ten years.[35]

The story of this feud was vividly recounted in *The London Chronicle*.

In the first duel, the two men fought with swords, and though both were wounded, Sheridan won the duel when Mathews lost his sword and pleaded for his life. But despite the blood-letting, this failed to settle the issue, and they fought a second duel, again with swords. Sheridan was seriously wounded. He recovered, and later married Linley.[36]

Seen in this context, *Percy* was a play with resonance for an often troubled time.

It offered conventional tropes: action, elements of mystery, violence, conflict, lovers' trials, and the like—but overarching all there was a didactic quality—one not hard to fathom in a writer who had been a teacher in early life. Here, it should be said More wasn't unique in bringing this to the theatre.

---

35 Hopkins, *Hannah More*, 27: "Among the lecturers who came to Forty-three Park Street were… Thomas Sheridan, father of the famous playwright…who gave a course on oratory, illustrating his points with readings from the scriptures and masterpieces of English literature…To young Hannah he was soul-stirring. [In 1763,] she expressed her girlish enthusiasm in a poem which asserted that he harmonized the ruffled soul…was as correct as science and as elegant as wit, as powerful as reason, as sweet as fancy, and so on. When a mutual acquaintance showed the verses to [Sheridan], he was struck with the young lady's intelligence and said he would like to meet her. This was the beginning of an acquaintance between him and Hannah, which included his delightful wife, Frances Sheridan, playwright and novelist, and later his son and his daughter-in-law, the lovely singer, born Linley."
    Given this, More would have been deeply grieved to hear that Richard Sheridan nearly died after his second duel. He had written the epilogue for More's third play, *The Fatal Falsehood*, in 1779. See Jones, *Hannah More*, 14. See also Alicia Lefanu, *Memoirs of the Life and Writings of Mrs. Frances Sheridan* (London: 1824), 247-248.

36 see *The London Chronicle*, October 3-6 issue (1772), 333. See also "Newspaper report about Sheridan's duels with Captain Mathews, 1772," archived online at: https://www.bl.uk/collection-items/newspaper-report-about-sheridans-duels-with-captain-mathews-1772

Perennially popular plays like Addison's *Cato*, which she knew well, had much of the same air, as in this famous line—

> *"'Tis not in mortals to command success,*
> *But we'll do more, Sempronius; we'll deserve it."*
> (*Cato*, act 1, scene 2, line 43.)

In concord with this plea for better aspirations, More would later write—

> *There almost inevitably runs, through the whole web of the Tragic Drama, a prominent thread of false principle. It is generally the leading object of the poet to erect a standard of* honour, *in direct opposition to the standard of* Christianity. *And this is not done subordinately, incidentally, occasionally; but worldly honour is the very soul, and spirit, and life-giving principle of the [conventional] drama.*
>
> *Honour is the religion of tragedy. It is her moral and political law…*
>
> Injured honour can only be vindicated at the point of the sword; the stains of injured reputation can only be washed out in blood.
>
> *Love, jealousy, hatred, ambition, pride, revenge, are too often elevated into the rank of splendid virtues, and form a dazzling system of worldly morality, in direct contradiction to the spirit of that religion whose characteristics are* "charity, meekness, peaceableness, long-suffering, gentleness, forgiveness."[37]

---

37 Hannah More, "Preface to the Tragedies," in *The Works of Hannah More in Eight Volumes*, v. 1 (London: 1801), 16-17. Italics added.

Added to this, More was grieved that anyone might conclude Addison's portrayal in *Cato* of a Stoic's suicide was a sanction of that practice—born of pride, and misbegotten ideas of false honour. It was tragic, "specious reasoning," to say—

> *What Cato did, and Addison approv'd,*
> *Must sure be right:—* [38]

Addison, More insisted, "could not avoid making his catastrophe just what he has made it, without violating a notorious fact [the dictates of authentic Stoic philosophy], and falsifying the character he exhibits."[39] Addison, in sum, was faithfully depicting a character, not commending the means or motives of that character's death.

Bearing all this in mind, More was counter-cultural and forward-thinking—crying out, through art, for a more humane England.

It took courage for her to countervail this spirit of the age in the theatre.

Percy was at once a story brought forward from legend; but also one that might have been influenced by the scandal, and More's horror, over Sheridan's duels—to say nothing of earlier plays, like *Cato*. There was much that fed into writing this tragedy, much that would have resonated powerfully with theatre-goers who knew the troubled context that was in the air, just as well as More did. All the same, her play's acclaim was pervasive—

> *The new plays of the season, preceding the production of*
> Percy, *had been failures; [John] Home's* Alfred *at Covent*

---

38   More, "Preface to the Tragedies," 30.
39   More, "Preface to the Tragedies," 31.

Garden had been withdrawn after three nights; The Roman Sacrifice *by William Shirley, and [Richard] Cumberland's* Battle of Hastings *at Drury Lane were both unsuccessful. London, ready for a novelty, went wild over* Percy...

With Mr. and Mrs. Garrick, Hannah attended her first London production, sitting in a dark corner of the manager's box.

Later that same evening, she wrote home from Garrick's study:

"He himself puts the pen in my hand, and bids me say that all is just as it should be...Mr. Garrick's kindness has been unceasing."[40]

The title page of the 1778 edition of Hannah More's tragedy, *Percy*, "probably the most successful English verse tragedy of its era."[41]

---

40 Hopkins, *Hannah More,* 78.

41 an assessment from modern playwright, James Armstrong, see: http://armstrongplays.blogspot.com/2016/07/hannah-mores-percy.html, accessed 15 February 2024

Here, it is worthwhile to pause and consider something. To turn the page of history, it assumes, in the bare recitation of dates and events, that Hannah More was always meant to have the triumph she experienced in the staging of *Percy,* and its success.

But such things are never foreordained, and they never unfold as though they were always meant to happen in just the way they did.

Certainly Hannah More, living the journey of her life, could not know her theatrical triumph would be what it became. But she invested much time and labour in working at her craft, aided by a phalanx of those who wished to see her develop and succeed as a playwright, David and Eva Garrick pre-eminent among these friends in the Bluestocking Circle.

Something else must be noted as well. Within four years of the time when her world was broken, as her prospects for marriage fell in ruins about her, More had seen her world mended in ways she could not have foreseen then—supremely in all that the triumph of *Percy* represented. She had become the toast of London, doing what she loved to do, and helped by a husband and wife team in the world of the theatre who had made her one of their own family. By any measure, that was a remarkable turn of events.

Yet following this watershed, resplendent moment there was a sombre reality to come, in something as-yet-unknown: even as More "achieved a triumph never to be repeated," David Garrick was to die "before her next play came on the boards."[42]

A poem she published in tribute to him, one year before his passing, tells the story of her gratitude for a sterling friend and literary mentor—

---

42 Hopkins, *Hannah More,* 78.

Peace!—To his solitude he bears,
The full-blown fame of thirty years;
He hears a nation's praise:
He bears his lib'ral, polish'd mind
His worth, his wit, his sense refin'd;
He bears his grove of Bays.

When others drop the heart-felt tear,
Because this Sun has left his sphere,
And set at highest noon;
I'll drop a tear as warm, as true,
I lov'd his beams, as well as you.
And mourn they're set so soon.

But all in vain his orb he quits,
Still there, in Memory's eye, he sits,
And will, till Time be done:
For he shall shine while Taste survives,
And he shall shine while Genius lives,
A never-setting Sun.[43]

In keeping with her devotion to poetry, and the acclaim of London society for her verse, More wrote another poem in celebration of the things she most admired, and sought after, in the Bluestocking Circle. Indeed, as one source has rightly noted, she "was the chief chronicler, as well as the poet laureate of the blues."[44] Her poem, *The Bas Bleu*, recreated occasions when some of the most gifted men and women in cultured London met—

---

43 *The Works of Miss Hannah More in Prose and Verse* (Cork: 1778), 141-142.
44 Ward and Waller, *The Cambridge History of English Literature*, volume 11, 363.

Hail, Conversation, heav'nly fair,
Thou bliss of life, and balm of care!
Call forth the long-forgotten knowledge,
Of school, of travel, and of college![45]

Evenings of the intellect, in place of the university education More was never able to have, won her keen allegiance. It was a master class, in company with the scholars, writers, and artists she knew in this famous coterie. She relished every minute in their company—

Ah! wherefore wise, if none must hear?
Our intellectual ore must shine,
Not slumber idly in the mine.

Let Education's moral mint
The noblest images imprint;
Let Taste her curious touchstone hold,
To try if standard be the gold…

But 'tis thy commerce, Conversation,
Must give it use by circulation;
That noblest commerce of mankind,
Whose precious merchandize is MIND![46]

And, if More's poem captured scenes so typical of the Bluestocking Circle, her friend Frances Reynolds, the painter whose brother, Sir Joshua Reynolds, crafted fine portraits of

---

45 *The Critical Review, or Annals of* Literature, April 1786 (London: 1786), 267, lines 232-235 of More's poem.

46 Hannah More, *Florio: A Tale, for Fine Gentlemen and Fine Ladies; and The Bas Bleu; or Conversation: Two Poems* (London: 1786), 83.

celebrities of the age, added to this number with a portrait she painted of More herself.

What More's feelings were, as her portrait was painted, were set within a letter home to her family, which reads, in part—

[London, 1780]

Instead of going to Audley Street, where I was invited, I went to Mrs. Reynolds, and sat for my picture. Just as she began to paint, in came Dr. Johnson, who stayed the whole time, and said good things by way of making me look well.[47]

One can well imagine the good-natured banter, and literary badinage, that flew about the room as Reynolds sought to capture More's likeness. Perhaps they talked of Milton and Addison, two of More's favourite poets—or perhaps More asked Johnson what it had been like to invest years of labour in creating his famous *Dictionary*.

One thing seems clear about this occasion: there was much about it that was festive and fortuitous. For the resulting portrait of More shows a young writer at work that caught most, if not all the things More had dreamt of attaining in her younger years, when all that she would know in literary London lay in the future. At her school-desk in Bristol, when she taught young women about art, literature, and the foreign languages she knew so fluently, she hoped that someday, her life might have a place in scenes like those written of in the books she asked her students to read—scenes that she herself had as yet only read about.

---

47 Roberts, *Memoirs…of Hannah More*, 63.

Now, she had a part in scenes like that, in company with fellow artists. Something of all this comes through in the painting Frances Reynolds created.

Hannah More as a professional author and "woman of letters," an 1838 engraving based on Frances Reynolds' portrait of 1780 (from the author's collection)

One telling description of this fine painting, and what it discloses, is given in the book *Brilliant Women: 18th-Century Bluestockings*, the Yale University Press companion book for an acclaimed National Portrait Gallery exhibit in London, from 2008. It states that

> *this painting by Frances Reynolds...attempts to present More as a professional yet genteel author. Quite exceptionally for a woman, she is shown in the act of writing. Her hand is at her temple, indicating that she is lost in thought, and she has the slightly dishevelled look reserved for people of genius...* [48]

As for the composition of the painting, it is noted that

> *the books behind [Hannah More] have large and heavy bindings to indicate the seriousness of their contents, and, by extension, the importance of More's own writing. The dignified library interior deliberately signals the distance between More's setting and a Grub Street hack's garret.* [49]

Here it is fascinating to recall that Samuel Johnson was present when More's portrait was being painted—still further, that in his early London days, Johnson was just the kind of hardscrabble writer the tag "Grub Street hack" implies. In Boswell's famous phrase, Johnson was then *"a mere literary labourer [writing] 'for gain, not glory,' solely to obtain an honest support."*

Seen in Frances Reynolds' painting, however, Hannah More was anything but this, and Johnson himself was there to insure (through animated conversation) that his young friend was seen to best advantage. Last of all, the writers of *Brilliant Women* state that the

---

48 Eger and Peltz, *Brilliant Women*, 77 & 79.

49 Eger and Peltz, *Brilliant Women*, 77 & 79.

pictorial conventions [in Frances Reynolds' painting of More] are not especially innovative; [but] what is new is their use to represent a respectable British 'woman of letters.'[50]

A *woman of letters.* More would have found that phrase deeply gratifying.

The NINE LIVING MUSES of GREAT BRITAIN.

The engraving modelled on Richard Samuel's painting of Hannah More and her compeers in London. Also shown are Elizabeth Linley, Angelica Kauffmann, Elizabeth Montagu, Elizabeth Carter, Catherine Macaulay, Anna Barbauld, Elizabeth Griffith, and Charlotte Lennox. More cannot be definitively identified in this image, but it is tempting to think she is the writer seated farthest to the left side of this image, dated c. 1779.

One event should, fittingly, close this chapter. Taking place just after the midpoint of the 1780s, More met a friend whose role in her life would prove as valuable and meaningful as any friendship she ever made. From that friend, William Wilberforce, an account of that first meeting survives. As he recalled—

---

50 Eger and Peltz, *Brilliant Women*, 77 & 79.

*I went, I think, in 1786 to see [Hannah More], and when
I came into the room, Charles Wesley rose from the table,
around which a numerous party sat at tea, and coming
forwards to me, gave me solemnly his blessing. I was
scarcely ever more affected.*

*Such was the effect of his manner and appearance, that
it altogether overset me, and I burst into tears, unable to
restrain myself.*[51]

Seldom in the page of British history has there more truly
been a meeting of kindred spirits. In the summer of 1787,
and in a letter written from her home in Bath, More spoke of
Wilberforce, and why, as one writer noted, she was "a great
admirer of his character"[52]—

*I find here a great many friends; but those with whom
I have chiefly passed my time are Mr. Wilberforce's family.
That young gentleman's character is one of the most
extraordinary I ever knew for talents, virtue, and piety.*

*It is difficult not to grow wiser and better every time
one converses with him.*[53]

Several humanitarian and cultural milestones flowed from
this storied friendship: in the fields of abolition, education,
literature, and Christian endeavour.

In time to come, none knew the extent and importance
of Hannah More's role in these undertakings better than
Wilberforce. Their collaboration, across many years, made a
great difference for good in British life. For More, Wilberforce

---

51 Wilberforce, *Life of William Wilberforce,* volume one, 248.

52 Thompson, *Hannah* More, 341.

53 Wilberforce, *Life of William Wilberforce,* volume one, 138.

was, in letters, *"my dear friend,"* while he signed letters to her with *"ever your affectionate friend."*

S.C. Wilks, writing in *The Christian Observer,* would say of them—

> *What Wilberforce was among men, Hannah More was among women...*
>
> *They were lovely and pleasant in their lives...two eminent servants of God, whom He was pleased to render an especial blessing to mankind by their writings, their active exertions, and their personal example.*[54]

To be described here, as they were, was a high compliment to both.

In the fifty years before Queen Victoria was crowned, there were few more influential or important figures in the national life of England.

Why this was so will be explored in chapters to follow.

William Wilberforce in 1789, three years after he met Hannah More, a detail of the frontispiece engraving from *The Life of William Wilberforce,* volume one (1838)

---

54 *The Christian Observer,* October 1833 (London: 1833), 632.

CHAPTER FIVE

'In the distress around me'

...the ordinary modern critic [assumes] that all women, in all ages, would have accepted the [idea] that the Byronic sort of romantic passion was the sole concern of their lives...

Women have had a great many other concerns...a great many other convictions.

[And at times,] they have been...blue-stockings keeping salons...

If you had said to Deborah the mother in Israel, or Hypatia the Platonist of Alexandria, or Catherine of Siena, or Joan of Arc, or Isabella of Spain, or Maria Theresa of Austria, or even to Hannah More or Joanna Southcott, that Byronic love was "woman's whole existence," they would all have been very indignant [and] asked in various ways whether there was no such thing as honour, no such thing as duty...no such thing as great studies or great enterprises...[1]

— G.K. CHESTERTON
The Illustrated London News (1931)

---

1   G.K. Chesterton, "On Love," in *The Illustrated London News,* vol. 88 (London: 1931), 720. The epigraph subtitle is from a January 4, 1827 letter Hannah More wrote to John Harford, in Alice Harford, ed., *Annals of the Harford Family* (London: 1909), 105.

*That Hannah More had worked assiduously to
alleviate poverty and to break down the isolation of the
poor is forgotten.*

*She was not…in the least indifferent to the poverty and misery
of [what were then called] the lower orders. She endeavoured to
make their distress known through her parliamentary friends,
and by her personal efforts to alleviate it…* [2]

— **M.G. JONES** (1952)

Benjamin Franklin, most certainly, was well aware of
Hannah More.[3]

On 9 March, 1787, he hosted a lecture in which her poetry,
and the inspiration for her philanthropy, were described by
his friend and fellow founding father, Benjamin Rush. With
a suasive plea for the importance of "sympathy in society," or
"sensibility," Rush told Franklin and the other guests gathered
in his Philadelphia home—

*It will not be necessary here to dwell upon all the
advantages of this principle in human nature. It will be
sufficient to observe, that it is the vice-regent of the divine
benevolence in our world. It is intended to bind up all the
wounds which sin and death have made among mankind.
It has founded hospitals, erected charity schools, and
connected the extremes of happiness and misery together
in every part of the globe.*

---

2   M.G. Jones, *Hannah More* (Cambridge: Cambridge University Press, 1952), 235-236.

3   in 1807, The Library Company of Philadelphia, founded by Franklin, listed seven works by Hannah More,
including two published in Franklin's lifetime: *Remarks on the Speech of Monsieur Dupont* (1793); *The
Works of Hannah More*, 8 vols (London: 1801); *Strictures on the Modern System of Female Education*,
2 vols (London: 1799); *Essays on Various Subjects* (London: 1778); and *Sacred Dramas* (London: 1782).

Above all, sensibility is the sentinel of the moral faculty.
It decides upon the quality of the actions, before they reach
that divine principle of the soul.

It is, of itself, to use the words of an elegant female
poet, [Hannah More]—

A hasty moral—a sudden sense of right.[4]

And More herself, along with her sister Patty, admired the celebrated Dr. Franklin. We learn of this from William Wilberforce, who visited Barley Wood with his wife and their two daughters, in October 1813, for a stay that they "very much enjoyed."

On 20 October, Wilberforce wrote about the Mores' interest in Franklin—

After breakfast, Miss Patty showed me her book of
handwriting of eminent men, many of them written on
purpose [to the More family,] and very curious.

[They included:] Edward VI, Queen Mary (William
III), Pope, Swift, Bolingbroke, and Atterbury. All the
Admirals, General Wolfe, etc. All the politicians [were
there as well:] Washington, Franklin, Prior, Priestley,
Burke, Fox, Pitt, Sir Joshua Reynolds. A beautiful letter
from Horsley, [and others from] Voltaire, Rousseau,
[and] Blackstone.[5]

---

4   Benjamin Rush, *An Enquiry Into the Effects of Public Punishment Upon Criminals and Upon Society: Read in the Society for Promoting Political Enquiries, Convened at the House of His Excellency, Benjamin Franklin, Esquire, in Philadelphia, March 9th, 1787* (Philadelphia: 1787), 6. Here, Rush quotes More's 1782 poem, "Sensibility." See *Sacred Dramas…To which Is Added Sensibility, A Poem*, by Miss Hannah More, (Dublin: 1784), 262.

5   Wilberforce, *Life of William Wilberforce*, vol. 4, 148-149.

By the time this diary entry was written, More had known Wilberforce for over twenty-six years. And the late 1780s were crucial years, for, as one biographer said—

There was a common subject, as well as common friends, to unite the two. In the spring of 1787 they met in London. When Wilberforce had publicly announced his intention of bringing the abolition of the slave trade before Parliament, Hannah More had written to a correspondent that she was absorbed in the subject,—

"This most important cause has very much occupied my thoughts this summer. The young gentleman who has embarked in it with the zeal of an apostle, has been much with me, and engaged all my little interest and all my affections in it."[6]

Even as More and Wilberforce sought the abolition of the British slave trade, More had been drawn, increasingly, to the evangelical wing of the Church of England. Wilberforce was there already, thanks largely to the influence of his spiritual mentor, John Newton.

As S.J. Skedd has noted, More had always been devout in her Anglican faith; but in the person of Newton she, like Wilberforce, found both a friend, and a wing of the Church, where she felt most at home—

Throughout her life [Skedd observes,] More steadfastly adhered to the orthodox trinitarian doctrines and episcopalian structure of the Church of England, yet in the 1780s her faith was both energized and transformed by

---

6   J.C. Colquhoun, "Wilberforce and His Contemporaries," in *The Christian Observer,* Nov 1864 (London: 1864), 838. Italics added.

evangelicalism...She sought out new acquaintances who shared her religious outlook and who became close friends and correspondents...[7]

More also read books popular among Evangelicals within the Church of England. Of these, Newton's *Cardiphonia, or, Utterance of the Heart*, had "deeply impressed" her. She wrote: "it is full of vital, experimental religion."[8]

Thus Newton "became perhaps her most important spiritual counsellor."[9]

This led, in time, to an important alliance of philanthropy that bridged two wings of the Anglican fold. For "together with her influential backers in the Anglican hierarchy, namely Robert Lowth, Josiah Tucker, George Horne, and Beilby Porteus," More's evangelical friends "urged her to use her talents and connections to further two evangelically inspired campaigns: abolition of slavery and reformation of manners." And in order to follow through on this, she moved, as it were, to a new base of operations. She "spent less time in London" in favour of Cowslip Green, Somerset, where she'd built a cottage in 1784.[10]

Earlier meetings in More's life now came into play as she took up her philanthropic mantle. In 1776 More met Charles and Margaret Middleton, "whose home at Teston, Kent, became the headquarters of the parliamentary campaign to abolish the slave trade in the late 1780s." And More's letters at this time reveal that "she and her fellow abolitionists canvassed MPs by letter and in person." At one such gathering, in April 1789, she showed the company present Thomas Clarkson's famous cross

---

7   Skedd, "Hannah More."

8   Roberts, *Memoirs...of Hannah More*, v. 1, 3rd ed., (1835), 188. "I like it prodigiously," More also said. "I have found nothing but rational and consistent piety."

9   Skedd, "Hannah More."

10 Skedd, "Hannah More."

section of a slave ship. John Newton's eye-witness accounts of atrocities inherent in the west African slave trade helped shape her abolitionist sympathies as well, and S.J. Skedd has stated his testimony "doubtless inspired her poetical contribution to the campaign." That poem was titled "Slavery," which "she wrote in great haste in January 1788 to maximize publicity" for William Wilberforce's first bill calling for the abolition of the British slave trade.[11]

More's poem was a powerful fusillade in verse, in which "she declared that the nation was shamed and compromised by its participation in the slave trade." In clarion tones, she urged her fellow Britons "to abandon such hypocrisy"[12]—

> *Shall Britain, where the soul of Freedom reigns*
> *Forge chains for others she herself disdains?*
> *Forbid it, Heaven! O let the nations know*
> *The liberty she loves she will bestow...*
>
> *What page of human annals can record*
> *A deed so bright as human rights restor'd?*[13]

Lines like these from More's poem derived much of their potency from the way they seemed to echo, in counterpoint, James Thomson's "Rule, Britannia" (composed in 1740). The refrain of this widely popular verse declared—

> *Rule, Britannia, rule the waves!*
> *Britons never will be slaves!*[14]

---

11 Skedd, "Hannah More."

12 Skedd, "Hannah More."

13 Hannah More, *Slavery: A Poem* (London: 1788), 18, a citation of lines 251-254 and 259-260 from More's poem.

14 *The Poetical Works of James Thomson* (London: 1849), 603.

More's commitment to abolition never wavered or waned. During "the long struggle to secure parliamentary abolition of both the trade and slavery itself; she subscribed to the African Institution, which replaced the Society for the Abolition of the Slave Trade in 1807." And also, in the late 1820s, she was "nominated to the committee of the Female Anti-Slavery Society at Clifton in Bristol."[15] All told, More's abolitionist commitment spanned nearly fifty years, covering a span from the mid-1780s through to passage of the bill abolishing slavery, which took place just before her death in 1833.

* * *

If More's meeting Wilberforce, and the vanguard dedicated to the abolition of slavery in the British Empire was a watershed event in the mid-1780s, one meeting just before that time seemingly held promise; but ultimately proved a false hope, and painful episode. For More, it was an event that drew forth her sympathy and generosity. Yet at the same time, it would show that she could be naïve, proud, and stubborn.

So to the story of her dealings with Ann Yearsley.

* * *

In the autumn of 1784, when More "was at the height of her literary and social fame in London," she returned to Bristol after visiting Elizabeth Montagu. It was then she was told about "an unlettered and wretchedly poor Bristol milkwoman," with a family of five children and a husband of "little capacity."[16] On hearing that this woman, Ann Yearsley,

---

15 Skedd, "Hannah More."
16 Jones, *Hannah More*, 73.

despite trying circumstances, had written verse which showed much promise, More's natural sympathy was aroused. A poor family with five children: was that so very different from the hardscrabble upbringing she had known? No, it wasn't.

More made further inquiries, read samples of Yearsley's verse, and learned that she—to all appearances—was "a deserving case," and a writer wrongly "buried in obscurity." So with the best of intentions, More decided to don the role of a patron, and take up Yearsley's case: she would "raise a subscription" from her literary and aristocratic friends to publish Yearsley's verse, and garner funds that could relieve her family's financial need.[17]

Telling Yearsley of this plan, More's idea must have seemed a godsend—a lifeline for a family that had struggled so much. For much of the next thirteen months, More became a teacher once again, and instructed Yearsley in "the rules of common composition," and other aspects of the poet's craft. She spent much time "translating and correcting" Yearsley's poems, and she wrote over "a thousand pages of letters appealing for subscriptions." Among the list of those to whom she wrote were no less than nine duchesses, which, apart from the wideness of More's charitable inquiries, showed the extent of "her own popularity with the great."[18]

And before she quite knew what was happening, More's inquiries led to Yearsley receiving invitations to meet the Duchesses of Beaufort and Rutland, Countess Spencer, and Elizabeth Montagu. Yearsley also received a handsome gift of books from the Duchess of Devonshire, and other gifts of money from prominent ladies. Elizabeth Montagu agreed to become a co-trustee with More of the funds that were raised.

---

17 Jones, *Hannah More*, 73.

18 Jones, *Hannah More*, 73.

Yet despite this kind decision from two members of the Bluestocking Circle, Montagu did voice a word of caution to More. She had learned from experience that sometimes, well-intentioned assistance like this sadly loosed "a little legion of demons, vanity, luxury, idleness and pride," which might "enter the cottage the moment poverty vanished."[19]

More listened, but decided to press on.

When Yearsley's first volume of poems was published, it won modest but noteworthy interest in London, and much acclaim in Bristol. Yearsley singled More out for praise as "the bright Instructress and Soother of the Soul," while Elizabeth Montagu was addressed in a grateful Prefatory Letter for the book.

Not long after, however, things began to sour.

The not-inconsiderable capital sum of £360 had been raised, one now worth close to £50,000. Managed rightly, the trustees of her subscription fund understood that this could easily provide "a permanent income" for Yearsley and her family. So they "invested the money in a 3 percent stock," and assumed powers under what was called a Trust Deed "to expend, apply and dispose of the principal and interest in such way and manner as they shall think fit for the benefit and advantage of Mrs. Yearsley and her children."[20]

However well-meant this was, and however prudent it might have been from a purely financial standpoint, Yearsley's pride was greatly wounded when she received a letter, along with this Trust Deed, asking for her and her husband's signature. "I felt," she was to write later, "as a mother deemed unworthy of the tuition and care of her family."[21]

---

19 Jones, *Hannah More*, 74.

20 Jones, *Hannah More*, 74-75.

21 Jones, *Hannah More*, 75.

This was all quite understandable, and looking through extant source accounts of what followed, one wishes some sort of reproachment could have been achieved.

But such was not to be.

Indignant, Yearsley asked to meet with More's sisters Mary and Elizabeth in Bristol, since More was herself then in London. Somehow, they persuaded Yearsley to sign the deed, and one would have thought there was an end to the contretemps.

But when More returned to Bristol in 1785, Yearsley and More had a stormy meeting, likely brought on by simmering resentment on Yearsley's part for what she had been led into.

Biographer M.G. Jones summarised it all—

Angry recriminations [then] ensued. Mrs. Yearsley demanded the return of her manuscripts. Miss More, embarrassed, informed her that they had been burnt at the printers. Unforgiveable words were spoken on both sides, and Hannah More, obstinately refusing to modify the deed, and admit Mrs. Yearsley as a joint-trustee, resigned from the Trust and refused further communication with her.[22]

As things unravelled further, friends on both sides took up arms, in print and among those sympathetic to either side. Public opinion and media sources alike entered the fray.

Then, Yearsley severed any remote hope of resolution when she publicly attacked More's character, alleging that More intended to abscond with the funds of her Trust to buy a home in the country. Adding cruel insult to injury, she then revived the story of More's broken engagement, and made a great point of saying that More got what she deserved as a "slighted

---

22 Jones, *Hannah More*, 75.

prude."[23] Whatever else More's failures in this might have been, Yearsley's conduct was beyond the pale. More could have responded in kind, but she didn't. In fact, she made no answer of any kind, in person or public, to Yearsley's bitter invective.

But More's letters to friends said much about the anger and humiliation she felt. The ingratitude of it all seems to have hurt most.

Eventually, the Trust was ended, the now £600 which had been accumulated turned over,[24] and Yearsley's financial security (as had been feared) was eventually lost.

Sadly she died well-nigh penniless, and "shadowed by domestic griefs," in 1806.[25]

As for More, many hard lessons were learned. And apart from any understandable naïveté, or impulsive good intentions at the outset of it all, she found that her stubbornness and pride were things she needed to guard against. Early in life she had shown commendable fortitude and determination in making an entrée in literary London. She had achieved hard-won success, and garnered wide acceptance among the cultured elite.

Yet the Yearsley episode revealed a vein of pride unsuspected. Chastened, she was no less resolved to find outlets for her philanthropy, born of deeply held faith,

She had seen her failings up close; but she would move forward, trying to be wiser for her experiences. It wasn't long before something new, and far more promising, developed.

* * *

---

23 Jones, *Hannah More*, 75.

24 Hopkins, *Hannah More*, 124.

25 Hopkins, *Hannah More*, 125.

In the autumn of 1789, William Wilberforce and his sister Sarah visited the Mores at Cowslip Green. During his stay, Wilberforce, fond of long walks in the country, was urged to go see the picturesque Cheddar cliffs. Biographer J.C. Colquhoun, describing this, said Wilberforce's return from that excursion was anything but what was expected. He'd seen much "distress and ignorance" among the poor families in and around Cheddar, and appalled by what he'd seen, he told the Mores that "he could not eat nor sleep after his visit, till a scheme for their improvement was prepared."[26]

His concern found voice in a phrase that later became famous: *"Miss Hannah More, something must be done for Cheddar."*

So a "method or possibility of assisting them was discussed, till a late hour." It was at length "decided in a few words," when Wilberforce told Hannah and Patty More—

"If you will be at the trouble, I will be at the expense."[27]

So began the work of educational reform, in the creation of schools and kindred philanthropies for the people near Hannah More's home. With funding from Wilberforce (and Henry Thornton as well), she and her sister Patty established a school at Cheddar which "quickly attracted 300 pupils." The sisters then "set up a second school, at Shipham; [and] within a decade, they were running twelve schools scattered across the Mendips." Heretofore, nothing like this had ever existed in Cheddar, or these other locales, nor had there been anything like them in all of England. As one biographer described it—

In keeping with their objective 'to train up the lower classes to habits of industry and virtue' the sisters also started evening classes for adults, weekday classes for girls to

26 Colquhoun, "Wilberforce and His Contemporaries," 839.
27 Thompson, *Hannah More,* 380-381.

learn how to sew, knit, and spin, and a number of women's friendly societies, where the virtues of cleanliness, decency, and Christian behaviour were inculcated.

From 1791 annual picnics were organized for the schools and societies, rewards for good conduct were handed out, and incentives of gingerbread or [one penny] were offered to the children for regular attendance at church.[28]

Over time, what began so modestly with Wilberforce's 1789 visit led to something in English life that had a wide influence in the British Isles—and beyond.

For, "at the height of their prosperity," the schools the More sisters established, "were attended by about 1,000 children." And by 1824, when the sisters had long since "delegated the work [to younger hands], there were 620 children in the remaining schools."[29]

In her life, More wrote best-selling books, which brought her fame. But her work to better the lives of the poor, and her collaboration with Wilberforce in these endeavours, set streams in motion that continue—to the present day.

For a Hannah More school still exists now, near where she lived.

---

28 Skedd, "Hannah More."
29 Stott, *Hannah* More, 103.

CHAPTER SIX

The Revolution in France

Hannah More, by all means.[1]

— **EDMUND BURKE** to Frances Crewe (circa 1794)

The Head beneath the Feet; they wear the Crown,
...we see the World turn'd upside down.[2]

— from **WHIG AND TORY** (1713)

But this ignis fatuus [will-o'-the-wisp] of liberty and universal
brotherhood, which the French are madly pursuing, with the
insignia of freedom in one hand, and the bloody bayonet in the
other, has bewitched your senses...

You are gazing at a meteor raised by the vapours of vanity,
which these wild and infatuated wanderers are pursuing to
their destruction...You mistake it for a heaven-born light,

---

1   Fitzwilliam and Bourke, eds., *Correspondence of the Right Honourable Edmund Burke,* volume 4 (London: Rivington, 1844), 259. See Stott, *Hannah More,* 149: "[*Remarks on the speech of Monsieur*] *Dupont* continued to make waves; Burke recommended it to Anne Crewe, the political hostess."

2   from *Whig and Tory...Poems Upon All Remarkable Occurrences,* second edition, (London: E. Curill, 1713), 9.

which leads to the perfection of human freedom, [but] you will,
should you join in the mad pursuit, soon discover that it will...
plunge you in deep and inevitable ruin.³

— **HANNAH MORE**, *Remarks on the speech of*
Monsieur Dupont: Made in the National Convention of
France (April 1793)

Following the Fall of the Bastille, and the rise of Revolutionary France, More took on a deeply important, influential, yet unexpected and ground-breaking role as an advocate of the established order in England. She defended England's traditions and way of government, in a time when the writings of Thomas Paine were disruptive, and threats of an importation of revolution from France were very real. At the same time, her books had been bestsellers, and helped to shape public opinion. She could make good use of that stature now.

During this crucial season of her writing life, More's friendships with Edmund Burke and William Wilberforce were underscored. She championed principles and views of what was unfolding in France kindred to those they articulated and published.

Indeed, even as More's forty-eight page text, *Remarks on the Speech of Monsieur Dupont,* proceeded "to make waves, Burke recommended it to Anne Crewe, the political hostess."⁴

In her writings she, like Burke and Wilberforce, urged her fellow Britons to work for better days "within the existing

---

3 Hannah More, *Remarks on the speech of Monsieur Dupont: Made in the National Convention of France* (London: Cadell, 1793), 6-7.

4 *Correspondence of Edmund Burke,* vii, ed. P.J. Marshall and J.A. Woods (Cambridge and Chicago, 1968), 426. See also Anne Stott, *Hannah More: The First Victorian* (Oxford: 2003), 149. See also Stott, *Hannah More,* 148: *Dupont* "was published by Cadell on 1 April [1793] with More's name on the title page." Two weeks later it went into a second edition. Soon after, it was translated into French. Before the year 1793 closed, a third edition was published in Dublin. In 1794 it was printed in America by Weld and Greenough in Boston.

social and political order,"[5] not throw away all that was good in English society (by emulating France's revolutionary purge of the *Ancien Régime,* or old order,) as much needed reforms were sought. Decrying "this desolating system," she said—

One instance of the prevailing cant [in France] may suffice, where a hundred might be adduced; and it is not the most exceptionable. To demolish every existing law and establishment; to destroy the fortunes and ruin the principles of every country into which they are carrying their destructive arms and their frantic doctrines; to untie or cut asunder every bond which holds society together; to impose their own arbitrary shackles where they succeed, and to demolish everything where they fail.[6]

More's book was modestly sized, and a long pamphlet really; but it packed a powerful rhetorical message. She sought to rally Britons to the ramparts of ordered liberty, and repel the "desolating system" that the leaders of revolutionary France, with their sympathizers in England, would put in place. There was no more urgent task for her to take up in 1793.

But, to begin, a start must be made with the fall of the Bastille...

* * *

More told something of that story, and her own thoughts at the time, in the pages of *Remarks on the Speech of Monsieur Dupont.* Looking back to 14 July 1789, and the portentous news that crossed over the channel from France, she'd written—

---

5   Anne Mellor, *Mothers of the Nation* (Bloomington: 2000), 13-14.

6   Hannah More, *Remarks*, 40.

What English heart did not exult at the demolition of the Bastille?

What lover of his species did not triumph in the warm hope, that one of the finest countries in the world would soon be one of the most free? Popery and despotism, though chained by the gentle influence of Louis the Sixteenth, had actually slain their thousands. Little was it then imagined that anarchy and atheism, the monsters who were about to succeed them, would soon slay their ten thousands...

Who, I say, that had a head to reason, or a heart to feel, did not glow with the hope, that from the ruins of tyranny...a beautiful and finely-framed edifice would in time have been constructed, and that ours would not have been the only country in which the patriots' fair idea of well-understood liberty...might be realized?[7]

Then, a little over one year later, on 1 November 1790, Edmund Burke published his classic cri de coeur, *Reflections on the Revolution in France*. In 1805, More wrote at length about the seismic impact of this book, and what it meant to her. It was a book, she said—

which, to the rhetoric of ancient Greece, and the patriot spirit of ancient Rome, unites the warmth of contemporary interest, and the dearness of domestic feeling; in which, to the vigour of a rapid and indignant eloquence, is superadded the widest extent of general knowledge, and the deepest political sagacity;—a work [as Milton has said,]

---

7   More, *Remarks*, 7-8.

Where old experience doth attain,
To something like prophetic strain:[8]

> *a work which first unlocked the hidden springs of*
> *revolutionary principles; dived into the complicated and*
> *almost unfathomable depths of political, literary, and*
> *moral mischief; penetrated the dens and labyrinths, where*
> *anarchy, [which] long had been mysteriously brooding,*
> *at length hatched her baleful progeny; [and] laid bare to*
> *view the dark recesses, where sacrilege, murder, treason,*
> *regicide, and atheism, were engendered.*
>
> *If[one] would hear the warning voice which first sounded*
> *the alarm in the ears of Britain, and which, by rousing to*
> *a sense of danger, kindled the spirit to repel it...peruse Mr.*
> Burke's Reflections on the French Revolution.[9]

More's fulsome praise for Burke's manifesto has added weight, when it is recalled that their political views diverged widely about the American War of Independence. Late in life, she told an American visitor, John Griscom, that "she had been much opposed to America during the revolutionary struggle."[10]

In the run-up to, and during the War of Independence, Burke repeatedly delivered "fiery pro-American speeches."[11] As one who "loved the King,"[12] this grieved and irritated

---

8   John Milton, *Poems Upon Several Occasions* (London: 1791), 93, lines 173-174 of the poem *Il Penseroso*, which reads in the original text: "Till old experience do attain/To something like prophetic strain." Given the different wording in line 173, it would appear that More is quoting from memory.

9   Hannah More, *Hints*, volume two, 202-203.

10 John Griscom, *A Year in Europe: A Journal of Observations*, volume one, (New York: 1824), 124. See also Robert Hole, *Selected Writings of Hannah More*, (Oxford: 2021), 239: "More was a bitter opponent of the American rebels and her relations with Burke cooled for a while this issue," also page 242: "Burke had been a close friend of More, but the pro-American stance in his *Speech on Conciliation with America* (22 March 1775) alienated her. His *Reflections [on the Revolution with France]*, was, of course, to restore him to favour."

11 Stott, *Hannah More*, 66.

12 R.B. Johnson, ed., *The Letters of Hannah More* (London: 1926), 16.

More, who cast him in her poem, *The Bas Bleu,* as Hortensius, "whose obsession with politics had made him 'Apostate now from social Wit.'"[13] As one scholar noted, "More had come to disagree with much of Burke's politics, in particular to deplore the violence of his language, [when] he was attacking the government's American policy."[14]

It was some time before their warmth of friendship was renewed.

That reproachment began at a London gathering in 1784, hosted by Elizabeth Vesey. Burke was present, and afterward More wrote: "I had a great deal of chat with Mr. Burke; and so lively, and so foolish, and so good humoured was he, and so like the agreeable Mr. Burke I once knew and admired, that I soon forgot his malefactions, and how often I had been in a passion with him for some of his speeches."[15]

Two years later, on 17 February 1786, all was right again. Following a "small party…of which Mr. Burke was one," during which "he appeared to be very low in health and spirits," More spent a good deal of the evening with him. Thereafter, she wrote: "he talked to me with a kindness which revived my old affection for him."[16] How complete this reproachment was may be seen in More's 1805 assessment of Burke's *Reflections*—

It was the peculiar felicity of this great, but often misguided man, to light at last upon a subject, not only singularly congenial to the turn of his genius, but of his temper also. The accomplished scholar, the wit of vivid imagination, the powerful orator rich in imagery, and abounding in

---

13 Stott, *Hannah More*, 66.

14 Stott, *Hannah More*, 131.

15 James Prior, *A Life of Edmund Burke* (London: 1891), 273.

16 Prior, *Edmund Burke*, 273.

classic allusion, had been previously displayed to equal advantage in his other works...He had never wanted genius—it would be hard to say he had ever wanted integrity—but he had often wanted that consistency which is so necessary to make the parts of a great character cohere to each other. A patriot, yet not unfrequently seeming to act against the interests of his country—a senator, never heard without admiration, but sometimes without effect; a statesman, often embarrassing his adversaries, without always serving his friends, or advancing his cause.

But in this concentration of his powers, this union of his faculties and feelings, the Reflections on the French Revolution, *his impetuosity found objects which rendered its exercise not only pardonable, but laudable.*

That [rhetorical] violence, which had sometimes exhausted itself, unworthily in party, or unkindly on individuals, now found full scope for its exercise, in the unrestrained atrocities of a nation, hostile not only to Britain, but to human nature itself. A nation not offending from the ordinary impulse of the passions, which might have been repelled by the ordinary means of resistance, but "committing the oldest crimes the newest kind of way,"[17] *and uniting the bloody inventions of the most selfish ambition...*[18]

For More, and Burke, there was something poignant in their renewal of friendship.

One scholar, J.G.A. Pocock, has said Burke "remained a lonely and distrusted figure" through his last decade (1787-97),

---

17 "Revel the night, rob, murder, and commit/The oldest sins the newest kind of way." – William Shakespeare, *Henry IV, Part 2*, act 4, scene 5.

18 Hannah More, *Hints*, volume two, 202-204.

and counter-revolutionary activists in the 1790s "relied less on Burke for their polemics than on William Paley, Hannah More, and other [writers] deep in Whig and Tory tradition."[19]

Whilst Burke became something of a pariah, More kept her respected place in society.

William Wilberforce confirmed the extent of Burke's unpopularity: "I had peculiar pleasure in his dinners with me," Wilberforce remembered. "He was a great man—*I never could understand how he grew to be at one time so entirely neglected*."[20]

By 1805, when More paid tribute to the literary importance of Burke's *Reflections,* and sought to honour his memory, she voiced deep concern with what the French wished to pull down (for the threat of Napoleon conquering England was still a very real one) and what his regime wished to put in its place. As she had written: "*dark recesses, where sacrilege, murder, treason, regicide, and atheism, were engendered*."

It was like the "fire and rolling smoke" of Milton's pandemonium, or the cautionary parable G.K. Chesterton wrote long years later, amid a time of unreasoning violence, when bombings by anarchists roiled Edwardian England—

Some people...pulled the lamp-post down because they wanted the electric light; some because they wanted old iron; some because they wanted darkness, because their deeds were evil. Some thought it not enough of a lamp-post, some too much; some acted because they wanted to smash municipal machinery; some because they wanted to smash something. And there is war in the night, no man knowing whom he strikes.[21]

---

19 Kevin Gilmartin, "Counter-revolutionary culture," in Pamela Clemit, ed., *The Cambridge Companion to British Literature of the French Revolution in the 1790s* (Cambridge: 2011), 131.

20 Wilberforce, *The Life of William Wilberforce,* v. 1, 159.

21 G.K. Chesterton, *Heretics* (London: 1905), 23. Italics added.

There were passages much like this in More's *Remarks on the Speech of Monsieur Dupont*. One section, in particular, drives this point home forcibly, evoking the Reign of Terror—

Little would a simple stranger, uninitiated in this new and surprising dialect, uninstructed by the political lexicographers of modern France, imagine that the peaceful terms of fellow-citizen and of brother, the winning offer of freedom and happiness, and the warm embrace of fraternity, were only watch-words, by which they, in effect,

Cry havoc,
And let slip the dogs of war.[22]

Scholar Robert Hole has rightly said that Burke's *Reflections on the Revolution in France* "sought to define a conservative set of values."[23] It did much to warn people in England of the dangers inherent in radical principles, and consequences they might lead to.

The same was true of More's *Remarks on the Speech of Monsieur Dupont*.

In it, she made an important, influential "contribution to the pamphlet literature of the Revolution." In the process also, she began a philanthropic effort. Her tract "was sold for the benefit of the exiled French priests in England,"[24] and she never received a farthing for it. Ultimately, the tract's sales garnered substantial, much needed funds.[25]

---

22 More, *Remarks*, 41. Here, More quotes line Shakespeare's *Julius Caesar*: Act 3, Scene 1, line 273.

23 Hole, Robert, "Hannah More on Literature and Propaganda, 1788–1799." History 85, no. 280 (2000): 613. http://www.jstor.org/stable/24425940.

24 Jones, *Hannah More*, 137.

25 Stott, *Hannah More*, 148. More's tract raised £240, or £29,000 today, slightly less than $38,000.

More used her pen to bolster the realm, amid war, and she aided refugees. For many Britons, men and women alike, she was a literary light and pioneer. Proof of it all came from a friend who well understood the good service she had done.

Not for nothing had Edmund Burke said to Frances Crewe, at this time—

"Hannah More, by all means."

CHAPTER SEVEN

Two Times of Controversy

She was, however, unable to avoid the interview...having once broken the ice, Macaulay was resolute for an explanation. Hannah More cannot be acquitted of some duplicity in her dealings with him...[26]

— VISCOUNTESS KNUTSFORD (1900)

...she may have won a moral victory over the Blagdon affair but her character, charitable works, and faith were vilified on a scale perhaps unprecedented for a woman...[27]

— S.J. SKEDD (2014)

As the 1790s turned to the 1800s, Hannah More was embroiled in two controversies: one concerning her immediate family, and the second, her reputation amid a time that drew national attention and prominence.

---

26 Viscountess Knutsford, *The Life and Letters of Zachary Macaulay* (London: 1900), 101.

27 Skedd, "Hannah More."

In the summer of 1795, a young Scot named Zachary Macaulay, the Governor of Sierra Leone, met More and her sisters when he was home on leave from the newly-fledged colony for former slaves in Africa. He was, as More knew well, a trusted colleague of William Wilberforce, Henry Thornton, and other philanthropists within the Clapham Circle.

At Thornton's behest, Macaulay set out to visit More, keenly interested in the schools she and her sisters had created. Once he'd arrived, More, for her part, was no less interested in meeting a young man "who had sacrificed so much" for the sons and daughters of Africa. During his visit, Macaulay met Selina Mills, a pretty teacher at the Park Street school, then in her late twenties. And for some years, she'd been a close friend of the More sisters.[28]

Macaulay and Selina Mills fell in love quickly, and he "reached an understanding with her."[29] It was then that Hannah More noticed this, and something Macaulay never expected took place. Unknowingly, he had entered a facet of the More sisters' lives where they wished to have no intruders. The warm welcome he had at first received turned to something quite the reverse, as he was soon to learn. Near the end of 1795, he stayed for several days in the More sisters' home in Bath. Selina Mills was also there, as it was the time of the Christmas holidays. Here Hannah More, "correctly interpreting some unguarded expressions on his first visit, had guessed at his feelings."[30] However, she was "reluctant to discuss the matter."

Yet when Macaulay insisted, More stated that "Selina was indifferent to him." This wasn't so, and "duplicitous; the truth

28 Stott, *Hannah* More, 194.

29 Stott, *Hannah* More, 194.

30 Stott, *Hannah* More, 194.

was she feared for [her sister] Patty's happiness should she lose her young friend to a man they hardly knew."[31]

Confused by all this, and confounded, Macaulay made ready to leave. It must have been a strained parting with the More sisters themselves (who had doubtless surmised what Hannah had), and the thought must have entered his mind that he might not be able to say much, if anything, to Selina as he left. That hurt deeply.

Yet as he passed downstairs to exit, and board the carriage that awaited him, he saw Selina in a side room, alone, and "weeping bitterly." In a thrice he was at her side, and as he sought to console her, he knew for certain what she felt. They both loved each other.

He could but stay a few moments; but as he left for the carriage that had arrived he, and she, could carry the knowledge of their declaration to each other, come what may. They'd need of that, for the More sisters' home was now one he left in turmoil.[32]

But this begs the question: why would More (and her sisters) act and feel as they did? Here, a recollection from Wilberforce's wife Barbara sheds light. For Patty More, it seems,

had endured a very painful trial, having relinquished an attachment very strong on her part, & which was mutual, in order to gratify her Sisters, who for some cause which I could never learn, could not endure her becoming the Wife of the individual for which she felt this decided predilection: her wishes were sacrificed to gratify her family, but the struggle was long and severe.[33]

---

31   Stott, *Hannah* More, 194-195.

32   Stott, *Hannah* More, 195.

33   Robin Furneaux, *William Wilberforce* (London: 1974), 171.

The upshot of what Barbara Wilberforce remembered is plain enough: at her sisters' behest—a painful demand that would brook no denial—Patty renounced cherished hopes for matrimony. Now, something very like that scenario was playing out again in the lives of the More sisters, save that Selina Mills was a surrogate sister, and not a blood relation.

As Anne Stott has noted perceptively—

the common factor in the two narratives is the possessive closing of ranks against marriage, seen as the mortal enemy of their special relationship. It was a breaking of the fellowship, a rift in the warm solidarity they had built up against a world all too ready to mock and despise single women.[34]

In appointing Selina Mills to run the Park Street school in 1789, the More sisters made her an "heir" to their hard-fought-for legacy, a unique position of trust—and a welcome into a very exclusive circle—which they alone had occupied heretofore.

To forsake that place, to leave their school, and leave their company—as someone who amounted to another younger sister—was for them highly disruptive. Macaulay, though first welcomed as a friend who'd won the trust of Wilberforce and Thornton, came to be deeply resented as a threat to what the More sisters had created for themselves—and what they saw as Selina Mills' future. For her to break away meant the ruin of many carefully placed plans.

Such might well have been (and was) a selfish, insular perspective; but few things in the More sisters' experience had ever threatened their sense of the way things were to be in such

---

34 Stott, *Hannah* More, 194.

a direct way. For so many years, they had thought, and spoken, with what was essentially "one voice" as a family. Over time, that mindset had become ossified and deeply entrenched, in ways not fully understood until a perceived threat to it all emerged.

Then, a flood of highly-charged emotion came to the fore, and seemingly all on a sudden—catching others unaware in its troubled wake.

Strong notions of what members of a family might, or might not do, ran powerfully in this era of history. Obtaining "family consent" for various matters was a pervasive thing. Often, it was something not given, or very easily granted.

Many did not question such a custom, or found it hard to break free of it.

All their lives, the More sisters stood together as a very self-contained, self-sufficient unit. All their lives they had made their way in a world where opportunities for women were highly limited. They had flourished, where few succeeded. That brought a mixture of pride, stubborn, resolute togetherness—and an all-encompassing, shared sense of purpose that was deeply felt and personal. Such traits can be a great strength, as in the Bristol school the More sisters created; but as is so often the case, great strengths can also become (if one isn't careful) a source of weakness, or troubled consequences in certain circumstances—as here.

And for all the times such a close bond could be felt as "confining," which it surely was at times among siblings; it was also extremely close and tight-knit—in ways others would find hard to fathom. Those who have known a family comprised solely of very close sisters will have some idea of how close and tight-knit such kinship can be.

To be admitted to such a family, and the prized, guarded fortress of this home, and then want to leave that family, was always going to be fraught, or seen as a betrayal, no matter how acceptable, polite, or solicitous a prospective suitor was, or whatever the reason for leaving might be. The five More sisters knew *they* would never leave their family circle—how could Selina Mills do so? And how, with what Patty More had given up, and what Hannah More had endured in her broken prospects for marriage—how could Selina (who may well have known about all this) ever think of leaving—the bare prospect of which dredged up a whole host of unpleasant and painful memories?

In the event, it was some time before anything like a resolution took place. Patty More made things especially difficult. A visit to Selina to try and find an understanding failed, as she spoke a great deal, and listened very little. Macaulay tried to reach an understanding with Patty, but in a moment of understandable frustration over the More sisters' duplicity and high-handedness, he said something meant to wound, and it did. Perhaps, he told Patty, "those women who possessed the greatest share of intrinsic worth did not seem to possess that degree of estimation in the eyes of men which they merited."[35]

Macaulay essentially told Patty to her face that, given their treatment of him and Selina, she and her sisters were unworthy of the regard in which many held them. He had called them out as deceitful hypocrites.

Meantime, Macaulay's return to Sierra Leone could not be delayed any longer. On 23 February 1796, he took ship from Portsmouth, not to return for three years. During that time, he had to solace himself with letters from Selina, which sometimes did not arrive for months after they were written.[36]

---

35 Knutsford, *Life and Letters of Zachary Macaulay*, 103.

36 Stott, *Hannah* More, 197.

Resigning his position at Sierra Leone in 1799, Macaulay was at last able to return home. Once in England, he was appointed a Secretary of the Sierra Leone Company (established to foster equitable trade with Africa). He soon went to visit his Clapham Circle friends at Battersea Rise (Henry Thornton's home). Meeting Hannah More there, he was relieved at least to find her showing "friendly attentions" to him, which were continued when she met the African children he'd brought to England to be educated. All this pointed to embarrassment and remorse over how she had managed things. She was reminded all over again of what she had at first liked and respected in Macaulay.

Several months later, and after all the storms their love had to weather, Selina Mills married Zachary Macaulay, in Bristol, on 26 August 1799. The More sisters, especially Patty, struggled at first with a welter of emotions, but slowly acquiesced.[37]

Meantime, Selina Macaulay, to her everlasting credit, ignored all that was going on in the sisterhood, and paid them a visit not too long after her wedding, at Cowslip Green.

Her magnanimity likely shamed them into something they should have seen from the first: she had been a great friend of the family, and would be so again, if they had the good sense to see it. A friendship that never should have been strained was restored.

That the Macaulays, Selina and Zachary, found it in their hearts to forgive and recover their old affection and respect for Hannah More may be seen clearly in one event of their family life: they named their fourth daughter (born in 1810) Hannah More Macaulay.[38]

---

37 Stott, *Hannah More*, 198.

38 Hannah More (née Macaulay), became Lady Trevelyan (1810-1873), and was the first wife of Sir Charles Edward Trevelyan. Her portrait is now kept in the National Portrait Gallery, and archived online at: https://www.npg.org.uk/collections/search/person/mp133213/hannah-more-ne-macaulay-lady-trevelyan

On receiving the news of her namesake, and that the Macaulays wished her to be the child's godmother, More wrote with a dash of wit much like her old and better self: *"I think it very hard on the poor babe to be obliged to carry about such an ugly name with her all her life."*[39]

Though no record of just how it unfolded survives, she had given time, and care, to mend the hurt she'd caused Selina and Zachary Macaulay.

In taking steps to make things right, she helped to bring a happier sequel.

For all concerned, it was the best resolution to a troubled chapter.

And, as will be seen later, Zachary Macaulay rallied to Hannah More's side at a time when she needed his help most. Seen in this light he, and his wife Selina, despite the hurt they'd suffered, could not have been better friends to her.

* * *

The second conflict from this time of More's life was the "Blagdon controversy." It concerned "the dispute between Hannah More and Thomas Bere, the curate of Blagdon, a village in the Mendip hills in Somerset, where she had set up a Sunday school in 1795." It began with what was "a purely local affair in 1799, blazed into national notoriety in 1801, and petered out in the summer of 1802."[40]

This was, in the words of one scholar—

---

39 as quoted in Stott, *Hannah* More, 198.

40 see the Abstract text for Anne Stott, "Hannah More and the Blagdon Controversy, 1799–1802," in *The Journal of Ecclesiastical History* (published online by Cambridge University Press: 01 April 2000).

the most problematic episode in [Hannah] More's career, seriously jeopardising her reputation as a loyalist [when Britain was at war with Napoleon's France]. According to M.G. Jones, her most substantial biographer, the controversy centred on two issues: 'whether the lower orders should be educated, and if so, by whom?', and 'Was Miss More a Methodist? Were her schools Methodist schools? Had she established them with or without the consent of the clergy in whose parishes the schools were set up?'[41]

In a word, was Hannah More, the writer who inveighed with Edmund Burke against the terrors of the French Revolution, somehow subversive in her philanthropic work among the "lower orders" near where she lived? In challenging the lack of education that had been the status quo before 1789, was she somehow creating settings that could lead to discontent, and something worse, over time? Or, if not what amounted to a closet revolutionary, was she not a champion of evangelical ideas that some in British society, not least many conservative Anglican clergy, viewed with open scorn and outright hostility?

So what began as a pamphlet war, launched by Bere, became a tawdry *cause célèbre*. Among the many unfounded accusations made by Bere was one alleging More had sought to get him removed from his curacy—a very trying thing, as she'd never sought to do anyone harm—quite the reverse, in point of truth.

So sides were taken; and Bere's acrimony issued forth repeatedly in print.

In time, the whole matter was "taken up by the London journals," rousing national interest when, according to one

---

41 see the Abstract text for Anne Stott, "Hannah More and the Blagdon Controversy, 1799–1802," in *The Journal of Ecclesiastical History* (published online by Cambridge University Press: 01 April 2000).

writer, some in the Church of England "saw it…as a symbol of Evangelical aggression."[42]

This view of the Blagdon controversy has been taken as well by scholar Mitzi Myers, who interprets the Blagdon controversy as "the public symbol of 'the whole conflict between Evangelical innovation and the status quo'"; More—tireless but pummelled—'self-consciously challenged customary oppression with a vision of charity as reform.'"[43]

And last, a recent study has concluded—

"The so-called Blagdon controversy was a pre-emptive strike by some high churchmen against the growing evangelical movement, represented by…Hannah More…and her friends in Clapham…For this reason it is a significant moment in the history of the late Georgian Church of England."[44]

* * *

Though a local tier of Anglican clergy, near Hannah More, might have felt threatened and offended by the prospect of such a prominent woman following "a vision of charity as reform," there were highly-placed prelates within the Church of England, not to say respected members of Parliament, like William Wilberforce, who defended her.

Finally, reluctantly, and from a wish to close the matter once and for all, More wrote in 1802 to Bishop Richard Beadon, who'd recently succeeded to the See of Bath and Wells. Her letter gives an overview of the whole matter, fully exonerating her from the charges of "sedition, disaffection, and a general

---

42 F.K. Brown, *Fathers of the Victorians* (Cambridge: 1961), 182.

43 Patricia Demers, ed., Hannah More, *Coelebs in Search of a Wife* (Peterborough: 2007), 19.

44 Mark Smith, Stephen Taylor, eds., *Evangelicalism in the Church of England c. 1790-c.1890* (Suffolk: 2004), 3.

aim to corrupt the principles of the community," that were so unjustly brought against her. More stated—

My Lord—

It is with deep regret that I find myself compelled to trouble your Lordship with this letter, though your known liberality of mind gives me more courage in taking a step which I should, in any case, feel it my duty to take; for, however firm my resolution has been never to answer a line to all the calumnies under which I have been so long suffering, yet to your Lordship, as my Diocesan, I feel myself accountable for my conduct, attacked as it has been with a wantonness of cruelty, which, in these mild times, few persons, especially of my sex, have been called to suffer...

A wish to keep my mind calm in a dangerous illness of some months induced me to read but very little of what has appeared against me. I can only notice such more material charges as have come to my knowledge. I do not mean to extenuate, much less to deny, any point in which I may have been to blame.

I shall only fairly state a few circumstances which have been violently exaggerated, or grossly misrepresented; the greater part of the charges being wholly groundless.[45]

More then told Beadon what her whole intent was in creating schools, and related charities, in villages near where she lived. She'd done so as a Christian who wished to live out the tenets of her faith, and the best traditions of the Church of England—

---

45 Thompson, *Hannah More*, 200-201.

I had so fully persuaded myself that I had for many years, especially in the late awful crisis [posed by revolutionary France], been devoting my time...to the promotion of loyalty, good morals, and an attachment to Church and State among the common people, that I was not prepared for the shock, when a charge of sedition, disaffection, and a general aim to corrupt the principles of the community, suddenly burst upon me. In vain have I been looking round me for any pretence on which to found such astonishing charges.[46]

More touched next on a chief allegation brought against her: breaking fealty with her lifelong commitment to the Anglican Church—

One circumstance [she said,] now made a ground for past accusation, is but recently brought forward...my being charged with having constantly attended and received the sacrament at [William] Jay's chapel at Bath for fifteen years.

The simple fact is this: The novelty and talents of Mr. Jay, a celebrated dissenting minister...were considered as such an attraction, that I, in common with a number of strict church people, frequently went to hear him preach.[47]

Apart from this, More said, she'd never let such attendance at Jay's chapel interfere with her proper observance of Sunday at Anglican services. Jay's chapel met

---

46 Thompson, *Hannah More*, 201.

47 Thompson, *Hannah More*, 201.

at six o'clock in the evening, an hour which did not interfere with the Church Service. It was not unusual to see, perhaps, near half a score clergymen, who, I presume, no more thought they were guilty of disaffection than I myself did.

I went, of course, to church as usual, except that the extreme nearness of this chapel drew me a few mornings, in severe weather, when my health was bad. At one of these times I unexpectedly found they were going to give the sacrament.

Taken by surprise, in a moment of irresolution, never having been used to turn my back on the communion at church, I imprudently stayed. How far this single irregularity, which I regretted, and never repeated, deserves the term of constant, your Lordship will judge. My eldest sister has been accused of denying it. She well might deny it, for she never knew it till now. I believe it to have been nine or ten years ago.

Again, I did not begin to reside part of the winter at Bath till about the beginning of 1791. I never go thither till near Christmas, and at the time alluded to I always left it, and went to London in February.

During a part of this short season I was generally confined by illness. When the interests of the Church became a question (I cannot be quite accurate as to the time, but I think it was either seven or eight years ago) I ceased entirely to go to Mr. Jay's. [48]

Having gone thoroughly over the accusations against her, More traced her dealings with Bere. They had, at the outset, been cordial—and indeed, meetings and dealings that took

---

48 Thompson, *Hannah More*, 201-202.

place at his request. The upshot was clear: she was the subject of unjust accusations from someone she had tried to help, and who had *asked* for her help—

> *How far this justifies the charge of fifteen years' constant attendance, your Lordship will judge. And is it unfair to request your Lordship to draw your own conclusion concerning the accuracy, as well as the candour of my accusers?*
>
> *It was subsequent to this that Mr. Bere thought so well of my principles, as to importune me, even with tears, to establish a school in his parish, lamenting its extreme profligacy, and his own inability to do any good to the rising generation.*
>
> *There was company present when he repeatedly made these applications, which I refused, pleading want of health, time, and money. I also declared my unwillingness to undertake it, unless it was the wish of the parish.*
>
> *He then sent his churchwardens as a deputation from the parish; [and] I yielded at last…I only name this to acquit myself of the charge of intrusion.*
>
> *As to connection with conventicles of any kind, I never had any.*[49]

In closing, More stated what should have been obvious to any fair-minded person, things that Beadon saw as such. Had More ever wished to break fealty with the Church of her youth, she would have had ample opportunities to do so.

---

49 Thompson, *Hannah More*, 202.

That she had not, when these opportunities were legion, or a source of attraction for many others, should have been adduced to her favour—

Had I been irregular, [she said,] should I not have gone sometimes, since my winter residence at Bath, to Lady Huntingdon's chapel, a place of great occasional resort?

Should I not have gone to some of Whitfield's or Wesley's Tabernacles in London, where I have spent a long spring for near thirty years? Should I not have strayed now and then into some Methodist meeting in the country?

Yet not one of these things have I ever done.

For an answer to the charge of my having ever made any application to get Mr. Bere removed from his curacy, I refer your Lordship to Dr. Moss and Dr. Crossman, [and] the declaration of both [that I never did,] in Dr. Crossman's printed letter to Sir A. Elton.[50]

Beadon accepted More's version of these events, and at last, it all was at an end.[51]

Those who opposed More were, if they persisted, going to inflict harm on themselves—rather than her. They may also have hoped damage already done through attacks in the press might have led her to curb her philanthropies.

But if so, they'd misjudged her. More, her sisters, and their philanthropic sponsors (like Wilberforce and Henry Thornton) weren't going to desist in charitable work. They would continue to do all they could.

And More had fine words like these, from Wilberforce, by way of encouragement—

---

50 Thompson, *Hannah More*, 202-203.

51 Stott, *Hannah More*, 249.

God bless you, and guide you. I adhere to my old opinion, that all these clouds, like the rack of the sky, will soon blow away, and leave all clear and calm.

With kind remembrances, Yours, ever affectionately, W. Wilberforce.[52]

In the end, the Blagdon Controversy was resolved in a way that vindicated More. She had not intended any slight, or harm, in doing what she could to provide for the physical and spiritual needs of poor, underserved people. But the cost of this conflict, and the storm of its duration, carried a fallout that never fully waned.

As one prominent writer has noted—

But she felt deep and lasting wounds too. Although in the "long-protracted trial" of the Blagdon controversy she prayed for her "enemies," trying "to indulge neither resentment nor misanthropy," she admitted to an unnerving erosion of confidence: "Battered, hacked, scalped, and tomahawked as I have been for three years, and continue to be, brought out of every month as an object of scorn, and abhorrence, I seem to have nothing to do in the world."[53]

Years later, Dr. Richard Valpy visited More, and learned first-hand about the pain she had endured, and still felt, when any mention of Blagdon took place—

---

52 Robert and Samuel Wilberforce, eds., *The Correspondence of William Wilberforce,* volume one (London: 1840), 234.

53 Demers, *Hannah More,* 130. Italics added.

Hannah More's "thorn in the flesh"…was the Blagdon controversy; [and] she [often spoke of it]…I was once sitting with her in one of her grottoes [at Barley Wood], over which she had inscribed pauperis Evandri tectum *[poor Evander's roof].*

I observed that the bleak hills of Mendip, opposite to us, [had] some resemblance to the country of Evander at the time of the embassy of Aeneas; but where, said I, is the den of Cacus [or den of thieves]?

"There," she instantly and emphatically replied, pointing to the tower of Blagdon.[54]

---

54 *The Christian Observer*, March 1835 (London: 1835), 167. Recollections from Dr. Richard Valpy. Italics added.

CHAPTER EIGHT

'Clear and beautiful intimations'

The imaginative side of [Longfellow's] temperament has commonly been attributed to his mother, who was fond of poetry and music, and a lover of nature in all its aspects—one who would sit by a window during a thunderstorm…"enjoying the excitement of its splendours." She loved the retirement of a country life, and found in it, in her own language, "a wonderful effect in tranquillizing the spirit, and calming every unpleasant emotion."

She played the spinet, until her daughter's piano replaced it, and apparently read [William] Cowper, Hannah More, and Ossian with her children.[1]

— T.W. HIGGINSON (1902)

When Alec looked out of his window the next morning, he saw a broad yellow expanse below. The Glamour was rolling, a mighty river, through the land. A wild waste foamy water,

---

1   T.W. Higginson, *Henry Wadsworth Longfellow* (Boston: 1902), 15. The chapter subtitle is taken from Hannah More, *Hints*, volume two, 219: "clear and beautiful intimations of happiness in a life to come."

looking cold and torn and troubled, it swept along the fields, where late the corn had bowed to the autumn winds. But he had often seen it as high. And all the corn was safe in the yard.

Neither he nor his mother regretted much that they could not go to church. Mrs. Forbes sat by the fire and read Hannah More's Christian Morals, and Alec sat by the window reading James Montgomery...[2]

— **GEORGE MACDONALD**, *Alec Forbes of Howglen* (1865)

...that long and luminous track, made up of minute and almost imperceptible stars...[3]

— **HANNAH MORE**, *Practical Piety* (1811)

The scenes above, from the lives of H.W. Longfellow and George MacDonald, show Hannah More as a cultural icon of the early 1800s. She was then, quite literally, a household name. And her poetic gift shone, amid prose, in the last epigraph line. It's one of those rare, arresting phrases that steal upon the memory with a sudden urgency.

It has the eloquence of a traveller who cared deeply about beautiful things.

More wrote these words when she was sixty-six—in a season, many said, that had taken its toll—and her writerly gifts had passed her by. They hadn't.

Time had slowed her step; but her gift for a lissom word was undiminished.

---

2   George MacDonald, *Alec Forbes*, volume two (London: 1865), 267.

3   Hannah More, *Practical Piety*, vol. 1, 6th ed., (London: 1811), 237.

These years saw a "more reflective side" to her writing, in three books published from 1811 to 1815.[4] Within them, her writing on faith flowered and flourished.

It may have reached its zenith. She not only wrote with depth about facets of Christian belief; she penned lines that reveal a prescient gift for words of spiritual counsel.

It was a gift much like that of her friend, John Newton, who had recently passed away. But where he placed his reflections in letters, in volumes like *Cardiphonia*, More used books themselves to converse with her readers; collectively, rather than one at a time.

In a way, these books were a literary echo of the 1770s and 80s, when she'd been so active in circles of conversation that made Bluestocking events welcome and meaningful—but there was one important difference.

Those meetings were limited, for only so many friends were present at one time. Now, writing her reflective books, More could widen the circle greatly—including friends she knew, but also readers whom she would never meet.

She'd found gifts of insight in her journey of faith, things that wisdom, reading, and meditation brought. Now, she could share these gifts in books that could travel far wider than she ever could—throughout the British Isles, and the English-speaking world.

It was a means to give, even as she'd been given.

Her three books were: *Practical Piety, or, The Influence of the Religion of the Heart* (1811); *Christian Morals* (1813); and her *Essay on the Character and Practical Writings of St. Paul* (1815). They were a trilogy: one more unlikely as she was so often ill when these books were written. In her December

---

4   Skedd, "Hannah More."

1812 Preface for *Christian Morals,* for example, she spoke honestly of the "hours of pain and suffering" under which it had been composed.[5]

"Suffering," she said, "is the initiation into a Christian's calling. It is [an] education for heaven."[6] Her words recalled the writings of Madame Guyon, or Thomas à Kempis. For sometimes, as they knew, wisdom and eloquence are born in hardship.

More's late-in-life books were not easily won.

* * *

Keeping to a reasonable length for this chapter, space will be devoted to just two of More's "reflective works," *Practical Piety* and *Christian Morals.*

The first, in theme and content, is something quite like C.S. Lewis' *Mere Christianity*—tracing key reasons for belief. *Christian Morals,* for its part, is a sequel, or companion text: exploring what Christians believe—and the guiding ideals for living a Christian life.

Yet, as one scholar has rightly said, *"this essential More— practical, confessional, self-aware, strong minded, compelling, adept at blending historical and contemporary references, and totally committed to the animating principle of faith—remains unread."*[7]

Such an insight takes in passages like the following, when More voiced persuasive words about her journey of faith: in a way she hoped readers would follow—

---

5   More, *Christian Morals,* vol. 2, ix.

6   Hannah More, *Practical Piety,* volume two, 8th edition, (London: 1812), 213.

7   Demers, *Hannah More,* 119. Italics added.

Christianity is not to be examined, nor the sacred Scriptures perused, as if they were merely to be believed, and remembered, and held in speculative reverence.

But, let it rather be impressed…that the Holy Scriptures are God's great means of producing…that awe of His presence, that reverence of His Majesty, that delight in His infinite perfections; that practical, affectionate knowledge of the only true God, and of Jesus Christ whom He has sent, which constitutes the rest, *the* peace, *the* strength, *the* light, *the* consolation *of every soul which attains to it.*[8]

And in passage two, with vivid words, More told readers of what it was to be

…taught to regard the oracles of God not merely as a light to guide her steps,

   but, as a sacred fire to animate and invigorate her inmost soul…[9]

Kindred to these reflections on Scripture, More also said of the Bible—

As the lawyer has his compendium of cases and precedents, the legislator his statutes…and every other professor his vade mecum [or "go with me,"] to consult in difficulties, the Christian, to which ever of the professions he may belong, will take his morning lecture from a more infallible directory, [the text] from which all practical excellence is deducible…and eternal in its obligation.

---

8   Hannah More, *Hints*, volume one, 222-223.

9   Hannah More, *Hints*, volume one, 223.

> *This sacred institute he will consult, not occasionally,*
> *but daily.*[10]

Passages like these show why *Practical Piety* and *Christian Morals*, within the canon of More's writings, ought to be better known and read.

* * *

In her Preface for *Practical Piety*, More wrote of a season many find as their generation becomes older, and friends of youth pass from the scene. Yet there were moments of solace and sweetness. Such was the time of her late sixties—

> *The Author may begin to ask with one of her earliest*
> *and most enlightened friends, [Dr. Johnson:] "Where is*
> *the world into which we were born?"* Death has broken
> most of those connexions which made the honour and the
> happiness of her youthful days.
>
> Fresh links, however, have continued to attach
> her to society.
>
> *She is singularly happy in the affectionate regard of*
> *a great number of amiable young persons, who may*
> *peruse, with additional attention, sentiments which*
> *come recommended to them by the warmth of their own*
> *attachment... [still further:]*
>
> *Is there not something in personal knowledge, something*
> *in the feelings of endeared acquaintance, which...if it does*
> *not impart new force to old truths, may excite a new*
> *interest in considering truths which are known?*[11]

---

10 More, *Christian Morals*, vol. 2, 217-218.

11 Hannah More, *Practical Piety*, vol. 1, 6th ed., (London: 1811), xiii-xiv. Italics added.

Though tinged by sad recollection, these lines disclosed the pen of a writer still young at heart. Needing solace, amid the passing of her friends, and trying changes in her life, More had immersed herself in the study of Scripture, and classic works of devotion.

They brought cordials from a renewing spring: comfort, beauty, and meaning.

Her return of gratitude was to write about them.

So, for younger friends, and readers she would never meet, More put pen to paper—in hope that some of the good she'd known might become theirs.

She drew deeply on her season of contemplation to speak about "the great truths of Christianity," and what she discerned in them.[12] They were vital, recurring themes.

Since ancient times also, they'd been pillars of revealing purpose.

* * *

Straightaway, in her Preface for *Practical Piety,* More described the reason for writing her book: "the world does not require so much to be informed as reminded."

So, she would cast herself in the role of a "remembrancer."[13]

But what did she mean by this? First, she saw the value of getting her readers' attention with a terse, arresting phrase.

But she also wished to make them think. Reminded about what? And why?

Then as to a "remembrancer," what did *that* mean?

---

12 Hannah More, *Christian Morals* vol. 2, second ed., (London: 1813), 282.
13 Hannah More, *Practical Piety,* vol. 1, 6th ed., (London: 1811), vi.

It had everything to do with avoiding the image of a dour, prim instructor, in front of a classroom. She wished to speak winsomely, of things familiar and welcoming.

Using the word "remembrancer," for example, More was drawing on the idea, present throughout the Bible, of taking time to reflect on redemptive teachings in its pages.

As she read and studied, preparing her book, she'd done just that.

She wished, conversationally, to say: "see what I've found— or rather, what I've been *reminded of* in my reading of Scripture. It's been a source of blessing. Why don't we walk on a while, and I'll tell you about it." More was a constant learner: and as a writer, she wished to share what she'd learned—so to meet other pilgrims on the way.

At the same time, she wished to offer salutary words for those who had yet to become Christians, and wondered what it was all about. Her purpose was to commend faith; while exploring teachings she'd found compelling.

In her Preface More underscored the intent of her book, saying it was a "slight sketch," or a text that "aims only at being plain and practical."[14]

This, in itself, was a refreshing change of tone. So many books of her time were prolix, heavy-going texts. To strive for a conversational voice was something rather rare.

But a more "vernacular" tone had been emerging for some time among writers in the evangelical Anglican fold. John Newton had shown this, with wide and influential effect, in his *Authentic Narrative* (1764) a book that would influence William Wordsworth in writing *The Prelude*.[15] And closer

---

14 More, *Practical Piety*, vol. 1, vii.

15 see Jonathan Aitken, *John Newton* (Wheaton: 2007), 60; see also Richard Gravil and Daniel Robinson, eds., *The Oxford Handbook of William Wordsworth* (Oxford: 2015), 605.

still to the writing of *Practical Piety*, William Wilberforce published his *Practical View of Christianity* (1797), a best-selling book many readers, including Newton, had praised for its conversational tone.

Indeed, on 7 June 1797, Newton had written to Wilberforce—

"My very dear Sir, I can converse with you as often as I please by your late publication, which I have now read through with increasing satisfaction a third time."[16]

Since Newton and Wilberforce were close friends, and More greatly respected them, it's not surprising she would write a book with traits kindred to theirs. She wished to till common literary ground, and address the same readership. But, at the same time, it must be remembered that More was herself a famous innovator, writing vivid, plain-spoken stories like *The Shepherd of Salisbury Plain*.[17]

Wilberforce understood this, and was one of many thousands who ardently admired *The Shepherd of Salisbury Plain* for its simply-wrought lines. In 1825, he stated his preference for More's tale, over other celebrated works of the time—

> *[17th October. I have been] hearing Walter Scott's* Heart of Mid Lothian *in the afternoon, and a little in the evening…20th [October.] much time taken, and interest too, in…Scott's* Heart of Mid Lothian. *Yet I only hear it in afternoon and evening. Much the best of his novels that I have heard. Jeanie Deans [is] a truly Christian character, and [the novel is] beautiful, as far as it goes. [Yet] I would rather go to render up my account at the last day, carrying*

---

16 Wilberforce, *Life of Wilberforce*, volume 1, 206.

17 More was an innovator in the development of the short story in literature. Her story "Betty Brown, the St. Giles's Orange Girl," has been set alongside others from Defoe, Swift, and Fielding in *The Penguin Book of the British Short Story* (London: Penguin Classics, 2015).

up with me The Shepherd of Salisbury Plain, *than bearing the load of all those volumes, full as they are of genius."*[18]

Artistically, More's tract had a woodcut-like quality. Yet it was a moving text, crafted with an artisan's skill—similar in métier to *The Pilgrim's Progress.*[19]

Each line, in common phrase, was "meant to tell."

Still, *Practical Piety* was quite different from *The Shepherd of Salisbury Plain* in scale and content. It was, of course, a work of non-fiction, rather than fiction—yet it did share the same aspiration to be conversational and accessible, the better to convey its message.

So More stated her wish "to be understood as speaking the language of sympathy."[20] She hoped her book, though of "slighter drapery,"[21] might, because of its less formal tone, serve to win a wider hearing.

* * *

Briefly, there are twelve chapters in *Practical Piety,* and though space doesn't permit time among each, highlights can be given here.

To begin with, More's title, *Practical Piety,* has a ring reminiscent of *Mere Christianity.* "Practical," or "mere,"— these are words of kindred description. They point to things essential. And inasmuch as C.S. Lewis had written of "the belief

---

18 Wilberforce, *Life of Wilberforce,* volume 5, 254.

19 G.B. Cheever, *Lectures on The Pilgrim's Progress* (London: 1846), 117: "Now if you wish for a commentary in plain prose on the sweetness of Bunyan's delineation of this Valley [of Peace], you may find it in *The Dairyman's Daughter,* or *in The Shepherd of Salisbury Plain."*

20 More, *Practical Piety,* vol. 1, xi.

21 More, *Practical Piety,* vol. 1, xii.

that has been common to nearly all Christians at all times,"[22] More did likewise. Her book, as she stated—

> *aims only at being plain and practical…contending solely for those indispensable points, which, by involving present duty, involve future happiness…[I have] avoided, as far as Christian sincerity permits, all controverted topics; [and] shunned whatever might lead to disputation rather than to profit.*
>
> *We live in an age, when, as [Alexander] Pope observed of that in which he wrote, it is criminal to be moderate. Would it could not be said that religion has her parties as well as politics! Those who endeavour to steer clear of all extremes in either, are in danger of being reprobated by both.*
>
> *[So I have] considered it as a Christian duty to cultivate a spirit of moderation…*[23]

Another point of common ground between More and Lewis rests in the respect each had for Richard Baxter, who coined the terms "meer Christian,"[24] and "mere Christianity."[25]

The nature of Lewis' debt is obvious, and his writing about it well known, as in his line: "the only safety is to have a standard of plain, central Christianity (mere Christianity, as Baxter called it)."[26] For her part, in *Practical Piety*, More called Baxter one of "the brightest luminaries of the Christian Church."[27]

---

22 C.S. Lewis, *Mere Christianity* (New York: 1952), vi.

23 More, *Practical Piety*, vol. 1, vii-viii.

24 Richard Baxter, *Church-History of the Government of Bishops and Their Councils* (London: 1681), 15. "I am a Christian, a meer Christian."

25 *The Practical Works of Richard Baxter* (London: George Virtue, 1838), 83. "The religion of protestants is mere Christianity."

26 See Lewis' 1944 essay, "On the Reading of Old Books," in *God in the Dock* (Grand Rapids: 1970), 201.

27 More, *Practical Piety*, vol. 1, 12.

And, if More's book was titled as it was, Baxter's *Practical Works* had been published in four volumes in 1707,[28] the "massy folios" of a set William Wilberforce read often.[29]

More likely had the same set, or a later edition, in her library.

So one could say that in her choice of a book title, More remembered Baxter in a meaningful way some seventy-seven years before Lewis was born: and she selected a book title with affinities to Baxter over one hundred and forty years before Lewis did.

Apart from *Practical Piety*'s affinity in spirit to *Mere Christianity*, a book of the modern era, it has a more direct tie to Wilberforce's treatise from 1797, *A Practical View of Christianity*.

Fourteen years separate the books; but whether in choice of title, stress on Christian essentials, the central place of "a thorough renovation of heart,"[30] or personal conversion, the books have much in common.

They were written in an atmosphere of literary friendship.

* * *

But to return to *Practical Piety* itself…

In chapter one, "Christianity an Internal Principle," More gave this opening line:

"Christianity bears all the marks of a divine original. It came down from heaven, and its gracious purpose is to carry us up thither."[31]

---

28 *The Practical Works of…Richard Baxter* (London: 1707).

29 William Wilberforce, *A Practical View of Christianity,* 2nd ed., (London: 1797), 380. Here Wilberforce wrote that Baxter's "practical writings, in four massy folios, are a treasury of Christian wisdom."

30 More, *Practical Piety,* vol. 1, 8.

31 More, *Practical Piety,* vol. 1, 1.

Here was an invitation to discover, and this chapter, perhaps the most important in the book, has much to commend it. Describing the "change in the human heart, one which the Scriptures declare to be necessary," More cast poetic imagery from the book of Genesis.

"The same spirit," she said, "which in the creation of the world moved upon the face of the waters, operates on the human character to produce a new heart and a new life."[32]

* * *

What followed from someone's assent to the redemptive plea of the gospel?

More used the imagery of light, charting the way for believers.

She said that "the affections and faculties" in redemption, are given "a new impulse," and the "understanding is illuminated." Further, in this season of new belief, aspirations win "a loftier flight…vacillating desires…a fixed object, [and heretofore] vagrant purposes a settled home." Last, she gave words of re-assurance and solace to those who had known brokenness, saying: the "disappointed heart [finds] a certain refuge."[33]

Her studies, and experience, taught her the language of the Christian heart.

Continuing on, More pictured the new life of a Christian in words of pilgrimage, as in the lines "a settled home," and "a certain refuge." She voiced compassion also for those of a prodigal or wounded heart, who had known what it was to wander lost (amid "vagrant purposes"), or had known what it was to suffer grief and disappointment.

---

32 More, *Practical Piety,* vol. 1, 3-4.
33 More, *Practical Piety,* vol. 1, 4-5.

To underscore this theme of compassion, she cited the theologian Richard Hooker, who said Christian belief was centred in "a Shepherd full of kindness, full of care, and full of power."[34] Then, to compliment this phrase, she gave a vivid image that might well have been indebted to her friend Edmund Burke's line, "What shadows we are, and what shadows we pursue," words that she greatly admired.[35]

So More explained that a Christian's understanding was "illuminated." Faith opened one's eyes "to realities, in the place of those shadows which he has been pursuing."[36]

These virtues notwithstanding, and as with any writer, some phrases in *Practical* Piety are less readable than others. At times, More's prose could be cumbersome, or overdone.

Perceptively, Harriet Beecher Stowe wrote that More's writing style was Johnsonian,[37] and while that style had many virtues, there were drawbacks—a tendency to what Wilberforce, speaking of the philosopher William Paley, called a *"turgid sesquipedality,* [to] describe that Johnsonian style by a Johnsonian epithet."[38]

In a word, able writers like More and Paley could go on a bit. So, contrasting outward observances, in place of hearts renewed by faith, More had written—

They are the accessory, but not the principal; they are important aids and adjuncts, but not the thing itself; they are its aliment, but not its life, the fuel but not the flame,

---

34 More, *Practical Piety,* 8. See also *The Works of...Richard Hooker,* vol. 2 (Oxford: 1839), 584.

35 More quoted this phrase in a letter dated 6 January 1789. See William Roberts. ed., *Memoirs...of Hannah More,* vol. 1 (New York: 1834), 303.

36 More, *Practical Piety,* vol. 1, 6.

37 H.B. Stowe, *Oldtown Folks* (London: 1870), 381; "The female principal, Miss Titcomb, was a thorough-bred, old-fashioned lady, whose views of education were formed by Miss Hannah More, and whose style, like Miss Hannah More's, was profoundly Johnsonian."

38 Wilberforce, *Correspondence of William Wilberforce*, 250.

the scaffolding, but not the edifice. Religion can no more subsist merely by them, than it can subsist without them. They are divinely appointed, and must be conscientiously observed; but observed as a means to promote an end, and not as an end in themselves.[39]

One gets the gist of it all; but this point would have been better served with just one metaphor, or contrasting image, like "the fuel, but not the flame," a fine and vivid phrase.

However, "turgid sesquipedality" was more rare than commonplace in *Practical Piety*. In the main, the book keeps admirably to its purpose of being conversational.

* * *

In this vein, and perhaps the best trait of *Practical Piety*, is that it shows Hannah More to be an accomplished writer of "spiritual counsel," a hallowed tradition in British literature.

Whether it was a terse, pithy aphorism, a line of telling imagery, the exploration of a biblical passage, a word of contrast to guide truth home, or the flight of an arresting phrase—she had the authentic voice of a spiritual counsellor.

This sphere of writing is one where More came into her own—a late-in-life flowering of writerly task. This is clear in one lambent passage, among the finest in Christian literature.

As the word lambent implies, this passage flickers with a soft radiance of faith—much as a candle did in homes like More's beloved Barley Wood—

---

39 More, *Practical Piety,* vol. 1, 71.

*Prayer is the application of want to Him who can only
relieve it; the voice of sin to Him who alone can pardon it.
It is the urgency of poverty, the prostration of humility, the
fervency of penitence, the confidence of trust.*

*It is not eloquence, but earnestness, not the definition
of helplessness, but the feeling of it; not figures of speech,
but compunction of soul. It is the 'Lord save us, we perish'
of drowning Peter; the cry of faith to the ear of mercy.*[40]

More also knew how to draw from the well of consolation,
saying that in the place of prayer, we may "look to the mercy of
the King,"[41] and God's loving character: "Our Heavenly Father...
bestows...the shining sun and the refreshing shower. [He] delights
in the happiness, and desires the salvation of all His children."[42]

And for all who sorrow, there was this hope, from the
Lord of Heaven—

"His heart is open to all the distressed."[43]

* * *

In chapter three of *Practical Piety,* More gave one of many
citations from great literary figures to explain a key teaching
of the Christian life. In this instance, she cited a line from
Shakespeare to capture the need for a "renovated heart." Only
those, she stated, *"who, as our great Poet says, are 'reformed
altogether,' are converted.* There is no complete reformation in
the conduct effected without a revolution in the heart."[44]

---

40   More, *Practical Piety,* vol. 1, 102.

41   More, *Practical Piety,* vol. 1, 108.

42   More, *Practical Piety,* vol. 1, 46.

43   More, *Practical Piety,* vol. 1, 42.

44   More, *Practical Piety,* 62; here More paraphrases Shakespeare's *Hamlet,* Act 3, scene 2: **Players:** *"I hope
we have reformed that indifferently with us."* **Hamlet:** *"O, reform it altogether."*

And, lest there be any misunderstanding as to why conversion was so important and necessary, More penned a passage that showed she'd more in common with C.S. Lewis than a shared affinity for the writings of Richard Baxter. This passage reads very much as though it could have come from the pages of *Mere Christianity*, as this comparison shows—

The mistake of many in religion [More wrote,] appears to be, that they do not begin with the beginning. They do not lay their foundation in the persuasion that man is by nature in a state of alienation from God. They consider him rather as an imperfect than as a fallen creature. They allow that he requires to be improved, but deny that he requires a thorough renovation of heart.[45]

Meanwhile, Lewis wrote in much the same way. The similarities of phrase and image here are quite striking: beginning in the right place, the fallen nature of us all, and the need to come to God with a penitent heart. The passages are almost interchangeable—

Christianity [Lewis said,] tells people to repent and promises them forgiveness. It therefore has nothing (as far as I know) to say to people who do not know that they need any forgiveness. It is after you have realised that there is a real Moral Law, and a Power behind the law, and that you have broken that law and put yourself wrong with that Power—it is after all this, and not a moment sooner, that Christianity begins to talk.[46]

---

45 More, *Practical Piety*, vol. 1, 8.

46 C.S. Lewis, *Mere Christianity* (New York: 2001), 31.

Turning to More's gift for a telling aphorism, the pages of *Practical Piety* often display that ability, as in this set of selected lines, which read in ways that linger in the memory—

The Bible never warns us against imaginary evil,
nor courts us to imaginary good.[47]

They too often judge others with little charity,
and themselves with little humility.[48]

...the world is insolvent...
it pays nothing of what it promised...[49]

He who has said 'Give me thy heart,'
will not be satisfied with less...[50]

As a poet, who'd written the lines so widely admired in *The Bas Bleu,* More's writing in *Practical Piety* led to moments when she cast poetry in prose. For an image of renewing faith, she said it was "watered by a perennial fountain."[51] And, in just six words, she communicated a world of meaning, speaking of "a heart devoted to its Maker."[52]

There was a kind of poetry as well, in the practice of philanthropy. So, More said, "Christian beneficence takes a large sweep. That circumference cannot be small, of which God is the centre."[53] Last of all, she cast a beautiful phrase,

---

47 More, *Practical Piety,* vol. 1, 21.
48 More, *Practical Piety,* vol. 1, 38.
49 More, *Practical Piety,* vol. 1, 65.
50 More, *Practical Piety,* vol. 1, 37.
51 More, *Practical Piety,* vol. 1, 69-70.
52 More, *Practical Piety,* vol. 1, 55.
53 More, *Practical Piety,* vol. 1, 42-43.

"repose of spirit" in a passage which spoke of things that can sustain Christians throughout their pilgrimage—

> *there is an inward peace in an humble trust in God, and in a simple reliance on His word; there is a repose of spirit, a freedom…for which the world has nothing to give in exchange.*[54]

* * *

In her excellent summary of *Practical* Piety, scholar M.G. Jones said the book was—

> *a…straightforward persuasive to the Christian life. It developed Hannah More's dominant conviction that Christianity brought happiness to all who accepted it…*
>
> *That it met the needs of young and old was affirmed by the amazing response of the public. Its sales exceeded those of [her novel] Coelebs, hitherto [her] best seller, by one edition and three thousand copies.*
>
> *It brought superlative praise from friends new and old.*[55]

* * *

Taking up her quill pen in 1812, after "the usual interval" she observed "between the publication of one work, and the commencement of another," More began a book that one early biographer called "a sort of sequel" to *Practical Piety*.[56]

---

54 More, *Practical Piety*, vol. 1, 25-26.

55 Jones, *Hannah More*, 199-200.

56 Roberts, *Memoirs…of Hannah More*, vol. 2 (New York: 1835), 196.

One wonders if she felt a certain pressure to come up to the level of what she'd written in *Practical Piety,* which the influential *Christian Observer* magazine reviewed in no less than 20-pages of two-columned text, coverage on a scale rarely given in its pages.

True, More had been an important and early contributor to this flagship publication of the evangelical wing of the Church of England. And while she wasn't quite a founder of the magazine, she was one of its most featured writers, sought out by William Wilberforce—who *was* one of its founders—to contribute articles he said were desperately needed to keep the newly launched magazine from foundering before it was well out of port.

Wilberforce was right about More's contributions and their importance. They were a key to the magazine's survival.

So, just ten years into the life of *The Christian Observer,* and under the editorship of More's friend Zachary Macaulay, this long review of *Practical Piety* ran. It was almost certainly written by Macaulay, though the review (per common practice) was unsigned.

At the outset of the review, a context for the appearance of *Practical Piety* was given. One sharp point of contemporary criticism was taken up, and spoken out against—

> *That [Hannah] More is an enthusiast, is often asserted; but the only evidence of the charge, which we have been able to discover, arises from the circumstance of her directing the energies of a powerful and enlightened mind to the best of all causes [the commendation of faith].*[57]

---

57 *The Christian Observer,* vol. 10 (London: 1812), 561.

Critics of this stamp had alleged that More was "an enemy to the exercise of reason." This idea was rejected forcibly, and out of hand, since the reviewer (Macaulay) had personal knowledge, based on a friendship of many years' standing, that More's writings "abound with the best specimens of reasoning, enriched and embellished with the most striking features of a fine imagination."[58] The reviewer then minced no words in saying—

Whether these and similar insinuations proceed from a wicked and malevolent motive, or are merely the result of ignorance and imbecility, we shall not pause to inquire; they are more than counterbalanced by the admiration and the love of the good and the wise; and these feelings of regard suffer no diminution by the publication of the volumes before us.[59]

Speaking next of *Practical Piety's* contents, the reviewer said the pages of More's book amply demonstrated that she "has her subject in full possession; observe[d] in all its bearings and relations." And here, it was said, "she possesses in an eminent degree the happy talent of a *popular* reasoner."[60] From this vantage point, the reviewer continued—

Her arguments are at all times easy of comprehension: there is nothing recondite, nothing perplexed: and they are all so adorned by liveliness of manner, propriety of allusion, and beauty of illustration, that none will complain of

---

58 *The Christian Observer,* vol. 10, 561.

59 *The Christian Observer,* vol. 10, 561.

60 *The Christian Observer,* vol. 10, 562.

weariness, and few will begin the work without giving it an entire perusal.

To [a person] of taste it will be recommended by its felicity of composition, and the familiarity which it bespeaks with the best models both of poetry and prose: [a reader] of reflection will be gratified by the development of character, and knowledge of the world contained in every chapter [as well as its] weighty observations.[61]

With fair-minded prose, the reviewer then described the shortcomings he perceived in *Practical Piety*, saying that "amidst a rich display of beautiful imagery, the metaphors are sometimes redundant, and sometimes not quite consistent." Also, "thoughts and expressions occur, which are beneath the usual elevation of the writer."[62]

But these rather incidental considerations, the reviewer said, only serve to prove

that "Practical Piety" is not a perfect composition…

the faults to be found in these volumes are few and trifling—the ordinary lapses of a great mind, intent upon great objects; and that nearly all of them have their origin in kindred excellencies—in the play of a fancy, which can summon images at command from all the regions of art and taste; in a power of illustration, which catches from almost every object the exact point of resemblance; in a flow of sentiments, which appear to rise without effort…These are excellencies, which, if they occasionally degenerate into faults, are sure to excite attention and to conciliate regard.[63]

---

61 *The Christian Observer,* vol. 10, 562.

62 *The Christian Observer,* vol. 10, 578-579.

63 *The Christian Observer,* vol. 10, 579.

The closing lines of *The Christian Observer's* lengthy review then bestowed a gracious and perceptive compliment. Some writers, "as they advance in years, [manifest] the ardour of youth, with the experience of age, [while] exhibiting the full power of splendid talents."[64]

Hannah More, the reviewer concluded, was one of them.

* * *

Notwithstanding its origin in a friendly quarter, More must have been deeply gratified to have received such a fulsome, prominent review. For she knew that no matter how fond he might have been of her personally, Zachary Macaulay was never a person to say something he did not mean, or forthrightly wish to say. Friend though he was to many contributors to *The Christian Observer,* he did not shrink from calling a spade a spade, if he felt a critique was warranted. Some few had written letters to the magazine over the years, noting just that fact.

More knew this, and could therefore be grateful that her book, written in a season of sickness, found a fine welcome in a setting she hoped it might.

Yet this very thing might have caused her to be somewhat diffident as she took up her pen to write the book she would call *Christian Morals.* Could she, as the modern phrase has it, "do it again"? Writers of advancing age often wonder that about themselves, and she would not have been human if the thought didn't cross her mind.

That this might have been so seems to have been borne out in a letter More wrote to her great friend Anne Kennicott at this time. This new book, she said—

---

64 *The Christian Observer,* vol. 10, 579.

is to be called Christian Morals. *I do not talk of it, except to one or two particular friends, because I do not like to have it discussed and to be questioned beforehand.*

I have not finished it. Whether it is worth finishing I hardly know, but Providence sometimes works by poor, weak instruments.[65]

If a faithful transcript of her thoughts, it's refreshing to read such a letter. It shows More to be a person who, like many an author, and however famous or "well-established," had moments of being unsure. And with hindsight, it's not always remembered that those well known to history wrestled with doubts and challenges throughout their lives. This kind of reflection, on reading More's letter to Anne Kennicott, is important to bear in mind.

* * *

Christian Morals, it must be stated, had more discursive lines than *Practical Piety;* but then, it also held moving lines of reflection. Some described God's sovereign care—in words that argue why this book shouldn't be neglected—

But, as soon as we clearly discern the mind which appoints, and the hand which governs, all events, we begin to see our way through them: as soon as we are brought to recognize God's authority, and to confide in His goodness, we can say to our unruly hearts, what He said to the tempestuous waves, Peace, be still.[66]

---

65 Roberts, *Memoirs…of Hannah More,* vol. 2 (New York: 1835), 196.

66 Hannah More, *Christian Morals,* vol. 1, second edition, (London: 1813), 36.

Speaking soon after of the ways of Providence, More found an eloquence that goes to sovereign places—where a reader might find a renewing, hopeful stay. Three passages show this, as a brief sampler, and show why *Christian Morals* became a bestseller—

1.

The various parts of the scheme of Providence are sometimes connected by a thread so fine as to elude our dim sight; but…it is never broken off. The plan is carrying on…[67]

2.

But if, after tracing Providence through many a labyrinth, we seem to lose sight of Him: if, after having lost our clue, we are tempted to suspect that His operation is suspended, or that His agency has ceased, He is working all the time out of sight…[68]

3.

…we are not cured of our incredulity till we again discover Him, bursting forth like the same river, which, having pursued its hidden passage through every obstruction, rises once more in all its beauty in another and unexpected place.[69]

In the first passage, More writes as though the threads of God's providential working are like those unseen in a tapestry: they are most certainly there, but not always discernible in the

67 More, *Christian Morals*, vol. 1, 68.

68 More, *Christian Morals*, vol. 1, 69.

69 More, *Christian Morals*, vol. 1, 69.

weave that makes the tapestry what it is. So, our insight as to God's ways is finite, as we are. But More sends that truth home in a way that offers reassurance and comfort.

In the second passage, More offers her own take, as it were, on biblical lines like those in 1st Corinthians 13:12, "we see through a glass, darkly." Left to our own devices, we easily lose our way; but we may safely trust to the knowledge that "all things work together for good to them that love God, and are called according to His purpose" (Romans 8:28). More is, in essence, saying: "We cannot see all ends, but God does, and that is enough. He will make a way, and often does, where we may not see one."

In the third passage, it is tempting to think that More borrowed imagery from what she knew of the sometimes hidden ways of water in the Mendip Hills. Walking there, all on a sudden, one might come upon a stream, though not able to see whence it began. So it is with blessings unlooked for in the Christian life. The ways of grace, and God's providence, are such that they may often take a believer by surprise—yet all the while, it is no less true that God's purposes are unfolding— they just have yet to be discovered.

As a writer skilled in spiritual counsel, and trained by years of study, More knew when to speak "a word in season." She was one of the ablest writers of her day in this tradition, as others, like John Newton, and William Wilberforce, were widely recognized to be. That is too often lost sight of today, but it was a prime reason why her books sold so well.

Readers knew they would find passages like these.

* * *

Other phrases in *Christian Morals* call the reader to discover more about them, such as: "the graces which embellish truth,"[70] "the renovation of hearts,"[71] or, perhaps, during a morning time with God, "to view Him in His bounties of creation."[72]

To read these lines is to see the great care More took over words of stirring imagery, or burnished turns of phrase. At times, she set brief lines of deep meaning, at other times, she traced a line of thought, as one might follow a path of implications.

That she was at home in either voice, is shown in these two examples—

...as no concern is so vast to encumber Omnipotence,
so none is too diminutive to escape the eye
of Omniscience.[73]

[Our] felicity does not, like that of secular ambition,
depend on popular breath— still, it subsists on
dependence. It subsists upon a trust which never
disappoints, upon a mercy which is never exhausted—
upon a promise which never deceives...[74]

Often, More's pen revealed pith and discernment. In one compelling line, she penned a cautionary tale for fair-seeming things that are deceptive, or harmfully misleading—

---

70 Hannah More, *Christian Morals,* vol. 1, second edition, 30.
71 Hannah More, *Christian Morals,* vol. 1, second edition, 24.
72 Hannah More, *Christian Morals,* vol. 1, second edition, 37.
73 Hannah More, *Christian Morals,* vol. 1, second edition, 75.
74 Hannah More, *Christian Morals,* vol. 1, second edition, 301.

To be enchanted with things that have
not much in them...[75]

And when it came to lines of paradox, set in words of spiritual counsel, More cast a thought about Christian character that G.K. Chesterton might well have envied—

There is a finer edge to his virtues, for
they are now sheathed in humility...[76]

At the same time, contemplative themes found their way into More's use of paradox, as when she wrote of "all the peace which springs from the large aggregate of little things."

Reading this, one can see her writing when the view from her window at Barley Wood disclosed the silver of a morning mist, rising from her well-tended gardens and groves.

That was her shining time; when good things found their way to the page.

* * *

Paradox was a keen, recurring device for More. Readers could always look forward to its appearance in her books, even as they wondered what form it might take next.

So, in looking to writers of classical antiquity, she observed: "that silence is one of the great arts of conversation is allowed by Cicero himself, who says there is not only an art, but an eloquence in it."[77] Elsewhere, she said memorably that "the

---

75 Hannah More, *Christian Morals,* vol. 2, sixth edition, (London: 1813), 303.

76 More, *Christian Morals,* vol. 2, 319.

77 Hannah More, *Essays on Various Subjects,* 4th edition, (London: 1785), 42.

soul on earth is an immortal guest,"[78] contrasting things transitory and eternal.

Both these lines were among the over sixty citations from More's pen in the classic book, *Forty Thousand Quotations, Prose and Poetical,* by C.N. Douglas, from 1917.

Among the highest tallies of quotes in this text from "standard authors of ancient and modern times," More ranked very high. Her tally was nearly tied with that of C.H. Spurgeon, cited sixty-four times, and she was cited far more often than John and Charles Wesley, who were quoted fifteen times altogether.

Meanwhile, Samuel Johnson was cited twenty-eight times, Daniel Defoe twenty-six, and Shakespeare, Milton, and Edmund Burke one hundred times each. Of famous writers in the genre of spiritual counsel, More was cited four times more often than Richard Baxter, quoted fifteen times. Meanwhile, Matthew Henry was cited twenty-one times. John Tillotson, the famous Archbishop of Canterbury, was quoted fifty-seven times.

Anthologies are of course subjective; but that said, for More to be this widely cited in a standard literary reference text is significant, nearly one hundred years after her passing: she was a major presence in a book kept in many homes and libraries.

To close a look at passages from More, cited in Douglas' book, three more examples may be given—each by turns memorable, and insightful:

---

78 Hannah More, Sacred Dramas, 5th edition, (London: 1787), 263.
     Thomas Jefferson's daughter Martha owned a copy of this book, a measure of Hannah More's wide influence in America. And see also N.D. Smith, *The Literary Manuscripts and Letters of Hannah More* (New York: Routledge, 2016): Extract, 8 lines, entitled 'Heavenly origin of the Soul' and beginning 'The soul, on earth, is an immortal guest', transcribed in the hand of Jane Jones Davies in a commonplace book. U. Penn. L., MS Coll. 325 MoH 128

The keen spirit seizes the prompt occasion.[79]

We are apt to mistake our vocation by looking out of the way for occasions to exercise great and rare virtues, and by stepping over the ordinary ones that lie directly in the road before us.[80]

*Love never reasons, but profusely gives: gives, like a thoughtless prodigal, its all,
and trembles then lest it has done too little.*[81]

* * *

There were also times, More explained, when Christians did well to follow streams of wisdom consonant with Christian teaching, but not exclusive to it, as in one reflection that referenced Socrates when speaking of "useful members of the great body of society"—

Like the great Athenian philosopher, [the Christian] does not so much aim to teach wisdom to others, as to put them in the way of finding it out for themselves.[82]

Likewise, to be well instructed in youth, More observed, "will give currency to good sense," and such good sense, in turn, "adds credit to virtue."[83]

---

79 Hannah More, *Sacred Dramas,* 14th edition, (London: 1805), 209.

80 Hannah More, *Coelebs in Search of a Wife,* volume one, 12th edition, (London: 1809), 217.

81 Hannah More, *Percy: A Tragedy, As It Is Acted In The Theatre-Royal In Covent Garden,* 2nd edition, (London: 1778), 7.

82 More, *Christian Morals,* vol. 2, 251.

83 More, *Christian Morals,* vol. 2, 250.

* * *

In *Christian Morals*, More stated that she set great store on critical thinking, or, to use the language of Scripture, learning to love God with the mind; giving high place to forming one's judgment based on careful consideration, and the dictates of conscience.

So, she wrote, the Christian "does not give up his independence of mind, when the superiority of the scheme of [an]other does not carry conviction to his judgment."[84]

Putting the matter to a point, she explained that the Christian "will transact business" with others in the world at large "with frankness and civility, but he will not follow them to any objectionable lengths."[85]

In another passage, More penned lines showing she was far from a naïf unacquainted with the writings of Machiavelli,[86] or the way things often were in the world.

Speaking after a reading of Machiavelli's *Discourses on Livy*, More observed—

...[the] thirst for human applause will be abated, when [the Christian] observes in those around him the unexpected attainment of popularity so soon followed by its unmerited loss. When he beholds the rapid transfer of power, it will, more than whole tomes of philosophy, shew him that "favour is deceitful."

---

84 More, *Christian Morals*, vol. 2, 250.

85 More, *Christian Morals*, vol. 2, 248.

86 Hannah More, *Hints*, volume one (London: 1805), 293. More writes: "Hear, then, the able but profligate Machiavel, 'Those princes and commonwealths who would keep their governments entire and uncorrupt are above all things to have a care of religion and its ceremonies, and preserve them in due veneration; for in the whole world there is not a greater sign of imminent ruin, than when God and His worship are despised.'" Here, More refers her readers to Machiavelli's *Discourses on Livy*.

He will moderate his desires of great riches, when he sees by what sacrifices they are sometimes obtained, and to what temptations the possession leads. He will be less likely to repine that others are reaching the summit of ambition, whether they achieve it by talents which he does not possess, or attain it by steps which he would not chuse to climb, or maintain it by concessions which he would not care to make.

The pangs of party, with which he sees some of his friends convulsed, and the turbulent anxiety with which they watch the prognostics of its rise and fall, keep him sober without making him indifferent.[87]

Given More's discerning view, one recalls the last line in G.K. Chesterton's trenchant defence of Jane Austen, and a key element of her greatness as a writer—

Jane Austen was born before those bonds which (we are told) protected women from truth, were burst by the Brontës or elaborately untied by George Eliot. Yet the fact remains that Jane Austen knew much more about men than either of them.

Jane Austen may have been protected from truth: but it was precious little of truth that was protected from her.[88]

At the same time, More's incisive reflections run in much the same channel as a line from her friend Wilberforce, who'd known a "long and stormy voyage in the sea of politics."[89] Speaking of Napoleon in early 1808, and his seemingly

---

87 More, *Christian Morals*, vol. 2, 246-247.

88 G.K. Chesterton, *The Victorian Age in Literature* (New York: 1913), 109. Italics added.

89 Wilberforce, *The Life of William Wilberforce*, volume 5, 332.

impregnable place on the world stage, Wilberforce said: "This man is manifestly an instrument in the hands of Providence; when God has done with him, He will probably show how easily He can get rid of him."[90]

Writing with wisdom about the need to rightly understand scenes from the past, More wrote of "the moral lessons of history"—

> *If we apply to our own improvement the...errors of which we read; if we are struck with the successes or defeats of ambition; the pursuits or disappointments of vanity; the sordid accumulations of avarice, or the wasting ravages of prodigality; if we are moved with instances of vice and virtue...if we read with interest of the violence of parties, of which both the leaders and the followers have been long laid in the dust; if we are affected, as every intelligent mind cannot but be affected, with these pictures of things, how much benefit may a well-directed mind derive from seeing them realized; from [as Shakespeare rightly said:] seeing the old scenes acted over again by living performers...*[91]

Here was a moving, clear-sighted, and eloquent reflection on the ancient phrase from Ecclesiastes: "there is nothing new under the sun," made new with a metaphor More drew upon from her time as a playwright, and settings from the stage. For she knew, only too well, as Shakespeare had written, "what's past is prologue."[92]

Yet with equal versatility, More could turn from a cogent discussion along lines that Solomon and Shakespeare knew to

---

90 Wilberforce, *The Life of William Wilberforce,* volume 3, 357.

91 More, *Christian Morals,* vol. 2, 222-223.

92 William Shakespeare, *The Tempest,* Act II, scene one, line 276.

a roster of aphorisms, or brief reflections, each showing her gift for wise, concise expression—with a skill reminiscent of Pascal, in the *Pensées*—or any of her own contemporaries, such as John Newton. Four examples show this—

1.

*much eventual good is educed by Him, who
by turning our suffering to our benefit,
repairs by grace...*[93]

2.

*We are not the creatures of casualty.
We did not come into this world by chance, or by
mistake, for any uncertain end, or any undetermined
purpose, but for a purpose of which we should never lose
sight, for an end to which we should have a constant
reference; that we might bring glory to God now, and be
received by His grace to glory everlasting.*[94]

3.

*But charity is a virtue of all times, and all places.
It is not so much an independent grace in itself, as
an energy, which gives the last touch and highest
finish to every other, and resolves them all into one
common principle.*[95]

4.

*Christianity is a social principle. He who has
discovered the use of time, and consequently the value*

---

93 Hannah More, *Christian Morals,* volume one, 2nd edition, 66.

94 Hannah More, *Christian Morals,* volume two, 2nd edition (London: 1813), 183.

95 Hannah More, *Christian Morals* volume one, 6th edition, (London: 1813), 184-185.

of eternity, cannot but be solicitous for the spiritual
good of his fellow-creatures. The one, indeed, is
indicative of the other.[96]

* * *

Too often, the passing of time can obscure deserving things.

It may be that *Practical Piety* and *Christian Morals* are two of the lesser known, seldom read books in Hannah More's oeuvre. But given the myriad gifts within them, they shouldn't be. Some of her best writing—in prose or poetry—resides in their pages.

In the winter years of her life, a sacred flame brought renewed and deepened faith, which led her to write. With fortitude, and despite painful seasons of recurring illness, she gave good things to the world.

---

96 More, *Christian Morals* volume one, 176.

CHRISTIAN MORALS:

BY

HANNAH MORE.

In moral actions, Divine law helpeth exceedingly the law of Reason to guide a man's life; but in supernatural, it alone guideth.   HOOKER.

FIRST AMERICAN FROM THE FOURTH
LONDON EDITION.

NEW YORK:

PUBLISHED BY EASTBURN, KIRK & CO.
86 BROADWAY, CORNER OF
WALL-STREET.

1813.

The title page of *Christian Morals,* one of Hannah More's most popular late-in-life books, from the 1st American edition, published on Wall Street in New York City

CHAPTER NINE

The 'Teens and 1820s

[The room] into which we were introduced, for the sake of a
more complete prospect of the country, contained her library;
which I should estimate at least at a thousand volumes.[1]

— **JOHN GRISCOM** (1818)

We then walked to Barley Wood. [My hosts, the Harfords,] very
kindly asked me to go upstairs. We saw…Hannah More's room.

The bed is where her sofa and desk used to stand. The old
bookcases—some of them, at least—remain. I could point out
the very place where the 'Don Quixote,' in four volumes, stood,
and the very place from which I took down, at ten years old,
the 'Lyrical Ballads.' With what delight and horror I read the
'Ancient Mariner.'[2]

— **THOMAS BABINGTON**, Lord Macaulay (1852)

---

1   John Griscom, *A Year in Europe,* volume one, (New York: 1824), 125.

2   Ernest Hobson, "Hannah More," an article in *The Westminster* Review" March 1907 (London: 1907), 308-309.

...the twentieth century observer has to remind himself that
inside all this cocoonery of words there was love, there was pain.[3]

— **E.M. FORSTER** (1956)

I feel very unwell and heavy; for I was obliged to
take laudanum last night, being in great pain.[4]

— **HANNAH MORE** (circa 1820)

In some ways, the later years of Hannah More's life were the most interesting years of her story. And why so? The answer is threefold, centred on the place of visitors, children, and friends in her life. These made for active, eventful years, memorable in many ways.

Then too, there was the wide extent of her influence in America: a side of her life that is both fascinating and revealing. All the while, there were colourful moments, scenes of active philanthropy, and poignant vignettes. Though eventful, her final years were at times difficult and deeply trying. Yet in the main, there were many things she treasured about these years: sources of gratitude for mercies given.

In sum, her life was anything but the supposed caricature of a person in their elder years; so often seen as far less noteworthy than the years of their earlier life.

To begin with, visitors made their way to Barley Wood, in astonishing numbers.

In May 1814, More wrote. "For the last month, I do not think we have had fewer than *forty persons*

---

3   E.M. Forster, *Marianne Thornton*, 71. See also Demers, *Hannah More*, 21.

4   *The Christian Observer*, March 1835 (London: 1835), 168n. This quote appears to date circa 1820.

a week, many of them strangers who brought letters from friends."[5]

Such visits continued, unabated, for many years, as William Wilberforce noted in late October 1822, in a letter to John Harford—

Elmdon House, near Coventry...My dear Friend...You are very kind in giving me an account of some of our friends within your circle. Our Barley Wood friend [Hannah] is a wonder to all of us. I heard from Macaulay two or three days ago...that she sees a constant influx of visitors, and is as animated and unsubdued as ever...[6]

In concert with this, one visitor, John Campbell Colquhoun, wrote in a memorable, present tense voice about his family's close friend: the lady of Barley Wood—

Of correspondents, too, there is no lack. England, Scotland, Ireland, and the United States, supply them; France, Denmark, and Russia add their quota. To Barley Wood, as to a place of pilgrimage, come a throng of visitors.

[Miss] More writes to Mr. Wilberforce, in 1825, that her levée from twelve to three is full, and that her young friend [Mary Frowd,] reckons her visitors at eighty in the week.[7]

A unique sidenote presents itself in J.C. Colquhoun. We learn something of him and his family, from More herself, in a letter from 17 November 1821 to Zachary Macaulay—

---

5 Harford, Alice, ed., *Annals of the Harford Family* (London: 1909), 101. Italics added.

6 Harford, *Recollections of Wilberforce*, 122-123.

7 "Mr. Wilberforce and His Contemporaries," *The Christian Observer,* November 1864, (London: 1864), 843. Italics added.

I had yesterday a most interesting family, Mrs. Colquhoun, etc.

She is the broken-hearted widow of the Lord Registrar of Scotland. She lost him and two grown-up daughters, almost together. Her son is now the most promising student at Oriel [College, Oxford].[8]

And here, a curious happenstance crosses Colquhoun's story. For he was the one time owner of Chartwell, the home near Westerham, in Kent, bought by Sir Winston Churchill in the early 1920s. Colquhoun had purchased the property in 1848.[9]

But Colquhoun had other claims to fame. Several times a Member of Parliament, he was the author of a number of political and religious works. He wrote a now-classic memoir: *William Wilberforce: His Friends And His Times* (published in 1866).[10]

In this work we find memories of Hannah More, and it's fascinating to note they were written at Chartwell. To see Colquhoun at a desk there, in the mind's eye, is to glimpse a unique picture of how details of More's life have come down to us.

But before Colquhoun published his book, these recollections appeared first in the November 1864 issue of *The Christian Observer* magazine. There, it was stated—

Her work on Practical Piety, *though more distinctly religious, ran speedily to ten editions; and her work on* Christian Morals, *also in two volumes, published about*

---

8   Arthur Roberts., ed., *Letters of Hannah More to Zachary Macaulay* (New York: 1860), 181.

9   from "Chartwell" an article by the International Churchill Society, at: https://winstonchurchill.org/resources/myths/leading-churchill-myths-chartwell/

10   T.F. Henderson, "Colquhoun, John Campbell," *The Dictionary of National Biography* (New York: 1887), 403.

two years after, [in 1813] was almost equally successful. Her last original work, termed Moral Sketches, *was written in 1819, when she had reached her 75th year.*

She had by this time [suffered the loss of] much domestic happiness. Her last and dearest sister had [died]. Yet this [final book] was characterized with the liveliness and point of her usual style...To these we must add her Essay on the Character and Practical Writings of St. Paul, *which was published in 1815...this was translated, under the direction of the Chief Justice of Ceylon, Sir Alexander Johnstone, into Cingalese, into which language and the Tamul several of her tracts and poems also found their way.*

To celebrate the abolition of slavery in Ceylon, she wrote, in her 74th year, a spirited poem [called The Feast of Freedom. *It was] translated, and recited with enthusiasm in Ceylon at the anniversaries of their liberty.*[11]

Bless the day that sets us free!
Hail the morn of liberty!
Our children's children still shall meet,
Fair freedom's birth to celebrate...

The twelfth of August then shall be
By us forgotten never;
From this bless'd period we are free,
For ever, and for ever.

Bless the day that sets us free!
Hail the morn of liberty![12]

---

11 *The Christian Observer,* November 1864, (London: 1865), 841-842.

12 Hannah More, *The Feast of Freedom* (London: 1827), 11-15.

Aside from Colquhoun's recollections, one friend who somewhat admired, but also sympathized with the flow of constant visitors to Barley Wood was S.C. Wilks, who recalled one conversation on a typical day—

> *"Oh, Mr. [Wilks]," said one of [Miss More's] sisters… "the sandwich-tray was up five times yesterday, to as many parties, and poor Hannah was quite worn out."*[13]

The "challenges" of hospitality notwithstanding, guests old and new found a hostess entering her seventies and eighties, who often surprised them with pungent displays of wit, or a seemingly-constant fund of anecdote.

John Harford, F.R.S., a long-time friend, philanthropist, and patron of the arts, said this of one visit with More, which had taken place at his home, Blaise Castle—

> *As an instance of her sprightly good humour, I remember her whispering to me, as she looked at a youth of fat and florid, but vacant countenance,*
>
> *'Can't you contrive to do some good to that young man who has so much of the corn, wine, and oil in his looks?' [She added,] when I next saw her,*
>
> *'How is our friend—Corn, Wine, and Oil?'*[14]

Harford was one of More's younger circle of friends, of which there were many. From him, an account of her first meeting with Samuel Johnson survives.

It reads much like a vignette from the pages of Boswell—

---

13 *The Christian Observer*, March 1835 (London: 1835), 167.

14 Harford, *Recollections of Wilberforce*, 274.

"After my marriage," Harford said, Hannah's "affectionate kindness was shared by my wife no less than myself… we often [stayed] at Barley Wood. [We] also had the gratification of receiving her, and [her sister] Patty at our own residence. It was on one of these occasions that she described to me her first interview with Dr. Johnson. It took place at the house of Sir Joshua Reynolds, in Leicester Square."

> 'I felt,' she said, 'a little trepidation at entering the apartment where he was, in consequence of something Sir Joshua said to me just before we did so about his occasional roughness of manner; but he received me with a kindness which quite removed any such feeling. He was caressing a parrot; and on hearing my name, he took my hand with the utmost cordiality, and addressed me in a few lines of one of my own poems.'[15]

Harford recounted still other memories of Dr. Johnson, described by his guest from Barley Wood—

> Hannah went on to tell me that on complaining to Dr. Johnson, how malevolently some of her writings had been attacked by the critics of the day, Johnson's sage reply was:
> 'Child, never mind them; don't you know that abuse is the second best thing? Praise may be the best; but oblivion is the evil.'
> Johnson delighted in her company; and when he was not in the best humour, she had a way of parrying his

---

15 Harford, *Recollections of Wilberforce*, 274.

thrusts which turned aside their edge, and provoked some pleasant sally which put all to rights again.

She told me that she was once staying in Oxford when Johnson was there, and that she was invited to be present at a féte given in his honour by some of the members of his college [Pembroke], when the sage was in the highest good humour and delighted everyone. He was not a little attached to some of his Oxford friends, speaking of whom he said to her—

'Child, we were a nest of nightingales.'[16]

Harford rounded out his recollections by telling of the times More spoke of another great friend from the years of London, and the Bluestocking Circle—

She often dwelt with admiration on the lofty intellect and brilliant conversational powers of Edmund Burke, and used to tell of the delight which he imparted to her own evening coteries in Park Street, Bristol, in the intervals of his canvass for that city, of which, as it is well known, he was for some time the distinguished representative.[17]

Aside from younger friends in England, like John Harford, there were many visitors to Barley Wood from America. One was John Griscom, a professor of Natural Philosophy from New York. On holiday in England, he wrote a long letter home, recounting it all—

---

16 Harford, *Recollections of Wilberforce*, 275. Italics added.

17 Harford, *Recollections of Wilberforce*, 278.

Burncoose, in Cornwall,
July 18th, 1818

The evening prior to my leaving Bristol, my kind host, and two of his daughters, proposed to accompany me to Barley Wood [to call upon] the justly celebrated Hannah More. [Her home] is in Somersetshire, 12 miles from Bristol, on the road to Bridgewater.

I could not but feel gratified with such a proposition, as there are few names… whose writings are held in higher estimation…both in England and America…

We arrived at Barley Wood, about noon, and were kindly and politely received by Martha More, the only sister…of the author. Their situation is delightful.

The cottage, as it is called, though covered with thatch, is exceedingly neat, and tasteful…Both within and without, [it] wears all the appearance of simple elegance.

It [is situated] on the gentle declivity of an eminence, and commands a view of the village of Wrington, a short distance below, a richly variegated country with an extensive horizon. The selection of this spot, the plan of the cottage, and the arrangement of the grounds [all reveal] taste and judgment.[18]

---

18 Griscom, *A Year in Europe*, 122-123.

A pastoral view of "Barley Wood," showing the extent of Hannah More's fine country home.

Then, as he awaited the arrival of Hannah More, Griscom had the opportunity to visit with her sister Martha—or "Patty," as she was called within the family circle—

In the short conversation we had with Martha More, before her sister joined us, the former spoke much of the latter, and appeared as much interested in the reputation of her works, and as highly to enjoy their celebrity, as the author herself could do.

The latter soon came in and took us by the hand, with great ease and urbanity...

A table was [then placed] in the middle of the room, around which we all seated ourselves...And as I was introduced...as an American, the conversation turned upon that quarter of the globe. The charitable and religious institutions of our country were inquired after by Hannah, [as] one who feels a lively concern for...every part of the world. She showed us a letter she had received from a deaf and [mute] child of [Dr. Cogswell] of Hartford, Connecticut, [with] a...letter from [T.H. Gallaudet,] the worthy principal of the institution, in that town, for the instruction of the deaf...

The letters had given her much pleasure.[19]

After this, Griscom learned of More's dedication to biblical literacy, and cooperative endeavours, in the spirit of mere Christianity. He also discovered his hostess had reserves of strength that many might not have suspected—

The cause of Bible societies [Miss More] has much at heart, and is decidedly opposed, though a firm church [of England] woman, to the restrictive principles advocated by some of the mitred heads of the establishment.

She had just given a notable demonstration of her zeal in this cause.

The anniversary of the Auxiliary Society of the neighbourhood, was held last week, and she and her sister gave a dinner and a tea entertainment to the whole company.

There were 103 persons who partook of the dinner, and no less than 300 that drank tea. As many as the cottage would hold, were accommodated in it; and the rest were served upon the lawn, around it.

Among them were thirty-seven clergymen, and the Bishop of Gloucester.

---

19 Griscom, *A Year in Europe*, 123.

Notwithstanding she is at the age of seventy-five, and has endured many attacks of disease, she [travelled], yesterday, twenty-two miles, to attend a Sunday school.

Her constitution, or, as she termed it, her "muscular powers," was very strong, for it had carried her, with the blessing of Providence, through the assaults of twenty mortal diseases.[20]

More then told Griscom something of her own history, starting with her views, long years before, of the War for American Independence. Stories of her early writings, and what led her to build her home, Barley Wood, came into the conversation—

She [said that] she had been much opposed to America during the revolutionary struggle, but admitted that we had many worthy characters amongst us...

Her Search after Happiness, *and* Sacred Dramas, *she told me, were the juvenile productions of seventeen; and written with the intention to counteract the growing custom of introducing into female boarding schools, plays of an improper tendency, and allowing them to be acted by the pupils.*

Her views, she thought, had been successful.

She and her surviving sister retired some years ago to this spot, which they found in a state wild and uncultivated. They selected it, for the beauty and healthiness of its situation; and had they surveyed all the south of England, it is questionable whether they could have found a situation more truly delightful.

---

20 Griscom, *A Year in Europe*, 123-124.

The village at the foot of the hill, contains an old Gothic church, and provides them with all the facilities [they need], at a convenient distance.²¹

As More talked, Griscom was drawn to works of art displayed in Barley Wood, and the contents of her well-furnished library. His recollections capture some of the best details we have of paintings she kept, and books she'd collected—

The house is large enough for all the purposes of domestic comfort and hospitality. The walls of the sitting room, below, are ornamented with the portraits of [her] most distinguished friends.

On our attention being turned to them, the characters of the individuals, and particularly their most valuable qualities, were adverted to by Hannah More, with a warmth and energy, which proved that age had not diminished the force of her early recollections, nor the ardour of her friendship. Among these favourites, I noticed particularly the likenesses of William Wilberforce, Elisabeth Carter... and [John] Henderson, the celebrated youthful genius of Bristol. In one corner of the room, was a picture which had been sent her from Geneva [a] scene from one of the most interesting passages of [her novel] Coelebs,— Lucilla, in the attitude of prayer, at the bed-side of her poor sick neighbour.

Her bed-chamber, into which we were introduced for the sake of a more complete prospect of the country, contained her library; which I should estimate at least

---

21 Griscom, *A Year in Europe*, 124.

at a thousand volumes...select and valuable works upon theology, and general literature.

She showed us a letter, from a Russian princess, written with her own hand, in broken English, solely to acknowledge the satisfaction and benefit which the works of Hannah More had afforded her. We were gratified too...seeing a translation of Coelebs, *in...German... and a splendidly bound copy...in French...presents from the continent.[22]*

Closing his letter, Griscom described what it was like to spend time at Barley Wood. He saw handicrafts made by the More sisters, with landscape features that Hannah had taken years to create. Her fondness for nature, and the flora around her home, shone through—

Industry [Griscom said, is] one of the habitual virtues of these worthy sisters.

Besides the numerous literary productions [of Miss More], and the extensive charitable offices in which they are engaged, everything within and about the cottage— the furniture, the needle-work, the flowers, bears the impression of taste and activity.

We pursued the windings of a gravelled walk...and reposed ourselves on seats in rustic arbours, from which glimpses are obtained of the...valley below. In an open spot, at one of the turns of the walk, was a neat, but plain monument, to the memory of Bishop Porteus, who had been [a close] friend; and in another place, a more costly

---

22 Griscom, *A Year in Europe*, 124-125.

stone was erected to the memory of John Locke. This was a present...from [Elizabeth] Montagu...

We all left Barley Wood, with feelings of much satisfaction from the visit. Mine was not diminished, by carrying with me a present of a copy of Christian Morals, *from the hands of the author, given as a [keepsake] of the visit, and in which she wrote my name, in an excellent hand, without spectacles.*

It is rare, indeed, to find so much vivacity of manners, at so advanced a period of life, as these ladies possess. They are fond of a country life.

Hannah remarked to us, that [now, at her age,] the only natural *pleasures which remained to her in their full force, were the love of the country and of flowers.*[23]

* * *

More's friendship with T.H. Gallaudet, mentioned above, has a story as well.

A pioneer in educating the deaf, he was also an evangelical clergyman. When he wrote his *Discourses on the Christian Faith*, it was dedicated to More.[24] There, he stated—

Madam...

Most of [the following Discourses] were delivered while I was [pursuing] in Paris, under the auspices of the venerable Abbè Sicard and his interesting pupil Clere...the object of qualifying myself to instruct an unfortunate and too long neglected portion of my country...the Deaf and Dumb...

---

23 Griscom, *A Year in Europe*, 125-126.
24 T.H. Gallaudet, *Discourses on...Christian Faith and Practice* (London: 1818), v-vii.

You were once pleased, Madam, to express a lively interest in the object which carried me to Europe, and it may afford you some pleasure to know, that it has so far been crowned with the smiles of a kind Providence [that,] six months after the commencement of the Asylum with which I am connected, it has begun...its benefit to thirty pupils.

In such a sphere...I shall deem myself truly happy in being made the instrument of leading one immortal mind to that Saviour in whose service your labours have been blessed with such a rich harvest of success. That He may long continue...your extensive usefulness, and shed upon you...the choicest consolations of His presence and His grace, is, Madam, the earnest prayer of one, who, with thousands of his countrymen, has long been taught to venerate your name and character.

By the time Gallaudet published his *Discourses,* he'd been corresponding with More for three years. One of her first letters to him read—

Barley Wood, near Bristol,
August 30th, 1815

Rev. Sir,—
Your very obliging and interesting letter would not have remained so long unacknowledged, but that the pacquet which inclosed it did not reach my hands till lately.
Of my high opinion of Miss [Lydia] Huntley's talents and piety[25] I shall say the less to you, as I shall thank her separately for her kind present, and shall also write a line

---

25 poet and philanthropist Lydia Huntley Sigourney, known after this time as "the American Hannah More."

to Mr. Wadsworth, both of which I trust, sir, you will have the goodness to convey to their respective addresses.

I shall also beg the favour of your calling on my bookseller, Mr. Hatchard, 190 Piccadilly, and deliver him the inclosed note.

You will be so kind as to charge yourself with one of the copies of my Essay on Saint Paul to Miss Huntley, as a present from the author; the other copy you will please to accept yourself, as a slight testimony of my respect for your character, and for the truly benevolent motive which brings you to England.

I hope it will please God to bless your pious labours, and to make you an important instrument of good in this way to your fellow-creatures, as I find by your friend you are providentially hindered by bad health from the exercise of your more immediate professional duties.

I pray God to give a blessing to your very meritorious undertaking!

It just occurs to me, that it may be useful to you to have an introduction to Mr. Macaulay; he is Editor of The Christian Observer, and is one of the most valuable, pious, and best informed men in this country, and, I think, takes an interest in the deaf and dumb.

Should business bring you to Bristol, I shall be very glad to see you.

My house is about eleven miles from thence.

I am, sir, with respect,
your very obliged,
Hannah More[26]

---

26 Heman Humphrey, *The Life and Labors of the Rev. T.H. Gallaudet* (New York: 1857), 55-56.

More wrote to Gallaudet again when she received her copy of his *Discourses*. She was especially thankful, apart from his book, to receive a letter from a young girl who was one of the deaf students he'd instructed in sign language, and taught to write—

Barley Wood, near Bristol,
28th April, 1818

Rev. and dear Sir, —

I would not return you my thanks for your kind letter and very valuable volume, till I had nearly finished reading your admirable Sermons. You are not one of that numerous class of authors whom it is prudent and safe to thank for their books before one has looked into them, *as the only way of preserving both one's veracity and good breeding.*

I declare my judgment is not bribed by your too flattering and most undeserved dedication, when I assure you, I think 'The Discourses' are of a very superior cast.

Though deeply serious, they are perfectly uninfected with any tincture of the errors of a certain new school in theology. Your style and manner are in thorough good taste, a garb in which I delight to see sound divinity arrayed.

By the blessing of God, I trust they will do much good...

I was going to point out to you the sermons with which I was particularly pleased; but I found the recapitulation would be almost universal. I would not [leave out] any.

I was charmed and deeply affected with the sweet letter of my dear little dumb correspondent! What heartfelt joy, dear sir, must it afford you to have been the honoured instrument of rescuing this, and so many other forlorn little creatures from a state of almost non-entity.

'Inasmuch as ye have done it to one of the least of these, ye have done it to me,' says our divine Master.

I have taken the liberty to convey to your hands, through Mr. Macaulay, a ten pound bank note, as a small token of my admiration of your admirable Institution, to be disposed of by you in such a way as your judgment shall direct for its benefit...

Adieu, my dear sir. May it please Him without whom nothing is strong, nothing is holy, nothing successful, to shower down his blessings on you, and on the great work you have, by so much labour...perilous voyages, and such great difficulties, accomplished...

May many of your pupils thank you in heaven for having been the favoured instrument of bringing them thither. I remain, with sincere esteem,

Your very faithful and obliged,
Hannah More[27]

Ten years after More's correspondence with Gallaudet, she had a visit from American clergyman William Buell Sprague, who would become famous for his collection of rare autographs and manuscripts—one of the finest in the United States.

In April 1828, however, much of this lay in the future. Sprague's task was to pen a letter to *The Christian Observer* in England, describing what it was like to meet Hannah More, and spend a day at her home.

---

27 Humphrey, *Life and Labors*, 84-86. Italics added.

Detailed in ways exceeding John Griscom's account, Sprague's store of memories is much worth quoting at length. It captures many details otherwise lost to the pages of history.

So his letter received its own introduction in *The Christian Observer*—

the above letter [this Introduction began,] is only one of hundreds that have been written by affectionate admirers of those two kindred minds [Hannah More and William Wilberforce]; but as it happens to be at hand, and as it conveys some particulars which may interest those who did not know Mrs. More personally, we subjoin it.[28]

Scarcely more than one sentence long, this introductory word tells a compelling story. Samuel Charles Wilks, editor of *The Christian Observer*, told readers he had received literally *hundreds* of letters paying tribute to the friendship of Hannah More and William Wilberforce. It was a famous friendship; noted for their collaboration, over many years, in many "concerts of benevolence."[29] At the same time, the fact that More's home had now become a place of pilgrimage was underscored, implicitly, in what Wilks shared.

This then, was the setting for Sprague's remarkable letter.[30] It began—

---

28 This letter appears, in toto, on pages 270-271 of the October 1833 issue of *The Christian Observer* (of London), and it would appear that the editor of *The Christian Observer* had a copy of Sprague's book, *Letters from Europe in 1828: First Published in The New York Observer*, at hand, from which the text of Sprague's letter was taken.

29 Wilberforce, *The Life of William Wilberforce*, v. 3, 374: from Wilberforce's letter to President Thomas Jefferson, 5 September 1808, in the National Archives online at: https://founders.archives.gov/documents/Jefferson/99-01-02-8773.

30 The very date of Sprague's letter is poignant. Just under three weeks after this, More left Barley Wood forever, moving to Clifton.

Bristol, April 1, 1828

My dear Sir—

If you are aware that Barley Wood, the far-famed residence of Mrs. Hannah More, is but ten miles from Bristol, you will not be surprised to know that I have given a day to visiting that delightful spot, and that incomparable woman.

This indeed constituted part of the plan of my tour from the moment that I determined to visit England; and having accomplished my purpose, I am happy now to be able to give you an account of one of the most interesting interviews I have ever enjoyed, while the particulars of it are fresh…

Yesterday morning, I set out…with my friend, Mr. H., for Mrs. More's residence.

As the morning was delightful, we had a fine view from some of the neighbouring hills of the city, and its environs, and particularly of Clifton, whose wild and beautiful scenery has called into exercise some of the most exquisite powers of the pen… After travelling over a delightful country, about nine miles, we found by inquiry that we were quite near the celebrated cottage, a sight of which, with its venerable inhabitant, was the object of our excursion; and we soon turned out of the main road, and followed rather an obscure path for nearly a mile, till we reached the gate of Barley Wood.[31]

Next, Sprague said he was fortunate in the timing of his visit, for More's health hadn't been good of late. Yet as it was, she was

---

31 *The Christian Observer*, October 1833, (London: 1833), 629.

well enough to receive a guest, especially one from America, a country from which she was always happy to receive news, and ask questions as to its leading citizens and undertakings.

Sprague captured this in what he wrote—

We were gratified to learn from the servant at the door, that Mrs. M. was in comparatively comfortable health; as we had heard of her having been recently ill, and were apprehensive that she might still be too feeble to receive company.

We were seated for a few moments in the parlour, the walls of which are nearly lined with the portraits of distinguished men, many of them Mrs. M.'s intimate friends.

I sent up my letters of introduction, and the servant soon returned with a request that we would walk into the apartment in which Mrs. M. was sitting.

When we entered the room, she rose and shook hands with us in a familiar and pleasant manner, which made me quite forget the embarrassment which I was prepared to feel on approaching so exalted a character.[32]

A gifted stylist, Sprague then crafted a prose portrait of More at this time of her life. With a keen eye for detail, he did not fail to notice she wasn't completely an invalid. Indeed, she ventured outdoors when fine weather and her health permitted—

She is rather small in stature, has a most regular and expressive countenance, and an eye which beams forth nothing but intelligence and benignity. She is now eighty-three years of age; and for the last five years has been

---

32 *The Christian Observer*, October 1833, 629.

confined to her room by bodily indisposition, except that in the Summer season, she has been occasionally carried out, and drawn by her servants in a hand-carriage about her grounds.[33]

As with nearly any visit to Barley Wood, it did not take long for More to speak of her friendship with Wilberforce. Sprague made this a highlight, and said More was especially grateful for the gift of Wilberforce's prayers during his visits—

She soon spoke of her "dear friend, Mr. Wilberforce," in connexion with the letter which I had brought from him; and when I told her that I had lately spent a most delightful hour and a half in his company, she replied that she had no doubt it was an hour and a half spent near the threshold of heaven. She observed that Mr. W. was one of her oldest friends; that his writings had produced a very beneficial effect on the higher circles in this country; and "his prayers," said she, "in my family, when he is here, are heavenly."[34]

After her tribute to Wilberforce, More told Sprague something of the history of Barley Wood, noting the memorial urns placed about the grounds of her home, and landscaped views she had created and arranged over the years.

Along the way, with a smile in her countenance, she gave a sly instance of her famous wit, followed just after with a philosophic theme on the passing of time—

---

33 *The Christian Observer*, October 1833, 629.
34 *The Christian Observer*, October 1833, 629.

When I remarked on the beautiful situation of Barley Wood, she replied that she should send her servant soon to conduct us over her little domain, and requested that we would particularly notice a monument that she had erected in honour of John Locke, and another to the memory of her "dear friend," Bishop Porteus; "but," said she, "you must first view the different prospects which I have from my house."

After pointing out to us some of the many beautiful objects to be seen from the room in which we were sitting, she conducted us into an adjoining apartment, which was her sleeping room; and pointing to an armed chair—

"That chair," said she, "I call my home. Here," looking out of a window, "is what I call my moral prospect [thus introducing a pun on her name. Then, she continued:] You see yonder distant hill, which limits the prospect in that direction. You see this tree before my window, directly in range of the hill. The tree, you observe, from being near, appears higher than the hill which is distant; though the hill actually is much higher than the tree.

Now this tree represents, to my mind, the objects of time; that hill, the objects of eternity. The former, like the tree, from being viewed near at hand, appear great; the latter, like the hill, from being viewed at a distance, appear small."[35]

Kindly inquiring after Sprague's health, the recovery of which had occasioned his visit to England. More spoke of her own struggles with debility. As Sprague observed—

---

35 *The Christian Observer*, October 1833, 629-630.

Speaking of...my health...the occasion of my present
absence from home, she advised me to be particularly on
my guard against undue excitement. "The disciples," she
observed, "could sleep in sorrow;" and she had found that
she could sleep far better after a day of affliction, than
after an interview which had caused much excitement.[36]

Remarkably, for a first meeting with a new American friend,
More told Sprague next something quite personal about her
writing habits, and what occasioned them—

Her own character through life, she said, had been marked
by impatience; not that impatience which would lead
her to be peevish towards her servants or others around
her; but that which led her to push on a work, when
she had commenced it, till it was completed; and to this
trait...especially, she attributed the fact of her having
written so much.[37]

Sprague then added More's reflections on her fading memory,
in ways that were both endearing and bittersweet. An author
for so many years, she now found her recollection of the very
books she'd written was declining. Yet even as their contents
became forgotten lines, she kept to her calling—

She remarked that she had never been able to quote from
her own writings; that her companion would often read
to her paragraphs from them, and she did not recognize
them as her own; and though her memory, in regard to
most subjects, seems to be very perfect, she assured us

---

36 *The Christian Observer*, October 1833, 630.

37 *The Christian Observer*, October 1833, 630. Italics added.

that she could not now recollect the titles of all her works; and having occasion to refer to one of them while we were sitting with her, she looked up to the book-case in which they were, and said,

"I do not remember the title, but it is something about Christianity I believe."

She presented me with her last work, on The Spirit of Prayer, saying that it was principally a compilation from her other works, and was dictated to a friend, while she was confined to her bed, and supposed herself near the gate of eternity...

she felt the importance of the subject so deeply, that she determined to send the work to the press, though the sale of it should be limited to fifty copies; but 8,000 copies were disposed of within less than six months.

She also presented me with another work of hers, which I had never seen before, entitled, Hints to a Young Princess; and accounted for its not having been printed in America, as her other works have been, from the fact that it was deemed inapplicable to our form of government; though, she remarked, that with the exception of forty pages, it applied equally to the education of all females in the higher walks of life.

Of the late Princess Charlotte, for whose benefit this work was particularly designed, she spoke as a most amiable, accomplished and promising character, and expressed the hope that she died the death of the righteous...[38]

---

38 The Christian Observer, October 1833, 630.

Sprague had no way of knowing, but More would soon leave Barley Wood forever, and move to Clifton. This adds poignancy, though unintended, to his account—

[Mrs. More] told us that the place on which she resides had been in her possession twenty-six years; that when she purchased it, it was in a wild, uncultivated state; and that whatever ornamental trees or shrubs we should see in walking over it, were planted by her own hand. As we passed round [it all,] we saw, at almost every step, some monument of the taste of this wonderful woman. We were particularly struck with the wild beauty of a 'Druidical temple,' as Mrs. M. called it, made of knots of oak, disposed in such a manner as to represent the most fanciful figures.

Mrs. M.'s dwelling, [Barley Wood,] is a thatched cottage, standing on...a gently sloping hill, overlooking the church and village of Wrington, a charming verdant vale... commanding a view of the Bristol Channel, and a beautiful range of hills which skirt the distant horizon. After going over her grounds, we returned for a short time to her chamber, where she had provided some refreshment for us...

[There,] she again entertained us by her delightful conversation.

On taking leave of her, she expressed the kindest sentiments, and, with an air of unaffected humility, [asked] me to remember her [at the] throne of mercy; [adding] that she attached great importance to intercessory prayer; [saying] she was a poor creature who needed an interest in the prayers of God's people as much as anyone.[39]

---

39 *The Christian Observer*, October 1833, 630-631.

To close, Sprague offered these valedictory thoughts—

...this interesting spot...I am sure, will be associated through life with some of my most delightful recollections... On leaving Wrington, we again passed Barley Wood on our return to Bristol; and I kept my eye on that charming spot, till it was hidden behind the hill, though my imagination still lingers about it with unabated interest.

I could not but reflect, when I heard Mrs. M. converse, and recollected what she had been, and saw what she was, that hers was one of the most honoured, useful and happy lives that the world has known. In her progress through life, she has diffused blessings at every step; and has probably contributed far more to elevate the standard of female education, and female character, than any other person living.

Her old age is rendered serene and cheerful by a review of her past life on the one hand, and by a firm trust in the Saviour on the other; and she is now waiting, in the bright hope of immortality, till her change come. Few indeed can hope to descend to the tomb like her, amidst the benedictions of a world; but there are none who may not aspire to that which constitutes her noblest distinction: a life of faith and piety.

I have extended the account of my visit to Barley Wood much beyond what I intended; but if any apology is necessary, you have it in the fact that it has made such an impression upon my mind [that I can] write and talk of nothing else.[40]

---

40 *The Christian Observer*, October 1833, 631.

Some years after his return from England, Sprague wrote a book inspired by More's example. It was titled *The Daughter's Own Book, or Practical Hints from a Father to His Daughter*. In its pages, he tenderly wrote to his twelve-year-old daughter Charlotte, whose mother had died when she was an infant—

If I should point you to the finest model of female manners which it has ever been my privilege to observe...I should repeat a venerated name, that of...Hannah More.

It was my privilege, a few years ago, to make a visit to [her] residence...a visit which I have ever since regarded as among the happiest incidents of my life.

At that time she numbered more than fourscore years; but the vigour of her intellect was scarcely at all impaired; and from what she was, I could easily conceive what she had been when her sun was at its meridian.

In her person she was rather small, but...of admirable symmetry. In her manners she united the dignity and refinement of the court, with the most exquisite urbanity and gentleness...She impressed me continually with a sense of the high intellectual and moral qualities by which she was distinguished, but...left me as unconstrained [in her presence] as if I had been conversing with my beloved child.

There was an air of graceful and unaffected ease, an instinctive regard to the most delicate proprieties...a readiness to communicate, and yet a desire to listen... united with the humility of the devoted Christian...

I rejoice that it is the privilege of all [readers] to know Mrs. More through her works; and I can form no better wish for you than that you may imbibe her spirit, and walk in her footsteps.[41]

The family of American founding father, Dr. Benjamin Rush, seen earlier, was also much indebted to Hannah More. Rush's son Richard, who was an Ambassador to England from the United States, wrote to More, praising her book, *Hints Towards Forming the Character of a Young Princess* (published in 1805). He then contrasted it with another famous text—

I think I see in it full as much of what is elevated, and more of what is practically useful, than in [Fénelon's] 'Telemachus.' I intend that my son shall read 'Telemachus' every year, from the time he is sixteen till he is twenty; and I am now truly pleased that he will have such a companion for your kind present.[42]

In Fénelon's text, Telemachus (or Télémaque), the son of Ulysses, was shipwrecked upon the island of the goddess Calypso, "Telemachus relates to her his varied and stirring adventures while seeking his father Ulysses, who, going to the Trojan war, has been absent from home for twenty years." In his search, Telemachus was "guarded and guided by the goddess Minerva, disguised as the sage Mentor."[43]

More's biographer, Henry Thompson, speaking of this letter, observed—

"The occasion which called forth Mr. Rush's letter is interesting. His father, Dr. Rush, feeling his health decline, wrote to Mrs. More, saying he could not quit the world,

41 W.B. Sprague, *The Daughter's Own Book* (Boston: 1833), 104-105.

42 Thompson, *Hannah More*, 238. Italics added.

43 Helen Rex Keller, *The Reader's Digest of Books* (New York: 1923), 827.

without thanking her for what she had written. Mrs. More immediately replied, but her letter did not reach America till after the doctor's death [in April 1813]. The letter quoted [above] was a reply to Mrs. More's."[44]

Richard Rush, while Ambassador to the Court of St. James, had the opportunity to meet others in More's wider circle of friends, William Wilberforce among them.

Such meetings added to his esteem for these philanthropic friends, and he wrote soon after meeting Wilberforce in 1818: "Most of the company were public professors of religion; always the more attractive, when in alliance with genius and accomplishments."[45]

These words were of a piece with Rush's letter to More from 1813, for at that time, he'd said essentially that, in the pages of her book, she was a "Minerva" to be preferred instead of the Mentor depicted in Fénelon's text. It was a literary compliment to remember; and one with an ambassador's imprimatur.

Nor was this the only correspondence associated with More and famous figures from the era of the early American republic. One very memorable letter was written when W.B. Sprague sent a gift copy of his book, *Letters from Europe, 1828* to John Marshall, Chief Justice of the Supreme Court. More and Wilberforce were given prominent character sketches, with passages of their conversation, gathered from Sprague's visits to their homes.

In reply, Marshall told Sprague, on 11 June 1829: "I am indebted to your goodness… Your animated description of the country, and of the magnificent edifices you had seen almost brought them before my view."[46]

---

44 Thompson, *Hannah More,* 238n.

45 Richard Rush, *A Residence at the Court of London* (London: 1833), 172.

46 John Marshall to W.B. Sprague, 11 June 1829, from *The Collector* magazine, September 1909 (New York: 1909), 109.

Then, warming to his theme, Marshall added a telling qualification—

however much I may be pleased with the topographical part of the work, I am still more interested in your description of living character. The reading world, in the United States, has long possessed a general knowledge of Mr. Wilberforce and Miss Hannah More, and this general knowledge, accompanied as it universally is with admiration, increases the admiration of being introduced to them in their private and retired scenes.[47]

Marshall's letter bore testimony to the place More held among readers in America during the first fifty years of the new nation. England and America had twice been at war with one another—during the War for Independence, and in the War of 1812. For many in both nations, feelings of bitterness might have persisted.

But More's writings, and her legacy as a reformer, won friends an ocean away.

* * *

More's life and writings also found favour in American academia.

Here, storied institutions like Harvard, Bowdoin, and Middlebury figure in the life of John Codman (Harvard, Class of 1802). His biography was written by William Allen, D.D., the former President of Bowdoin, with reminiscences by Dr. Joshua Bates, past President of Middlebury. Both men, leaders of New England culture, knew of Codman's great respect for Hannah More as a writer, abolitionist, and reformer.

---

47 *The Collector magazine*, September 1909, 110.

All his life, Codman had a great love for England, and the spiritual heritage of the British Isles. Briefly told, his story is as follows.

Born at Boston, in 1782, Codman was educated at Andover Academy and Harvard. After his graduation, he began the study of the law with his kinsman John Lowell of Boston.

Just before his father died in May 1803, leaving an ample fortune, he expressed a wish that his son become a minister. Codman honoured this wish, abandoned the study of the law, and began preparing himself for the ministry.

In 1805 he visited Europe, and pursued his theological studies in Scotland. He spent three years abroad, visiting many places in Great Britain. In 1807, he obtained at Bristol a license to preach, and was invited to preach at the Scotch Church of Swallow Street, London, where he officiated about a year. He returned to New England in May 1808.

In November 1824, he took a sea voyage to Charleston, South Carolina, for the benefit of his health, and spent several months there, in company with his wife and one of her cousins. On the 1st of February 1825, all three set sail for Liverpool, where they arrived the 22nd. They spent about five months in Europe, including a short visit to Paris.

Among the celebrities they visited were the Thomas Chalmers, D.D., at St. Andrew's, Scotland, and Hannah More at her home, Barley Wood. In later years, and visits to England, Codman attended the anniversaries of many religious and philanthropic societies at London. He spoke at meetings of the British and Foreign Bible Society, the Religious Tract Society, the London Missionary Society, and the Congregational Union of England and Wales.[48]

---

48 information gleaned from *The New England Historical and Genealogical Register,* October 1894
   (Boston, 1894), 409-412.

Codman was thoroughly in step with many endeavours More championed.

* * *

We are indebted to Codman, as a friend of England, for an important account of his visit to Barley Wood. It contains vital information. On the morning of 4 May 1825, Codman and his travelling party set out for "the residence of Mrs. More." On their arrival he presented his card, and was told that "she would see us with pleasure." As Codman remembered—

> We were then conducted to her bed-chamber, [and] found her seated in an easy-chair. She rose at our entrance, extended her hand, and gave us a most cordial reception. Her person interested us exceedingly.
>
> She has a fine countenance, full of animation, and expressive of everything kind and benevolent. She wore a plain lace cap, with a wreath of white ribbon in front, and her hair was slightly powdered.[49]

Codman was seated next to More. As they conversed, "her countenance brightened," and "she occasionally laid her hand upon his arm"—a gesture "expressive of the interest which she felt in the subject of conversation."[50]

When Codman indicated he hadn't seen her most recent work, *The Spirit of Prayer,* More at once handed him a copy, saying, "I will make you a present of it. It was compiled during my late illness, and was intended as a death-bed present to my friends."

---

49 William Allen, *The Memoir of John Codman* (Boston: 1853), 129.
50 Allen, *Memoir of John Codman*, 129-130.

The Spirit of Prayer was a deep, discerning, eloquent book—set with gems of faith. In its pages, More wrote of "the vast dimensions of the love of Christ." Words of solace lived in her reflections, such as "extraordinary grace is imparted for extraordinary trials." She'd learned that for herself, all along her journey. And last, she conveyed a world of meaning when she wrote, "wherever we are, still we are in God's presence."[51]

Codman then learned something of More's physical debility at this time—

[as she] wrote [my] name on the leaf, without using her glasses, for which she said she seldom had occasion, she remarked that it had pleased God to deprive her of both taste and smell, "which," she said, "you may think somewhat afflictive; but no, for I have been doomed for the last eight years to live upon medicines, and I can see the kindness of my Heavenly Father in continuing to me the two intellectual senses—seeing and hearing, while He has deprived me only of those which, under existing circumstances, would have been a source of misery."[52]

Yet after this sombre moment came another, both happy and memorable—

On a table before her [Codman wrote,] lay a box made of mulberry wood, which, [was crafted] from a tree planted by the hand of Shakespeare. We read aloud, at her request, the lines...inscribed upon it:

---

51 Hannah More, *The Spirit of Prayer,* third edition, (London: T. Cadell, 1825), 171, 205, and 75.

52 Allen, *Memoir of John Codman,* 130.

I kissed the ground where Shakespeare's ashes lay,
And bore this relic of the bard away. 1767.[53]

Looking round More's room, after examining this gift from David Garrick, Codman noted what the room was like, in fine detail—

The room in which she received us was furnished in a very simple manner.

One part of it contains her library, and in the other part there is a bow with three windows, down to the floor. In this bow, a large number of beautiful plants and flowers were arranged. Beside her was a table, composed of parts of the different kinds of trees growing at Barley Wood, all of which she had planted with her own hand, excepting one, which was put into the ground by her friend, Bishop Porteus, and was distinguished from the rest by its peculiar colour and texture.[54]

Then came a resplendent moment, as telling as it was a change of subject from what had been the stream of Codman's recollections. It was fleeting, but powerful—

Something had previously been said on the subject of slavery in our southern States, and Mrs. More remarked, that if she could live to see that evil remedied in our country...she could say, "Now let Thy servant depart in peace."[55]

Peaceful, pastoral lines brought a close to Codman's account—

---

53 Allen, *Memoir of John Codman*, 130.

54 Allen, *Memoir of John Codman*, 130.

55 Allen, *Memoir of John Codman*, 130.

*As we were leaving, Mrs. More begged us to walk about
her grounds, and visit the monuments which she had
erected to the memory of Locke, and of her friend [Bishop]
Porteus. We walked through a winding path, bordered by
shrubbery, with here and there a little rural house, which
had been erected for the accommodation of Mrs. More
and her friends, in their rambles through this delightful
solitude. Near where we stood, on the top of the hill, was the
monument to Locke presented by [Elizabeth] Montagu...*[56]

In addition to John Codman's recollections, there were others
from someone many regarded as More's literary representative
in America, Samuel Goodrich, the wealthy author and
publisher who issued the first complete American edition of
More's *Works* in 1827.

Prior to this, in May 1824, and after weathering a hurricane
at sea near Ireland, Goodrich arrived in England, and toured
the country. He recalled—

*[I] departed for Bristol, taking the...cathedral at Salisbury
and the Druidical ruin of Stonehenge in my way. Having
reached that city and seen its sights, I hired a post-coach,
and went to Barley Wood, some ten miles distant. Hannah
More was still there!*

*The house consisted of a small, thatched edifice, half
cottage and half villa, tidily kept...garnished with vines and
trellises, giving it a cheerful and even tasteful appearance.*

*Its site was on a gentle hill, sloping to the southeast,
and commanding a charming view over the undulating
country...including the adjacent village of Wrington,*

---

56 Allen, *Memoir of John Codman*, 131.

with a wide valley sloping to the Bay of Bristol, the latter sparkling in the distance, and bounded by the Welsh mountains, in the far horizon. Behind the house, and on the crown of the hill, was a small copse, threaded with neat gravel walks, and at particular points embellished with objects of interest. In one place there was a little rustic temple, with this motto [from Virgil:] Audi Hospes, contemnere opes—

[that motto reads in full: "Have the courage, my guest, to scorn riches; make yourself, too, worthy of deity, and come not disdainful of our poverty."][57]

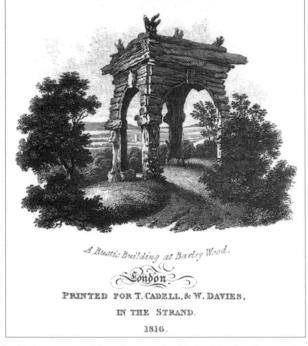

A Rustic Building at Barley Wood.

London

PRINTED FOR T. CADELL, & W. DAVIES,
IN THE STRAND.
1816.

The "little rustic temple" on the grounds of Barley Wood, with its overlook of the countryside, the title page image from More's *Poems* (1816)

---

57 Virgil, Aeneid: Books 7-12 (Cambridge: 2001), 87. The Barley Wood temple motto cites lines 364-365 from Virgil's *Aeneid*, Book VIII.

in another [place], there was a stone monument, erected to the memory of Bishop Porteus, who had been a particular friend...A little further on, I found another monument, with this inscription: "To John Locke, born in this village, this monument is erected by Mrs. Montagu... and presented to Hannah More." *From this sequestered spot, an artificial opening was cut through the foliage of the trees, giving a view of the very house, about a mile distant, in which Locke was born! In another place was a small temple built of roots, which might have served for the shrine of some untamed race of Dryads.*[58]

Next, Goodrich offered vivid memories of More's appearance and manner—

Mrs. More was now seventy-nine years of age, and was very infirm, having kept her room for two years. She was small, and wasted away.

Her attire was of dark-red bombazine, made loose like a dressing-gown. Her eyes were black and penetrating, her face glowing with cheerfulness, through a lace-work of wrinkles. Her head-dress was a modification of the coiffure of her earlier days—the hair being slightly frizzed, and lightly powdered, yet the whole...of moderate dimensions. She received me with great cordiality, and learning that I was from Hartford, immediately inquired about Mrs. [Lydia] Sigourney, [T.H.] Gallaudet, and Alice Cogswell...

---

58 S.G. Goodrich, *Recollections of a Lifetime*, volume two (New York: 1856), 163-164.

Of the latter [a young deaf-mute girl who had written to her,] she spoke with great interest.[59] She mentioned several Americans who had visited her, and others with whom she had held correspondence.[60]

Throughout this time, More was animated, and keenly interested in all that Goodrich had to tell. In return, she recounted chapters of her literary history—

Her mind and feelings [Goodrich observed,] were alive to every subject that was suggested. She spoke very freely of her writings and her career.

I told her of the interest I had taken, when a child, in the story of The Shepherd of Salisbury Plain, *upon which she recounted its history, remarking that the character of the hero was modelled from life, though the incidents were fictitious.*

[I also learned that] her tract, called Village Politics, by Will Chip, *was written at the request of the British Ministry, and two million copies were sold the first year. She showed me copies of* Coelebs in Search of a Wife— *the most successful of her works—in French and German, and a copy of one of her sacred dramas—*Moses in the Bullrushes—*on palm-leaves, in the Cingalese tongue— it having been translated into that language by the missionary school at Ceylon. She showed me also the knife with which the leaf had been prepared, and the scratches made in it to receive the ink.*

---

59 Gardner Hubbard, *The Oral Method [for the Deaf] in America* (Washington: 1898), 16: "in 1816 the parents and friends of a little deaf girl in Hartford, Connecticut, sought for her some means of instruction, it was found that there were no schools for the deaf in America. This little girl was Alice Cogswell, daughter of Dr. Cogswell, a prominent citizen of Hartford. Her situation excited the sympathy of many friends..."

60 Goodrich, *Recollections,* 164-165.

She expressed a warm interest in America, and stated that Wilberforce had always exerted himself to establish and maintain good relations between Great Britain and our country. I suggested to her that in the United States, the general impression—that of the great mass of the people—was that the English were unfriendly to us.

She said it was not so. I replied that the Americans all read the English newspapers, and generally, the products of the British press; that feelings of dislike, disgust, animosity, certainly pervaded most of these publications, and it was natural to suppose that these were the reflections of public opinion in Great Britain. At all events, our people regarded them as such, and hence inferred that England was our enemy.

She expressed great regret at this state of things, and said all good people should strive to keep peace between the two countries: *to all which I warmly assented.*[61]

As his time as Barley Wood drew to a close, Goodrich recalled—

My interview with this excellent lady was, on the whole, most gratifying.

Regarding her as one of the greatest benefactors of the age...indeed, one of the most remarkable women that had ever lived...I looked upon her not only with veneration but affection. She was one of the chief instruments by which the torrent of vice and licentiousness, emanating from the French Revolution and inundating the British Islands, was checked and driven back...She was even, to a great

---

61 Goodrich, *Recollections,* 165-166. Italics added.

extent, [a] reformer of British morals and manners—as
well among the high, as the humble...

    I felt that I owed her a special debt, and my visit...was
almost like a pilgrimage...[62]

Other recollections, aside from summer-time scenes, survive
in the writings of novelist Anna Maria Hall. With a painterly
turn, she rendered scenes of Barley Wood when England
was shrouded with snow. In answer to "a note of invitation"
from More, "written by her own hand," Hall began her much-
anticipated journey.[63] As she remembered—

In the month of January, 1825, during a fall of sleet and
snow, we left Bristol to [visit] Hannah More...close to
the...village of Wrington in Somersetshire...

    [Her] great work in life had been accomplished, [her]
lessons had been [my] guides from youth...and [her]
friends were the...immortalities of a gone-by age.

    Her Strictures on Female Education *had been [my]*
Polar Star from infancy...

    The snow was deep on the ground, and the friends
with whom we sojourned said it was madness to set out...
on such a morning, particularly as [Miss More's] hours
of reception were but from twelve till three...But we were
decided, and the journey of some ten miles was passed
in speculations as to what she would say, how she would
look [and] what we should say [to] Hannah More, [who'd]
written Practical Piety *and* Christian Morals, *who had*
suggested to royalty how a Princess should be educated...
been complimented by Dr. Johnson...exchanged wit with

---

62 Goodrich, *Recollections*, 166-167.

63 Hall, *Pilgrimages to English Shrines*, 49.

*Sheridan, [and] enjoyed the social eloquence of Burke. [For
years, she'd] been the honoured counsellor of Porteus and
Wilberforce, and the familiar friend of David Garrick...*

*All that she had written...all we had heard of her,
gathered about our memory as the wheels rolled softly in the
snow; or, sinking deeper, crackled upon the frozen paths.*[64]

Other thoughts came to mind as the carriage made its arduous
way. Hall remembered More's philanthropic work, and how,
with fortitude, it was continued; despite many physical trials,
or seasons of prolonged illness—

*[driving on,] we counted up the schools which owed their
existence, not only to her money and influence, but to her
[industry], and that while struggling with infirm health...*

*At length, we saw the chimneys of Barley Wood above
the trees, and driving along between high hedges...whose
bright leaves occasionally pierced through masses of snow,
we drew up with a frosty crash at the door of the school
master's daughter.*

*It was a pretty cottage, simply and purely rustic; even
in winter, it looked cheerful, with its eaves where swallows
build, its covering of English thatch, [and] pillars hewn
from the adjacent wood...*[65]

Alighting from the carriage, for a few brief moments in the
winter chill, Hall and her travelling party stepped into Barley
Wood gratefully—

---

64 Hall, *Pilgrimages to English Shrines*, 50-51.
65 Hall, *Pilgrimages to English Shrines*, 51-52.

A country serving girl gave us entrance; and we stood for a moment in the hall...

We were kept waiting for a few minutes in the parlour, in which were hung several old and interesting engravings. The stillness and torpor of a frosty atmosphere had hushed all external noise, save the cold chilling whistle that moves no leaf...

The snow was cleared away from the porch, and food for...wild birds had been strewed within the circle; several...were still there, and the [snow] was marked with the impress of their feet; [the] slender toes of the...lark, the broad foot of the wood-pigeon, the deliberate prints of the thrush and the blackbird—[all] told of the considerate charity that [looked] to their wants...Once a glittering shower of crystals fell from a...bough, and a flock of starlings wheeled up, but to return again to the same spot.

While watching these...birds, a demure-looking servant ushered us up-stairs, and though all was so still without, within we heard voices and the very merry laugh of a child—a glow...diffused through the half-opened door, [created by] the heat and light which are so delightful after a chilling drive.

When we entered, a glance showed...the room was not too large for comfort... the walls were lined with books, [and] a group...of three ladies and a little boy were round a table, upon which there was an abundant supply of cake and wine...

To the cake, the little fellow was doing ample justice; and a diminutive old lady was in the act of adding another piece to that already upon his plate...

She moved to meet us, [and] it was the least possible movement, but it was most courteous. Instead of black velvet, Hannah More wore a dress of very light green silk—a white China crape shawl was folded over her shoulders...

Her white hair was frizzed, after a by-gone fashion, above her brow, [and] backed, as it were, by a very full double border of rich lace; [the image] was as dissimilar from the picture painted by our imagination as anything could well be; such a sparkling, light, bright, 'summery'-looking old lady...[66]

Just then, Hall saw a display of the love and keen interest More had for children—

[As] the visitor and her son took their leave; 'Mrs. Hannah' stooped and kissed the boy, not as old maidens usually [do,] with a kiss of necessity, or a kiss of compliment: she took his...face between her hands, and looked down upon it for a moment, as a mother would; then kissed it fondly more than once...

'And when you are a man, my child, will you remember me?'

The boy's eyes glanced from her to the remnants of the cake...

'Well, remember the cake at Barley Wood,' she said, reading his thoughts [as] her own, and laughing.

'Both,' replied the little fellow... 'It was a nice cake, and you are so kind.'

'That is the way I like the young to remember me,' she replied, 'by being kind*—then you will always remember old Mrs. Hannah More.'*

'Always, Ma'am,' he answered...as he returned her gaze...

---

66 Hall, *Pilgrimages to English Shrines*, 52-53.

'I'll try and remember it always,' he repeated, and then there was another kiss.[67]

There was another, rather Dickensian moment. Hall captured it with her pen—

'What a dear child,' said Mrs. Hannah after they were gone, 'and of a good stock—that child will be as true as steel! I so enjoyed his glance at the cake; it was so much more natural he should remember that than an old woman so very little taller than himself…

[He is] a dear child—I hope he may be spared to his lonely mother'--and her eyes were in an instant suffused with the light of coming tears, as if there had been something sad in that young mother's history [that she knew of and tried to help with].[68]

Curiosities from far places, and literary items, were next on Hall's home tour of Barley Wood. The first set of items was perhaps the very last thing she expected to see—

There were some South Sea curiosities scattered about the room, as if they had been recently examined. [Mary Frowd,] the lady who was residing with [Mrs. Hannah], her tried friend and companion, directed our attention to these things…

While the venerable lady drew nearer to the fire, [this friend, seeing] our interest …showed us translations of many of her works…the eleventh edition of one, the tenth of another, and so on: every spot in the room was

---

67 Hall, *Pilgrimages to English Shrines*, 54. Italics added.
68 Hall, *Pilgrimages to English Shrines*, 54.

distinguished by having some treasure in its keeping, and every article of virtù had its story…One in particular attracted us—an inkstand made of Shakespeare's real mulberry tree, the gift of David Garrick.

It was impossible not to congratulate her on the possession of such mementos.[69]

And here, Hall heard a revealing and forthright admission from her hostess—

'Yes,' *[More] said,* 'this place is in itself a great blessing from the hand of Heaven, and the trees you praise are well grown, and have taken deep root; and old as I am, there are times when I feel it a duty to be careful lest I become too deeply rooted myself in a soil sanctified by friends and friendships!'[70]

Something of what More's voice sounded like, and her habit of expression at times caught Hall's eye. Her hostess wasn't one to stand on ceremony; instead, she carried herself with good humour, and humility, in the evening of her years—

Her voice had a pleasant tone, and her manner was quite devoid of affectation… she spoke as one expecting a reply, and by no means like an oracle. And those bright immortal eyes of hers—not wearied by looking at the world for more than eighty years, but clear and far-seeing then,—laughing too, when she spoke cheerfully…

---

69   Hall, *Pilgrimages to English Shrines*, 54.
70   Hall, *Pilgrimages to English Shrines*, 55. Italics added.

Her friend [Mary Frowd]⁷¹ said she had been fatigued sooner than usual that morning by visitors; but would recover and be herself presently. She drew close to the fire, and seemed inclined to repose or to muse, we could hardly tell which…

It was a privilege to look at her for the few moments she 'rested,' and to think of all she had done; when so far from education being, as it is now, 'the fashion,' it was something so new as to be considered dangerous, particularly to women…⁷²

During More's impromptu siesta, Hall noted other things about her appearance—

Her brow was full and well-sustained, [and] though her eyes were half-closed, her countenance was more tranquil, more sweet…than when those deep intense eyes were looking you through and through…

Aged as she was, she conveyed…no idea of feebleness; she looked, even then, a woman whose character, combining…thought and wisdom, as well as dignity and spirit, could analyse and exhibit in language suited to the intellect of the people of England, the evils and dangers of revolutionary principles.⁷³

---

71 "When Hannah's fourth and last sister died, Mary Frowd went to live with her as companion, housekeeper and co-worker. They lived together for fourteen years. In September 1833, as Hannah More was dying (aged 88), Mary Frowd knelt at her bed and read to her from the Bible. Hannah said: 'I love you, my dear child, with fervency. It will be pleasant to you twenty years hence to remember that I said this on my deathbed.' Mary Frowd received £1,120 in Hannah More's will." See note Number 2 in the leaflet "St. Mary's next St. John's Churchyard," produced in partnership with Friends of St Mary's Churchyard, (2019).

     See N.D. Smith, *Literary Manuscripts and Letters of Hannah More*, 4: HM "appointed her 'dear friend' Mary Frowd as joint executrix."

72 Hall, *Pilgrimages to English Shrines*, 55-56.

73 Hall, *Pilgrimages to English Shrines*, 56.

That thought prompted a recollection of More's stalwart defence of ordered liberty in England, when the threat of invasion by France in the years of the reign of terror were at their height. Women were not, of course, allowed to take up arms; but More had done much to help rally her fellow Britons in their crowded hour. And Hall understood this—

How bravely had that woman stood in the gap during the crisis of England's moral [and] political peril, and sent forth in the Cheap Repository, *tracts after tracts, that were devoured by the people...How fine and brave and true was her exposure of the speech of Monsieur Dupont, ringing, as it did, with the...clangour of atheism throughout Europe; and how noble her [charitable] sacrifice of the sum produced by its sale (£240)[74] to the relief of the[Catholic] French emigrant clergy,—a [deed] again proving her practical piety, for her dislike [of its] tenets...whose ministers she [aided] and protected, was well known. There were no traces of the sarcasm she evinced in her clever story of* Mr. Fantom...[75]

The wintry world around Barley Wood held a magic all its own; though few such days survive in written accounts from this time. Hall's prose was a rare and welcome exception—

It had ceased snowing, and though the sun cast what seemed rays of fire through the atmosphere, without dispelling the thick, [frosty] substance that hazed the air, we resolved to brave the cold, and see the monuments

---

74 £28,000 today's currency, as calculated by the Measuring Worth site.
75 Hall, *Pilgrimages to English Shrines*, 56-57.

erected in [Barley Wood's] pleasure-grounds to the memory of Locke and Porteus.

We felt as if breathing icicles, but we persevered, and knew that beneath that expanse of snow lay the lawn, where [Hannah More] had assembled [on fine, festive occasions], those best monuments of her Christian love— [children from] the schools [she founded, and governed,] according to the light of the period…

A beautiful sight it must have been, when some of the most able and best in the country came to witness [these] gatherings…

We returned, shivering, from our scramble through the snow. [Our] hostess had [awakened, and] become quite herself.

[She left] her seat by the fire, and insisted upon our occupying it.

[After this,] she spoke with fervour and affection of the advantages she received from her long friendship with [Bishop] Porteus, and laughed while she said that [Horace Walpole,] Lord Orford, had called [the Bishop] her 'Father Confessor'…

She seemed quite alive to the on dits [rumours and gossip] of Clifton, and referred to her long residence at Bristol more than once; she spoke with animation of Wilberforce, and his exertions on behalf of [West Indian slaves].[76]

Thoughtfully, Mary Frowd was the kind catalyst for a conversational time machine—prompting More to reminisce about her early London days. As Hall stated—

---

76 Hall, *Pilgrimages to English Shrines*, 57 & 59.

Her friend [Miss Frowd] drew her back from...'modern times' to Mrs. Thrale, and Mrs. Carter, and Dr. Johnson, who, she said, was never at all 'savage' to her, though once he nearly made her cry concerning an apology she offered for [reading books by Catholic writers]...Then she spoke of Garrick, and the expression of her countenance became more earnest, more affectionate, than it had been at the mention of any other name.

Certainly, her eyes in youth must have been glorious; for even then, they were dark, and, almost painfully, penetrating—*except when softened by emotion: when she spoke of this great Master of his Art, they expressed the utmost tenderness.*

'Ah,' she said, 'if he had been alive, it would have been indeed a trial to have retired from the world!' She considered him in every way a man of extraordinary genius: her reverence for Garrick was...true 'Hero-Worship:'...

How beautiful it [was] to see this enthusiasm outliving its inspirer, and animating with fresh life the slow pulsations of age.

'I should have liked,' she said, 'to have looked upon his face once more, but they only showed me his coffin.'

Her friendship for Mrs. Garrick only terminated with that venerable lady's life.[77]

But More was not done with her store of memories, when she finished speaking of the Garricks. Caught up in a flow of fond recollection, she bestowed further gifts.

It all made for a lovely, often moving close to Hall's visit—

---

77   Hall, *Pilgrimages to English Shrines*, 59-60. Italics added.

After a moment's silence she smiled, and [said]—

'I must show you some mementos of my wicked days.'

She opened a bureau, and took out some cards and a play-bill: the cards were admissions for the new play of 'Percy;' the bill, the list of the players who performed therein—amongst them, David Garrick!

It was curious to see these in the hands of the author of 'Percy' after the lapse of so many years. 'It was a great temptation,' she said, 'to write for such an actor; no one now can form any idea of what it was. He not only was all you could imagine, but the reality of whatever he undertook. Then such a face!

Can you wonder at my thinking so seriously of the passing away of all these things, when I believe I am the only one living of all who are named on this paper?' She folded the play-bill and cards together as they had been, and replaced them carefully...

...[I] would gladly, for the sake of one so great in her day...do pilgrimage anew to...Barley Wood, [the] home of her affections...[78]

* * *

Yet not all was pleasantness, or poignant, in the constant stream of visitors to Barley Wood. At times, its occasionally taxing nature came through, and there were moments when More found it all just a bit much. As one writer has noted—

Barley Wood became a place of pilgrimage for all professing Christians with the leisure to call. At the end

---

78 Hall, *Pilgrimages to English Shrines*, 60-61.

of 1809 she estimated that she had received double the number of visitors in the previous twelve months than she had in 1808. [And] in a letter to her friend Mrs. Kennicott [some years later,] she stated that in one day alone she had received nineteen visitors of whom she did not know six.

In 1816, [she drew on vivid biblical imagery to convey something of her chagrin at receiving so many callers, saying in one letter to] Wilberforce, visitors 'come to me as to the Witch of Endor, and I suppose I shall soon be desired to tell fortunes and cast nativities.'[79]

And yet...

More seems very much to have seen it all as a blend of Christian duty, or charity, and a way (when visits proved interesting and animating) to experience something like the literary salon culture she'd known in London, in the 1770s and 80s.

In truth, only someone genuinely "young at heart" could take such constant pleasure, in the main, spending so much time with visitors. The best things outweighed the trouble.

Noting this, one writer has said—

Hannah made herself available to guests for a variety of reasons. She offered one string of crisply logical explanations. "If my visitors are young, I hope I may perhaps be enabled to do them some good; if old, I hope to receive some good from them. If they come from far, I cannot refuse to see them after they have incurred (though so little worth it) so much trouble and possibly

---

79 Crossley Evans, *Hannah More*, 25.

expense to visit me; and if they live near, I could not be so ungracious and so unkind as to shut out my neighbours."[80]

There was something else about these "salon days." Many knew that More's books cast a wide net among readers. As a person, and as a literary figure, she lived in their pages. Yet visitor memories of Barley Wood show that she lived vividly in that setting also—in ways as telling as any book she ever wrote. It was a very appreciable kind of influence, present among old friends, or those who only met her once.

Still, there were times when none but old friends knew the difficulties often present when More received callers. S.C. Wilks, editor of *The Christian Observer* in the 1830s, was one friend who'd known More for years. In his March 1835 review of a book by a friend both he and More knew well, Wilks wrote of a time when More carried on valiantly, despite one trying recurrence of physical debility—

Hannah More shone very brightly [during most visits]. She was just the woman to manage the intellectual part of a rustic fête; while she never forgot the less refined duties of...hospitality. [I] was present...at Barley Wood before and after [one] meeting, with the busy preparations of housekeeping for so large an assemblage.

It was a fine summer's day...many guests...dined in the house, and twice that number took tea and coffee on the lawn. Hannah...had been ill the day before; and on [my greeting] her, on the morning of the meeting, with some alarm, as to how she would be able to get through the fatigues of the day, she said:

---

80 Demers, *Hannah More*, 8.

"I feel very unwell and heavy; for I was obliged to take laudanum last night, being in great pain; and to make sure of some rest I took a double dose; but it had not the effect of sending me to sleep, so that I am very tired and stupid this morning. I never count more than a hundred; for if I do not fall asleep then, it is loss of time, and I turn my thoughts to meditation. But I get so little rest now, that I begin to think sleep a vulgar error; and as for pain, I never was absolutely free from it for ten minutes since I was ten years old."

This seemed a bad beginning for a fête; yet she received her guests as if nothing had happened; she found something to say to every person whom she knew, or who was introduced...everybody felt gratified by her... attention...were it but a passing...remark, a kind question, [a] playful recommendation to a jelly, or to beware of a "saucy pudding."[81]

Crossing the ocean again to America, the daughter of lexicographer Noah Webster (creator of the classic text, *Webster's Dictionary*), said this of Hannah More, and her writings, in the home she knew growing up. It was reminiscent, in its way, of Barley Wood—

[Father] found a large double house, half-finished, on a gentle eminence opposite the "green" in the picturesque town of Amherst. He purchased and finished it.

There were ten acres of meadow land about it, which he greatly improved.

---

81 *The Christian Observer,* March 1835, (London: 1835), 167. Italics added.

I think it was the convenience of the house, and its pleasant situation, which decided him to take Amherst as his abiding place. But not this alone.

There were some men of education there and the pastor of the "decent church, which topped the neighbouring hill," good old Dr. Parsons, and his stately wife, the sister of Chief Justice Williams, were congenial friends...

Once accustomed to the quiet of the village life, [our family was] very happy there.

The daughters of the Parsonage, and my sisters, used to read together the best books of English literature, and for amusement in the long winter evenings would act the simple plays of Hannah More [from her book of Sacred Dramas].[82]

Of the fine moments in this book, one widely popular with American readers, were these stirring lines, from More's drama about Daniel, the paragon of the Old Testament—

...and may the Spirit of Grace,
Who stamp'd the seal of truth on the bless'd page,
Descend into thy soul...[83]

Nor was Hannah More solely an important presence in this Webster family memory. She was the subject of a literary source citation in *Webster's Dictionary*. In the revised London edition of 1864, the following definition is given—

---

82 E. Fowler, *The Life of Noah Webster* (New York: 1912), 108-109.

83 Hannah More, *Sacred Dramas: Chiefly Intended for Young Persons* (London: 1782), 208.

prosaist. noun. [cf. French, prosateur, Italian, prosatore.] A writer of prose. Usage: "Then comes Hannah More, an estimable prosaist." Isaac Taylor.[84]

* * *

From this, it is jarring to leave S.C. Wilks' recollections, or *Webster's Dictionary*, for the story of another visit to Barley Wood—one from 1819. William Wilberforce described it in a letter to his brother-in-law James Stephen, written on 19 September: "Of the uncertainty of life, we have just now had a fresh instance in the death of…Patty More."[85]

"Patty sat up with me," [Wilberforce wrote in his Diary on 9 September], "till near twelve, talking over Hannah's first introduction to a London life, and I, not she, broke off the conference; I never saw her more animated. About eight in the morning when I came out of my bed-room I found Hannah at the door— 'Have you not heard Patty is dying?'

They called me to her in great alarm, at which, from the ghastliness of her appearance I could not wonder. About two or three hours after our parting for the night, she had been taken ill." She lingered for about a week.[86]

"Ghastliness" expressed the ravaging, terrible pain Patty experienced. It was beyond enduring at times, and her cries, before laudanum could be administered, were harrowing.

---

84 *The New Illustrated Edition of Dr. Webster's Unabridged Dictionary* (London: 1864), 1050.

85 Wilberforce, *Life of William Wilberforce*, volume five, 32.

86 Wilberforce, *Life of William Wilberforce*, volume five, 32.

Her death, on 14 September, brought a merciful end; and her grief-stricken sister had at least the faith-borne consolation of hearing her speak of heaven.

In the time after Patty's passing, More knew what it was to dwell on the banks of the Acheron, or "river of sorrow." She had friends, like Wilberforce, and Mary Frowd, who could help her navigate the first storms of grief. But the lowering skies of its recurrence never left her. She carried on, without any of her sisters, for the remaining fourteen years of her life.

* * *

The friend whose book prompted *The Christian Observer* review from S.C. Wilks was Dr. Richard Valpy, the Oxfordian scholar who served for many years as Headmaster of Bury St. Edmunds school. During one 1829 visit, Valpy recalled that More, though for many years opposed to Roman Catholic Emancipation,[87] had a change of heart.

As Valpy described it—

[Hannah More] was originally, and long opposed to [this step]…

She reasoned on that subject with great mildness and candour; but her sister Patty was very violent. I argued… with the former, but I seldom ventured to mention the subject to the latter. But some time before the decision of Parliament [on the question, Miss] More told me that so many of her friends, whose sincerity and disinterestedness she admired—such as Mr. Wilberforce, Sir Thomas

---

87 The Roman Catholic Relief Act of 1829 removed most restrictions on Catholicism in the British Isles, and allowed them to serve in Parliament.

Acland, and others whom she mentioned—were in favour
of that measure, that she must abandon her opposition.[88]

This was a telling turn. It's a commonplace that the old seldom change opinions or convictions late in life. But here, More wasn't intransigent or unyielding. She had a teachable heart, at least in this, and was willing to change her opinion, given the views of people like Wilberforce and Acland, whom she deeply respected.

Born in 1745, the very year that Bonnie Prince Charlie, the Catholic pretender, had led a rebellion to reclaim the British throne, Hannah More could be forgiven for holding a lifelong antipathy toward a faith so closely associated with one who'd literally threatened her King and country. But over the course of her long life, though she ardently disagreed with Catholic teaching, she read books by Catholic authors. Very memorably, and as recorded in a later edition of Boswell's *Life of Samuel Johnson*, she was chided by the great lexicographer in 1781 for her reading of Catholic writers—

"He reproved me," [she wrote] "for reading Les Pensées de Pascal, *alleging that as a good Protestant I ought to abstain from books written by Catholics. I was beginning to stand upon my defence, when he took me with both hands, and with a tear running down his cheeks [addressed me],*

'Child,' said he, with the most affecting earnestness, 'I am heartily glad that you read pious books, by whomsoever they may be written.'"[89]

---

88 *The Christian Observer*, March 1835, (London: 1835), 169. Recollections from Dr. Richard Valpy.

89 G.B. Hill, ed., *Boswell's Life of Johnson*, volume four, (New York: 1891), 102n.

As late as 1825, as Anna Maria Hall noted after her visit, More's dislike of the tenets of Catholicism "was well known." And yet, as Hall also noted, More had in the 1790s donated the entire proceeds from the sale of her book, *Remarks on the Speech of Monsieur Dupont,* to the relief of French Catholic clergy who'd fled the reign of terror. Now, that kind act had a sequel, in 1829, when she set aside her lifelong opposition to ending the restrictions on Catholicism in Britain, and granting them political power in Parliament.

Time, reflection, and the counsel of friends, can bring a new wisdom in life.

There was also a part of her that remained "young at heart," and that was never more in evidence than in her dealings with children in her elder years. She loved young people. They remembered how well, and how colourfully she did.

Of all the young people she knew and influenced, Marianne Thornton, her "beloved goddaughter,"[90] is the one of whom most is known from surviving papers.

By way of setting the stage for this side of More's life, the story of one appellation, given in friendship, is apropos.

A playful air of chivalry, and a beloved book, *The Faerie Queene,* was behind it all.

In 1789, William Wilberforce wrote to More: "Your labours [to educate the poor] can only be equalled by Spencer's lady knights, and they seem to be much of the same kind too, I mean, you have all sorts of monsters to cope withal." At this, Wilberforce's biographer sons observed, "The monsters were, however, all subdued by this intrepid lady knight, supported by her generous champion—the 'Red Cross knight' was his familiar name with [their mutual friend,] Mrs. Montagu."[91]

---

90 Stott, *Hannah More,* viii.

91 Robert and Samuel Wilberforce, *The Life of William Wilberforce,* volume one, 249.

Marianne Thornton was Wilberforce's young cousin, and in letters to her, More's wit and humour often had free rein. In one she called their mutual friend, Sir Thomas Acland, "the recreant knight of Devonshire." In another, she wrote with a playful, high disregard for grammar: "When I think of you, I am gladerer and gladerer and gladerer."[92]

Here is where E.M. Forster enters the story, as a courier of family heritage.

A good many years after Hannah More's passing, Marianne (Forster's great-aunt) set down her childhood memories of Barley Wood. Forster published many of them, including: "There never was such a house, so full of intellect and piety and active benevolence."[93] Other recollections were a little mosaic of fond moments. Marianne recalled being

sent off by ourselves, or with some village child, to buy chickens at the next farm, and when we returned dragging along our purchases, how we were fed with strawberries and cream, and told to lie down on the hay whilst Charles, the Coachman, Gardener, Bailiff and Carpenter, made us a syllabub under the cow.[94]

Marianne, inventive and spirited, was not above taking advantage of her loving godmother. "She was in many ways a charming companion for children," Thornton wrote—

but she had very little power of resisting either persuasion or fun, and I early found I had more much influence over her than I had over my mother. As I grew older I learnt not

---

92 Forster, *Marianne Thornton*, 140.

93 Forster, *Marianne Thornton*, 46. See also Stott, *Hannah More*, 291. A syllabub is a whipped cream dessert, most often flavoured with white wine or sherry.

94 Forster, *Marianne Thornton*, 47.

to take advantage of this. I have this year [1857] revisited
that Paradise of my childhood, Barley Wood, and fancied
I could once more see the venerable forms, and hear the
kind greetings of the 5 hospitable sisters.[95]

Forster contributed to the narrative of his aunt's friendship
with More.

Clapham, and places called "Battersea Rise," the home of
Marianne's family, and "Broomfield," that of Wilberforce, were
the setting: "Next door [to her parents] for a time lived the
friend of friends, William Wilberforce. He and Hannah More
were the two [family friends] whom she took over from her
parents when they died [in 1815]."[96]

Beyond this, Forster added: "Since Dr. M.G. Jones' excellent
book on Hannah More, it has been possible to get a clearer
view of that *'bishop in petticoats,'* and to realise her warmth
and charm. Marianne adored her."[97]

Forster then cited this passage, from Marianne's
Recollections—

[Hannah More was] the friend par excellence of my
mother, the woman who held that rare place of having
been my father's nearest associate, and most confidential
counsellor before his marriage, and then became the
nearest and dearest tie she had out of her own family, to
my mother...

I should [say] Hannah More and her sisters, for my
parents loved them all, and though Hannah...was the most
celebrated, they always thought Patty her equal in talent

---

95 Forster, *Marianne Thornton*, 46.

96 Forster, *Marianne Thornton*, 41.

97 Forster, *Marianne Thornton*, 45. Italics added.

and goodness. 'May is coming, and then Hannah will be with us,' was one of the earliest hopes of my childhood, and when she did arrive, I always felt I had a fresh companion just my own age, and ready to sympathize with all my pleasures and troubles.

Her health was always very bad, and often prevented her going out for weeks together, and when this was the case and I was too young to go to Church, I was delighted at being left under her care on a Sunday.

How well I remember sitting on her bed whilst she discoursed to me about Joseph and his brethren, and all the wonderful adventures of the children of Israel, with such eloquence and force that I fancied she must have lived amongst them herself.[98]

In More's company, Marianne could always look forward to stories of literary life in London—people she'd read about, whom More had known well.

How deep Marianne's affection ran was clearly evident in an eloquent, moving tribute that closed this portion of her *Recollections*—

Hannah...was always ready to talk about the literary set with whom she passed her youth. Many an evening...she amused me by describing Johnson and Burke, Horace Walpole, Mrs. Montagu and the many [figures] I had read of in Boswell['s Life of Johnson], *and for this reason, I suppose no period in history interests me so much.*

At our last two visits to Barley Wood she was alone living of all the band of sisters. She was too ill even to

---

98 Forster, *Marianne Thornton*, 45-46.

leave her bedroom, but her flow of spirits never failed, her sufferings of body seemed conquered by her cheerfulness, and her love of all she had ever known, her interest in their welfare, her enjoyment in their society was as great as ever.

One night her maid came to send me out of her room, saying her mistress would be tired, and must be put to bed, she being then confined to it the greater part of the day.

While Mary went down for something, [Hannah] said—

'We have not had our half hour talk out, and it does not tire me a bit; hide behind the window curtain, and come out when Mary fancies she has shut me up.'

No girl of 16 could have enjoyed the trick more.

But she too is now lying in Wrington Churchyard... Barley Wood has passed into other hands; but God has indeed given them a better name than sons and daughters.[99]

For Marianne, one vignette of the happy days she'd known seemed to stand for all the others. It was, amid a mélange of memories, loving and beautiful and prosaic.

Her vivid prose brought a long-ago scene at Barley Wood to life—

I can now imagine our arrival at the door covered with roses, and 'the ladies' as they were always called, rushing out to cover us with kisses, and then take us into the kitchen to exhibit us to Mary and Charles, the housemaid and coachman, then running themselves to fetch the tea things...Patty allowing no one but herself to fry the eggs for 'the darling', the brown loaf brought out, the colour of

99   Forster, *Marianne Thornton*, 47-48.

a mahogany table, baked only once a week—of enormous size, but excellent taste.

Then the 2 cats, called 'Non-resistance' and 'Passive obedience', who were fed by us all day long, and then the next day crowns of flowers were made for ourselves, garlands for the sheep; the peas we were set to pick, and then shell, perched upon the kitchen dresser, while Sally made the room resound with...merry stories of the cottagers round.[100]

Beyond this telling store of fond memories, More's pattern of faith did much to guide Marianne's walk as a Christian. E.M. Forster captured this—

[Marianne's parents] left twin comforters behind them in the persons of William Wilberforce and Hannah More. From 1815 to 1833, [the year these cherished friends] died, she had these two precious relicts to guide her spiritually.[101]

Among the many bequests More left her, by way of their friendship, Marianne also inherited philanthropic concern for those in need. Forster readily discerned this, and wrote gratefully about it. More was neither Marianne's blood-relation, nor his, but she had guided something noble, and fine, into their family heritage—

Under the influence of her parents and of Hannah More, [Marianne] had tried to teach poor children while she herself was only a child, she had gone into primitive

---

100 Forster, *Marianne Thornton*, 46-47.
101 Forster, *Marianne Thornton*, 125.

schools of the early century and helped. It was her duty, and it was also a pleasure.

She had never been afraid of the poor, and she had too much faith in human nature to foresee that education might be a hindrance to happiness.[102]

* * *

More's friendship with Marianne Thornton was uniformly happy, undisturbed by any occurrence of later years. Her kindness, in childhood, to Thomas Babington, Lord Macaulay, the son of Zachary and Selina Macaulay, was no less great. However, their friendship was troubled later by his ardent support of Parliamentary Reform, early on in his career in the House of Commons.

Prior to this, she'd thought him a "jewel of a boy," and that warmth of affection was returned in kind. When young Macaulay began and excelled in his studies at Trinity College, Cambridge, More wrote to rejoice with his parents over the success of their "wonderful son." The capstone of these university days came when Tom Macaulay won the Chancellor's Medal for his poem *Pompeii* in 1819. More wrote that his lines of verse were "really worthy of any poet of any age." Her praise was born of affection; but also of a poet's love for another gifted poet's skill and achievement.[103] Meanwhile, she told Zachary Macaulay of her intent to leave his son "the bulk of my Library," a bequest of great value and many magnificent texts.

But it was not to be.

---

102 Forster, *Marianne Thornton*, 134.

103 Jones, *Hannah More*, 221.

Eleven years later, in 1830, amid the flurry of acclaim after his election to Parliament, Macaulay visited More, and let his fervor for Parliamentary Reform get the better of him. At More's time of life, age eighty-five, such sweeping changes to England's electoral system were a bridge too far for her to cross. Yet Macaulay, when the subject came up, held forth as he might have done in a speech before the House of Commons, with a good deal of ardour. Whatever the merits of this issue, More was offended. She was alarmed as well at the thought of her protégé becoming radical in his political views, as she would have seen it.[104]

Too late, young Macaulay realized his error. The damage was done, and More revoked the bequest of her books to him. He would have to solace himself with the gift volumes she had given him heretofore; and though these were fine, important books, they were far less than the great library he would have had if he'd been more circumspect in his visit.

Seven years later, Macaulay spoke of this, and his abiding regard for More, in a letter to Macvey Napier, when asked if he'd ever planned to write a literary assessment of More—

Dear Napier...

I never, to the best of my recollection, proposed to review Hannah More's Life *or* Works. *If I did, it must have been in jest.*

She was exactly the very last person in the world about whom I should choose to write a critique. She was a very kind friend to me from childhood. Her notice first called out my literary tastes. Her presents laid the foundation of my library.

---

104 Jones, *Hannah More,* 221.

She was to me what Ninon[105] was to Voltaire,—begging
her pardon for comparing her to a bad woman, and yours
for comparing myself to a great man.

She really was a second mother to me. I have a real
affection for her memory.

I therefore could not possibly write about her unless
I wrote in her praise; and all the praise which I could
give to her writings, even after straining my conscience
in her favour, would be far indeed from satisfying any of
her admirers...[106]

How bittersweet this was, and remained, is seen in a letter
Macaulay wrote in 1852. It was then he visited Barley Wood
for the first time in many years.

Just prior to that sojourn, travelling close by, he'd written:
"saw dear old Barley Wood from the road."[107] On 14 September,
he was able to return for his last visit there—

A beautiful day. After breakfast Ellis and I drove to
Wrington in an open carriage and pair. We first paid a
visit to the church...

We then walked to Barley Wood. [My hosts, the
Harfords,] very kindly asked me to go upstairs. We saw...
Hannah More's room.

The bed is where her sofa and desk used to stand. The
old bookcases—some of them, at least—remain. I could
point out the very place where the 'Don Quixote,' in four
volumes, stood, and the very place from which I took

---

105 a salonnière during the reign of Louis XIV, Ninon de Lenclos was a courtesan who had liaisons with prominent people.

106 T.B. Macaulay, *Miscellanies*, volume four (Boston: 1900), 221-222.

107 Ernest Hobson, "Hannah More," in *The Westminster* Review" March 1907 (London: 1907), 309.

down, at ten years old, the 'Lyrical Ballads.' With what delight and horror I read the 'Ancient Mariner.'[108]

At the same time, More's commitment to philanthropy did not lessen with the years. There was much for her to do to help those in need, and she found a wide range of ways to do what she could. John Harford, prominent in her younger set of friends, had a near view of these years, since his home, Blaise Castle, was just fifteen miles away from Barley Wood, or within a day's travel by coach. He recalled More's faith, and devotion to charity—

To do good to others had long become the leading principle of her life…

    to attract the souls of those over whom she had any influence…into the school of Christ, was, therefore, her daily aim.[109]

This "be not weary in well doing" aspect of More's life was the focus of a forthright and detailed letter written to Harford on 26 May 1814. She was honest about the cost such commitment to philanthropy entailed for two sisters in their late sixties, and often in poor health. These incessant charitable endeavours were not an easy undertaking. And here too, More's irenic love of "mere Christianity" was also much in evidence. As she wrote—

In the Bishop of St. Asaph I have lost one of the oldest of my Episcopal friends.

    He always showed me great regard, and used to comfort himself that I was not a Calvinist, tho' he said

---

108 Hobson, "Hannah More," 309.
109 Harford, *Recollections of Wilberforce*, 279.

I associated with those who were. Poor man, he knows now that there are no narrowing names, nor party distinctions in heaven.

More than fourteen years ago, I voluntarily quitted the great and the gay, the wise and the witty world.[110] I made the sacrifice cheerfully, from the conviction that we ought to endeavour to interpose an interval between the world and the grave.

But I reckoned without my host, or rather without my guests, when I looked for anything like retirement. For the last month I do not think we have had fewer than forty persons a week, many of them strangers who brought letters from friends.

It is not of the quality, but of the number that I complain. Talking wears me out, especially as I sleep so little.

Patty works as hard as the healthiest, and has herself cut out and prepared 700 articles of clothing for the children in our schools, and is now regulating and feasting near 300 of our poor women, for whom we are now vesting in Trustees' hands, preparatory to our deaths, above a thousand pounds.[111]

A sense of matronly falderal and botheration, all colourfully feigned, was the subject of a letter More posted to Harford on 18 September 1821. After much cajoling, some good-naturedly, if rather relentlessly inflicted, she had consented to allow H.W. Pickersgill, of the Royal Academy, to paint her portrait. The kind importunity of friends had won the day—

---

110 as used here, the word "gay" means blithe, or light-heartedly heedless.

111 Harford, *Annals of the Harford Family* (London: 1909), 101.

Mrs. Macaulay will neither let me sleep in my bed or rest in my chair, "if Mr. Harford is not written to." Indeed, I never did write to you with such an ill-will nor consent to a business so contrary to my feelings and my judgment.

It is no small sacrifice: why should this "lump of clay" be thought worthy of having the remembrance of its bent form and corrugated visage preserved [in a portrait] for a little space after it has gone hence, and is no more seen? But if I must submit to the despotism of friendship, you must have the goodness to communicate to Mr. Pickersgill Sir Thomas Acland's idea of sketching the two copies first, that both may be originals, and then giving them a separate finish.

My stubborn rejection of Mr. Gwatkin's request, a friend of fifty years, and then yielding to the affectionate importunity of dear Sir Thomas, I should feel to be unkind, unless both have the same advantage, if such a word may be used on such an occasion.

All this is Shakespeare's veritable Much Ado about Nothing.[112]

More's postscript was just as sprightly in character—

P.S.—I will try with all my might not to think of the Artist till I see him.

Don't tell him so! He would think it so savage. Say how long he will be employed here? Think of a week out of my little fragment of life.[113]

---

112 Harford, *Annals of the Harford Family,* 102-103.
113 Harford, *Annals of the Harford Family,* 103.

Five years later, in a letter to Harford from 23 August 1826, More showed she'd lost none of the irreverent, or impish sense of fun, that flowed into letters to close friends.

Juggling financial tasks, greeting welcome guests, keeping less welcome guests at bay—venturing outside when her health and the weather permitted—it was all of a piece with what she'd written in her letter. She even told Harford to bring a pair of pruning shears with him on his next visit, to help her trim ivy from the windows of Barley Wood.

Harford must have laughed aloud as he read this letter to his wife Louisa. He may well have said something like, "Now, this is classic Hannah More!"

Never make an apology to me [her letter stated,] for sending any visitor. The Smythes were very agreeable. Remember you have carte blanche. *I do not say this to many.*

Shakespeare was much in the right when, in enumerating the ills of life, he put the law's delay in company with the pangs of despised love and the proud man's contumely.[114]

*At the end of three weeks, I cannot get the instrument for conveying a scrap of ground somewhat bigger than a tablecloth. They talk of twenty sheets! I need not have been in such haste to sell stock. You have done me a service—*le void.

Don't you remember saying, "The next beggar that comes, set him to work"?

One came the next day.

[Our coachman] Charles set him to work with a wheelbarrow, telling him he should have a shilling and

---

114 Here, More is referring to lines 71-73 of *Hamlet*, Act 3, scene one: For who would bear the whips and scorns of time/Th' oppressor's wrong, the proud man's contumely/The pangs of despised love, the law's delay,

three meals. He drove his barrow manfully, but on peeping into it, Charles only saw a few ounces of gravel.

At night he took his money and engaged to come next day.

We have, however, never heard of him again; but the good thing is, that we have never since been pestered by a single beggar!

I have at last yielded to incessant importunity, and have been carried up the garden in a Sedan, attended by a large cavalcade. I found the wood so pretty that it is well I should not see often what I must so soon leave.

Can you and your chère moitié *[dear half] come on Monday and stay the night? Let me know, that I may do my best to keep off interlopers.*

Bring with you the learned eye and the lopping hand. I have been lopping a good deal myself to-day—from every window—and think I have done very prettily.

Whether [you,] the great professor in the art, will think so, remains to be seen.[115]

The plight of local miners and farmers was of great concern to More in a letter she wrote to Harford on 4 January 1827. She described steps she'd taken to help them. For her, no better use could be found for the royalties she'd earned from her best-selling books—

I suffer much from this frost, but have a greater trial awaiting me in the distress around me. My Shipham schoolmaster tells me the Copper Company have bought a little ore from Shipham; oh! that they would buy much! They sit heavy at my heart.

---

115 Harford, *Annals of the Harford Family*, 105.

They now live on the potatoes we planted in such abundance; but [they] cannot buy a loaf of bread. I sent out and bought their own potatoes while they were tolerably cheap, and have had them buried in a pit, that they may have some for seed [next year].[116]

But good use of the royalties she'd earned wasn't the only publishing concern that More had at this time of her life. She told Harford about another worry in March 1828—

I am at present, through the intervention of my able and judicious friend, Mr. Macaulay, endeavouring to settle all affairs past and present with Mr. Cadell, but he is a hard man, tho' considerably richer than Croesus, and so narrowly watchful of his own interests that I could not deal with him myself, for myself.

My poor works have been so long published, and, I am thankful to say, have had so much wider circulation than many far better books, *that I have now £400 to receive, but he pays me by such small, shabby instalments, that I may be dead before I receive it!*[117]

Here, humility and rueful wit mingled with concern over finances that might lead to a curbing of her charitable work, or home economies she hadn't foreseen. But once again, Zachary Macaulay was a friend of friends. More thanked God for his kindness.

---

116 Harford, *Annals of the Harford Family*, 105.
117 Harford, *Annals of the Harford Family*, 106. Italics added.

CHAPTER TEN

A Kind Coalition

...settled down as a lively and delightful saint,
living at Barley Wood, Wrington, Somerset.[1]

— **MARY ALDEN HOPKINS** (1947)

By those who attach value to the minutest circumstances
connected with genius... we shall be forgiven for adding that
almost every tree [at Barley Wood] has been planted by [Miss]
More's own hand, and that a little cabinet-table, from whence
has issued many a sheet for the edification of mankind, is
elegantly inlaid with small diamond-shaped pieces of wood,
from the trees of her own rearing...[2]

— **LYDIA HUNTLEY SIGOURNEY** (1827)

For many readers, Hannah More's life and writings furnished an example they sought to emulate. Many times they told her so, via letters, confirming that she continued to have an

---

1   Hopkins, *Hannah More*, 2.

2   *The Works of Hannah More: With a Sketch of Her Life, by L.H.S.*, iii.

influence for good. These brought intervals of solace, and good cheer, during the trying times of illness, and mourning, that came to her in this season of her life.

Often, she had occasion to pen a reply, and "continue the conversation," as it were, from the table made of many trees. This table, and the letters she wrote, were symbols of the ways her influence travelled to far places in the world.

And for this, her special room at Barley Wood was a point of origin.

It's a part of her legacy now too little appreciated. Her books, correspondence, time with visitors, and her friendships more generally, led to rich and meaningful events.

Tracing them is an important and revealing task.

To recount one instance of the impact of More's writings, Susan Fenimore Cooper, the daughter of novelist James Fenimore Cooper, said this of her father and Hannah More, as an English "woman of letters"—

[As I was growing up,] there came sailing into the harbour of New York, with each returning month, one or two packet ships, from London or Liverpool, their arrival in the lower bay being duly announced on Wall Street…

Among bales of English calicos and broadcloths, there never failed to be some smaller package of far greater and more lasting value—some volume fresh from the London press, high in merit, full of interest, a work whose appearance had been already heralded, and whose arrival was eagerly expected by every reader in the country.

Perhaps it was a romance of the Waverley series, still a delightful mystery as [to] their [authorship by Walter Scott,] a brilliant canto of Byron, or a charming social tale

by Miss Edgeworth, or a valuable religious work by Mr.
Wilberforce, or Miss More.[3]

Even as the Coopers were a famous literary family, and had
a standing order for books from England, another American
had a greater role in commending Hannah More's books: the
writer and poet Lydia Huntley Sigourney. "One of the first
American women to succeed at a literary career," she, over
the course of many years, "used proceeds from her writing
to contribute to charitable causes," among them "peace
societies, Greek war relief, and the work of missionaries at
home and abroad."[4]

Born in Norwich, Connecticut, in 1791, Sigourney (the
only daughter of a gardener) was called the "Sweet Singer of
Hartford." As her family was of humble means, the kindness
of her father's employer was especially welcome, for Lydia was
able to attend private school with this employer's assistance.
Over time that kindness paid dividends Hannah More
would have recognized as kindred to her own: helping those
in need.

And why so? In 1814, when she was twenty-three, Lydia
founded a Hartford school for girls. And there, she "taught
a deaf student, Alice Cogswell, to read and write."[5] A year
later, she published her first book, *Moral Pieces in Prose*
and Verse.

In 1819 she married Charles Sigourney, a wealthy widower
with three children. She published several volumes of poetry
and essays in subsequent years, her verse often "engaging

---

3   S.F. Cooper, *Pages and Pictures from the Life of James Fenimore Cooper* (New York: 1865), 16.

4   see "Lydia Huntley Sigourney," posted by the Connecticut Women's Hall of Fame, at: https://www.
cwhf.org/inductees/lydia-huntley-sigourney

5   E.D. Sayers & D. Gates, "Lydia Huntley Sigourney and the Beginnings of American Deaf Education in
Hartford," *Sign Language Studies*, (Summer 2008), 369.

Native American and anti-slavery concerns within a religious context."[6]

This led to her receiving another sobriquet, apart from the regional one she held. As H.E. Perrin, an Irish traveller in America, wrote from Dublin in March 1834—

last November, as I passed through the town of Hartford in...New England, I called on Mrs. Sigourney (the Hannah More of America), and finding that she took a great interest in the Deaf Institution of her own town, I [spoke of the institution] at Claremont.[7]

Sigourney must have cherished this, unsought though it was, for she revered the name of Hannah More. As she wrote to biographer William Roberts in March 1835—

...the name of...Hannah More has here been on [my] lips from infancy as "a household word," [then too,] her works have travelled with the family of the emigrant to the utmost cabins of our scarcely-settled West...

[I have] been encouraged in my earliest intellectual efforts by letters from that distinguished lady, and occasional presents of her works...[8]

Here was literary confirmation that, as in England, More was able to write successfully for Americans of all walks of life, and be read widely by them. Her success in the British

---

6   the quotations in the two paragraphs preceding are from a Poetry Foundation article at: https://www.poetryfoundation.org/poets/lydia-huntley-sigourney

7   *The Eighteenth Report of the National Institution for Deaf and Dumb Poor Children...19th May, 1834* (Dublin: 1834), 86.

8   Arthur Roberts, ed., *The Life, Letters, and Opinions of William Roberts, Esq.,* (London: 1850), 163.

Isles had been replicated in the United States, even in homes on the frontier.

Beyond this, Lydia Sigourney did far more to acknowledge her literary debt.

She wrote a prefatory memoir for *The Works of Hannah More: Complete in Two Volumes,* (Boston: S.G. Goodrich, 1827). It was one of the first complete editions of More's writings. A copy of this important set is now kept at Harvard University. Its title page held a woodcut complementing Sigourney's memoir: to convey a message about its contents.

The woodcut shows Barley Wood, in a vista under a sky of scudding clouds—driven on a summer's day. The image conveys life and purpose. To the right is More in earlier years—a woman of letters and philanthropist—walking to a carriage with one of her sisters, perhaps to visit a school they founded. At a glance, American readers saw something of the England she knew, and the guiding purpose faith had for her life and writings.

Here, words from her book *Christian Morals* could well have been a caption. For there, she wrote tellingly: "and to others benignity, philanthropy, and kindness."[9]

* * *

---

9   Hannah More, *Christian Morals* (New York: 1813), 307.

A woodcut detail of Barley Wood (1827), showing More and one of her sisters, walking to their carriage.

The panoramic "view" by John Knight (1820) which inspired the 1827 woodcut for More's *Complete Works*. The rustic temple John Codman saw in 1824, with its inscription from Virgil, is to the middle right.

Lydia Huntley Sigourney, the poet, educator, and philanthropist called "the Hannah More of America." This engraving first appeared in *The National Portrait Gallery of Distinguished Americans* (1839)

Returning to Lydia Sigourney, we learn that her brief memoir was written with a view to present "to the American people a new edition of the works of an author…who has so long contributed to their instruction and delight," and give "a few remarks respecting her."[10]

What followed may have been the first memoir of Hannah More written in America. Brief though it was, taking up just four pages of a very large folio edition, Sigourney conveyed many things to Americans in the 1820s that they may not have known—

Hannah More…born in 1745, [was born] near Bristol… Her talents and virtues gained not only the patronage of

---

10 *The Works of Hannah More: With a Sketch of Her Life, by L.H.S., complete in two volumes,* (Boston: 1827), iii.

men of taste and science, but the firm friendship of some of the most illustrious names [in] the annals of Great Britain.

After continuing for many years in the interesting work of education, [she and her] sisters retired to Barley Wood in Wrington, near Somersetshire, where a beautiful cottage and grounds were arranged and ornamented...[11]

Sigourney then said that More, at eighty-two, was yet a vital force for good—

She still continues to exercise hospitality [and] charm, by the vivacity of her conversation, [and] the multitude of guests who seek the honour of a personal interview...

The youngest [visitor] finds her...manner...dispelling the awe [which] her talents had inspired, [and] the stranger who approaches Barley Wood...leaves it cheered by... benevolence...The following...description...is from the pen of an American gentleman, who visited her in the spring of 1824—

"Mrs. More is rather short, but...she has the brightest and most intellectual eye that I ever saw in an aged person; it was as clear, and seemed as fully awake with mind and soul, as if it had but lately opened on a world full of novelty..."[12]

Sigourney then traced the stature of More's writing in American culture, anticipating her letter to William Roberts in 1835—

---

11 *Works of Hannah More, With a Sketch by L.H.S.*, iii.

12 *Works of Hannah More, With a Sketch by L.H.S.*, iv. Italics added.

The diffusion of the works of [Hannah] More has in some measure kept pace with their intrinsic value. It may almost be said that their "speech has gone forth to the ends of the world"...Portions of them have been transfused into the languages of France, Germany, and Ceylon. In this far country of England's planting, they have been extensively, and warmly appreciated, [and now] incorporated with the elements of a young nation's literature...Companions of the Bible, they have travelled with the family of the emigrant to our uncultivated wilds, and forest frontiers.

There, where the woodman's axe wakens echoes... Practical Piety *[is read] by the evening fireside, [or]* The Shepherd of Salisbury Plain...*[13]*

Near the close of Sigourney's memoir, she paid tribute to More, and the twofold way her life and writings found readers the world over. Sigourney began by saying—

If as [Hannah More] has asserted, "there is between him who writes, and him who reads, a kind of coalition of interests, a partnership of mental property, a joint stock of tastes and ideas," how great must be her satisfaction , who over so wide a field has sown...

If some faint love of goodness glow in me...
I first caught that flame from Thee...[14]

---

13 *Works of Hannah More: With a Sketch by L.H.S.*, v-vi.

14 lines in tribute to Samuel Richardson, in *The Works of Hannah More in Prose and Verse*, volume one (Dublin: 1789), 263.

A blessing the most desirable in this life, most powerful over the destinies of the next, has been granted [Miss More], that influence of mind over mind...entering alike the palace and the cottage...[15]

Others, besides Lydia Sigourney, were called "the Hannah More of America." One of them was Margaret Mercer. Her story appears in a presidential biography: George Morgan's *Life of James Monroe* (1921). Mercer's legacy lies in her endeavours as an abolitionist and educator. Tracing her family heritage, we learn first that her father—

John Francis Mercer [born in 1759] studied law with [Thomas] Jefferson, and was in the Continental Congress of 1782-85. In the latter year, he married Sophia Sprigg of "Cedar Park," [in] West River, Maryland...He was a delegate to the Federal Constitutional Convention, [a Member of] Congress...and Governor of Maryland in 1801.

His daughter, Margaret Mercer, freed the slaves of "Cedar Park," and established a school for girls. She was known as "the Hannah More of America."[16]

Archival sources identify another "Hannah More of America," yet enigmatically, her name cannot be verified precisely. She is, in the page of history, simply "Miss Hinsdale," and one of her students, Almira Lincoln Phelps, penned this tribute to her memory—

Nancy Hinsdale, born April 16, 1769...was the eldest daughter of Rev. Theodore Hinsdale. The Pittsfield Female

---

15 *The Works of Hannah More: With a Sketch by L.H.S.*, vi.

16 George Morgan, *The Life of James Monroe* (Boston: 1921), 69n.

Academy, under her direction, was founded and became distinguished as...the mother of all Pittsfield seminaries.

[This] writer was the pupil of her cousin, Miss Hinsdale, in the year 1812, whom she ever regarded with love and veneration, often viewing her as the Hannah More of America.

Like that venerable woman ...she was courteous, benevolent, [and] learned...

If she did not write scores of books, [Miss Hinsdale] preached sermons to the young, trained them in the way they should go, and always exercised great influence in the sphere in which she moved...[I] esteem...it a privilege...to offer this tribute to the blessed memory of a saint-like woman... titled to a place among the benefactors of a past age.[17]

* * *

On 18 April 1828, about a year following the American edition of her *Complete Works*, with its celebration of her writings, More faced a trial that was completely unexpected.

But for the kindness of close friends, it might have been too much for her to weather at eighty-three. For increasingly, she was infirm and in precarious health.

Briefly, the story was told by E.M. Forster. Describing the setting for an image of More that he inherited from his great-aunt Marianne Thornton, the image showing More with her pet squirrel—and happy with her books and letters, Forster stated—

---

17   A.L. Holman, ed., *Hinsdale Genealogy* (Lombard, Illinois: 1906), 93.

It must be Barley wood, for she is very old—Barley Wood where she hoped to die, but her servants mishandled and betrayed her.

"I am driven, like Eve, out of Paradise," she said, "but unlike Eve, not by angels."[18]

The "domestic tragedy" ending Hannah More's days at Barley Wood was one of greed, lies, deceit, and theft. Over many years, More's kindness to her servants, which extended to their education in some cases, as well as much-needed employment, had become proverbial in and around the village of Wrington. Yet for years prior to April 1828, those who served at Barley Wood, entrusted with More's care, began quite literally to spend her out of house and home, pilfering the resources of her home and home farm.

Trusting, and unaware, More had no idea that the servants with whom she had family prayers each evening would, once they put her to bed, go through reams of costly fine food and wine (which they had ordered). They used her possessions, and kitchen quarters below stairs, to stage clandestine fêtes, dances, and (some evidence indicates) lovers' trysts. Their theft and deceit meant that Barley Wood expenditures greatly exceeded More's income.

Rumours eventually began to swirl, and they reached the ears of Zachary Macaulay. In an act of great friendship, showing his regard for her, Macaulay wrote a letter telling More everything her servants had done. Soon after, he journeyed to

---

18 E.M. Forster, "Mrs. Hannah More," an essay in *The Nation and the Athenaeum,* 2 January 1926 (London: The New Statesman Ltd., 1926), 493. Forster's image of More may have been drawn by Marianne Thornton, or perhaps her sister Henrietta, who created a drawing of the oval library at Battersea Rise in Clapham that looks much like the drawing of More at Barley Wood. See E.M. Forster, *Marianne Thornton* (London: 1956), 32. That the squirrel shown in this image was a pet is confirmed in Stott, *Hannah More,* 328. Stott states More also kept caged birds: a welcome source of cheer, as More could only rarely venture outside.

Barley Wood, and in person, he produced witnesses to all that had been taking place.[19]

The theft and deceit were bad enough, but their dangerous neglect of More's care was no less dire. Anyone of sense could see that when her servants left her home to take part in "night revelries in the village,"[20] no one was there to summon a doctor's aid if her health ever took a turn for the worse. She would be left to her fate.

It was a thoroughly sordid tale—all brought upon an elderly woman who had done nothing to deserve such treatment.[21] Quite the reverse.

Scholar Anne Stott has detailed an instance of More's constancy and kindness—

She had taken his daughter off Charles Tidy's hands when he was too poor to look after her properly; she had educated this daughter, given her a home, and recently spent £120 [a sum equal to several thousand pounds today] apprenticing her to a milliner.

(She might have done even more had the young woman been as ambitious and as academically inclined as she had been at her age.) She had kept on a larger staff of servants than she needed because she could not bear to turn them out onto an uncertain labour market.[22]

---

19 for this summary, I am indebted to Jones, *Hannah More*, 226-227.

20 Knutsford, *Life and Letters of Zachary Macaulay*, 448.

21 Stott, *Hannah More*, 327. Here, to counter any "tendency to assume that More must have somehow 'deserved' her misfortune," among those wondering if her treatment of servants somehow warranted her being "repaid with negligence and deceit," Stott states clearly: "All the evidence points the other way."

22 Stott, *Hannah More*, 327. The UK Inflation Calculator states that £120 in 1830 would be £12,683 today.

With great sadness, all More's servants were discharged. Her carriage, her horses and Barley Wood were sold. Her friends helped her move to Windsor Terrace, Clifton.[23]

On the day she left, 18 April 1828, More was "escorted by a dozen gentlemen of the neighbourhood" who were present, while her things were being removed, to guard against any further theft, or reprisals from servants who had been summarily discharged.[24]

One symbol of this sad departure was the roof-tower bell that had been rung on so many festive occasions—its rich tolling sound carrying far over the surrounding hills.

When More left Barley Wood for the last time, she would no longer hear that bell. She had chosen it, watched its installation, and thrilled to think it was a special part of her new country home, in 1801. For over twenty-five years, she had been reminded, each time it tolled, that her home was a gift of the books she had written. She, unlike so many women who were becoming writers, had earned enough income to build such a home. It became a cherished haven for her, and a centre for philanthropy. She loved the way this bell sounded for cherished hours at Barley Wood. It held a music all its own.

And she'd no reason, heretofore, to think this would ever change. But it had.

It was as one writer said, "troubles fall on her, in the evening time."[25]

---

23 Crossley Evans, *Hannah More*, 20 & 23.

24 Jones, *Hannah More*, 227.

25 S.C. Wilks, in *The Christian Observer*, November 1864 (London: 1864), 843.

Barley Wood in the 1800s, showing the roof-tower bell (top centre image) that rang for many festive occasions. This photograph appears in Marion Harland's biography, *Hannah More* (1900), facing page 202

Something of More's grace and fortitude during this time, and just after, is evident in a letter she wrote to William Jay, the famous dissenting minister from Bath. It was the last letter Jay ever received from her. To him, it was a missive that "pleasingly display[ed] traits of her more private character," and afforded "proof of her kind and constant friendship."[26]

Writing from Clifton, on a fine Saturday in 1829, More had stated—

My dear Sir,—

I know not how to express the gratitude I feel for the very excellent works you have had the goodness to bestow upon me. To feel deeply their inestimable value, and to offer my fervent prayers to the Almighty Giver of every good gift, are all I can do.

---

26   G. Redford & J.A. James, eds., *The Autobiography of William Jay,* 3rd edition, (London: 1855), 342.

May He enlighten and strengthen me more and more by the constant perusal.

Your last bounty, the new edition of your Prayers, *with the valuable additions, is a great additional treasure. We fell upon it with a keen appetite this morning, and I hope I shall be the better for it as long as I live.*[27]

Then came a felicitous scene, set at the start with More's mention of a name that was decidedly Tolkienesque. In telling Jay about her devotional reading, she referred to—

My truly pious friend Mr. Elven, who is my chief spiritual visitor, said, when I showed him your volumes, "Mr. Jay has more ideas than any man I ever knew."

I could not prevail on myself to keep this remark from you.

I thought my hard necessity to leave Barley Wood was a great trial; but it has pleased my gracious God to overrule it to my great comfort and benefit.

I was there almost destitute of all spiritual advantages.

Here I find four ministers of great piety, who are much attached to me, and who supply my want of public attendance at church...

I hope you will have the goodness to remember me at the Throne of Grace; no one stands more in need of your prayers than, my dear Sir,

> *Your very faithful*
> *And highly obliged*
> *Friend and Servant,*
> *Hannah More*[28]

---

27 Redford & James, *William Jay*, 342.
28 Redford & James, *William Jay*, 342-343. Italics added.

In tandem with the 1829 letter More wrote to William Jay, another of her younger friends, J.C. Colquhoun, penned a series of recollections describing things he saw during More's final years at Windsor Terrace. These memories have an elegiac, bittersweet quality, set with quotes from More herself that are often moving. Colquhoun published them in November 1864, in the pages of *The Christian Observer*.

"She enters a new home," he began—

a home of peace; for friends gather round her, and admirers flock to her; so many, that, with the weight of eighty-three years on her, she is forced to set bounds to the stream; she reserves for herself two days [to receive visitors] in the week entire.[29]

Next Colquhoun spoke of the remaining friend who was cherished most in the latter years of More's life. Here, his words were as much a tribute to that friendship as they were to More herself, and Colquhoun's great regard for her.

This passage began with an affirmation of More's abiding trust in God—

One Friend she has long proved, and He does not fail her now. He has been by her [sick] bed, and her path, and has guided all her steps.

Now, as strength declines, she turns to Him and is at peace.

Thankfully she recounts her blessings; not the least among them are her friends, and of these the oldest, her tried friend, Mr. Wilberforce.

---

29 Colquhoun, "Wilberforce and His Contemporaries," 844.

"My guide," she says in 1828, "philosopher, and friend."

To him she addresses in that autumn one of her last letters, recounting to him her blessings, her residence, her quiet, worldly cares contracted, wants all supplied, young eyes to see for her, young voices to read to her, young heads to care for her, and young hands to minister to her wants. It delights her with "immense joy" to think that she will see him once more, and she pours forth for his preservation her loving prayers.

A year later, we find her in the excitement of the Oxford election, working with her wonted energy for the return of [Sir Robert Inglis,] "the champion of Protestantism:" no girl more eager, no girl more triumphant in success.

In 1831, she again saw Mr. Wilberforce; she walked in her room, leaning on his arm, and talked with delight, light and playful as ever, of present interests and future hopes.

Once more they met, in 1832; but then the veil was over the sky, and the mind was under a cloud. At the sound of the well-known voice, she rallied. But the memory began to fail, and the mind could not always answer the helm.[30]

In the days of her declining health, More struggled at times with mental clarity. Friends, like Colquhoun, found it difficult to see her this way; yet he saw the humility and courage that graced her struggle. He described it by saying—

Yet the eye was bright, and the heart glowed with love.

Asked if anything could be done for her—

---

30 Colquhoun, "Wilberforce and His Contemporaries," 844.

"Nothing," she said, "but love me, and forgive me when I am impatient."

At times, she felt painfully the confusion of her mind.

She could not now entertain her friends, nor could she help the sufferer [as she had done, when news reached her of those in need].

Faire des heureux, [make people happy,] had been her motto, and she could not bear to forsake the pleasant labour. At times she wept—"but if I shed tears, they are tears of gratitude, and from a sense of unworthiness."

[Still, there were bright moments and good days.]

At times [her] mind revived; she led her friends to the windows of her room, and gazed with rapture on the landscape, holding them by the hand, hardly suffering them to go, and asking them soon to return. In these moments her thoughts were expressed in words as bright as in her day of power: "You behold," she said, "a dying creature.

Pray for me; I cannot describe the comfort and support I find from these words, 'I know that my Redeemer liveth,'—not I believe, or I hope; but I know. What confidence!

I live in the Psalms. 'The heavens declare the glory of God;' how I love that Psalm!

I have lived a long life, I might have lived a more useful one; but I have a gracious Saviour, and His peace is in my heart. I feel His presence with me."[31]

Witness to More's final days, Colquhoun captured their pathos and hope—

---

31 Colquhoun, "Wilberforce and His Contemporaries," 844-845. Italics added.

Her memory became very uncertain, but she was still able to take an interest in a letter which told her that Princess Victoria, the heir to the throne, had recently received a gift of her works, and that her mother...was deeply impressed with their value.

At the close of 1832, her mental and physical powers declined dramatically. She refused food and became touchingly aware of her mental confusion, although her religious sentiments remained firm. She died on the 7th September 1833, in her 89th year, calling with her last breath for her beloved sister: "Patty,—Joy!"

She was buried beside her sisters in the churchyard at Wrington.

As the cortège left the city of Bristol, all the church bells were ringing to mark her departure to her last resting place.[32]

We may close with a phrase that, in its way, evoked More's love of Barley Wood in days gone by. But beyond this, it looked with greater meaning, and in metaphor, to the rest she'd gone to. In a letter written to Lord Orford, long years before, she recalled words from Edmund Burke. They spoke to her, with meaning and beauty.

She scribed them with her pen, upon the page, as words she'd taken to heart.

In a very real way, they'd become her words too, looking to the far country of God's making, and the peace upon its hills that always remains. So she wrote of

"the soft quiet green, on which the soul loves to rest!"[33]

---

32 Crossley Evans, *Hannah More*, 23.

33 Peter Cunningham, ed., *The Letters of Horace Walpole*, volume 9 (London: 1861), 115n.

These words were a kindred echo of a line she had written,

"I am going to a place of rest."[34]

---

34 *The Works of Hannah More, in Eight Volumes,* volume four (London: 1801), 323; a quote from More's tract, "Tis All for the Best."

The Mural and the School

Then again, a few years later, when the perspective of time has lengthened, all stands in a different setting. There is a new proportion...

History, with its flickering lamp, stumbles along the trail of the past, trying to reconstruct its scenes, to revive its echoes, and kindle with pale gleams the passion of former days.[1]

— **SIR WINSTON CHURCHILL** (1940)

Hannah More was the most influential woman living in England in the Romantic era. Through her writings, political actions, and personal relationships, she promoted a successful program for social change from within the existing social and political order.[2]

— **ANNE MELLOR** (2000)

---

1   Andrew Roberts, *Churchill: Walking with Destiny* (New York: 2018), 617.
2   Anne Mellor, *Mothers of the Nation* (Bloomington: 2000), 13-14.

Hope is one of the Theological virtues. This means that a continual looking forward to the eternal world is not (as some modern people think) a form of escapism or wishful thinking, but one of the things a Christian is meant to do.

It does not mean that we are to leave the present world as it is…the English Evangelicals who abolished the Slave Trade… left their mark on Earth, precisely because their minds were occupied with Heaven…[3]

— **C.S. LEWIS** (1952)

In 1952, the year M.G. Jones published her now classic study, *Hannah More*, another book, C.S. Lewis' *Mere Christianity*, appeared in print. Both books, though it might not have been apparent to many at first, shared a common point of interest in Hannah More.

For in the epigraph above, Lewis paid tribute to More, and her fellow philanthropists, for their abolitionist endeavours. Their inspiration, as Evangelicals, for the making of a better world flowed from faith—or, as Lewis phrased it, "because their minds were occupied with Heaven." How discerning Lewis was in saying this found a precise point of confirmation in a passage from More's text, *Christian Morals*.

There, she'd written enigmatically of those "who might have made the world a better thing than they found it, employ[ing] their…powers of intellect in studying how they might please God, by promoting the best interests of His creatures."[4]

So More had for many years striven to invest her gifts and talents this way. Indeed, her life bore testament to this: through education, the written word, and philanthropy.

---

3   C.S. Lewis, *Mere Christianity* (New York: 2001), 134.
4   More, *Christian Morals*, vol. 2, sixth edition, 223-224.

She did her part to help end the slave trade, and much else besides. For that, she has a living claim on our memory. It endures, even as our knowledge of her time grows.

So we do well to remember her; but not as a perfect soul, for no one ever is.

Yet she was a great one.

* * *

In October 1840, as autumn tints coloured trees in Somerset, a ceremony took place honouring what Hannah More achieved. It was led by the Bishop of Gloucester and Bristol, James Henry Monk, of Trinity College, Cambridge, former Regius Professor of Greek, and a current member of the House of Lords. With him were a set of dignitaries and local leaders gathered to celebrate "the Hannah More Schools." They were a symbol of her legacy, and one of the telling things that would live on after her passing.

On the platform were assembled "his Lordship, the Bishop of Gloucester and Bristol; J.S. Harford, Esq., A.G.H. Battersby, Esq., the Rev. T.F. Jennings…minister of the parish; a large body of the clergy; the gentlemen of the building committee, and others. In the centre of the room was a numerous company of ladies and gentlemen."[5]

A contemporary account continues the story—

On [Oct. 7th,] the infant-school in St. Philip's which completes the [undertaking] known as the Hannah More Schools, was opened under the auspices of the Right Rev. the Lord Bishop of Gloucester and Bristol.

---

5   *The Christian Guardian and Church of England Magazine,* November 1840 (London: 1840), 438.

The Institution...now consists of two large schools—one a boys' and girls' daily school; and the other the infant-school above mentioned, and a neat cottage for the persons who have the charge of the buildings.

The boys' and girls' school at present receives as many as 500 pupils, and the infant-school can accommodate full as large a number. The school-room is a really elegant building in the Gothic style, seventy feet in length and twenty-two in breadth...[6]

Then, stepping to the dais, after "appropriate prayers" had been offered, His Lordship told those assembled, with a knowing smile and dash of diplomatic aplomb—

I am just told it is expected I should express my sentiments...I had not anticipated that it would be necessary; and what I have to say is therefore... unpremeditated.

We are met for the purpose of opening the last portion of the monument erected to the memory of Hannah More, a name which will ever be honoured as long as English literature shall endure...

[Hers is] the name of one who, (if she had not acquired honour and celebrity by her writings), has by her liberality, her example, by the whole tenour of a long life, [won] for herself a fame which far transcends, in my opinion, the highest literary reputation.

She devoted her talents, her extraordinary talents...to the important task of improving the state of society during the [era] in which she lived.

---

6   *The Christian Guardian*, 438.

Not merely did she devote herself to the instruction of the wealthy and…those of her own station, but she applied her talents and her energies to that neglected portion of the community, the children of the poor.[7]

Here, His Lordship paused a moment, as he recalled the momentous times of More's life, how things had been, and how they had changed. He'd seen much of it all.

"When she began her labours," he said—

the practice of educating the poor was not so general as it is now. There was not then, as now, day, Sunday, and national schools in almost every parish. We all trust they may become even more universal and common; and they are in a great degree to be attributed to the enlightened, the liberal, the zealous exertions of Hannah More.

If, then, we had deliberated as to what monument should be erected to that illustrious lady, could imagination conceive one more appropriate than the [creation] of schools in a poor part of this populous city?…

Not only will the schools be beneficial to the city and neighbourhood, but the Committee, by associating them with the name of Hannah More, have done far more than they could have done under other circumstances. We can indeed build schools and endow churches in other parishes, but is not a permanent and enduring good obtained in the name in which these schools are founded?[8]

Next, His Lordship offered closing words, in a personal vein, vividly explaining the nature of his own debt to More—

7   *The Christian Guardian,* 438.
8   *The Christian Guardian,* 438.

I never had the honour of seeing that illustrious lady, but I speak as having children of my own, and as one acquainted with her works even from my nursery, and I declare no author ever possessed more power over the human mind, a power she always exercised in the cause of virtue and religion…

Posterity will declare also that, as respects classical excellence, she out rivalled all contemporary female genius.[9]

One hundred and fifty-nine years after James Henry Monk paid tribute to More's life and legacy, historian M.J. Crossley Evans provided a capstone that His Lordship would have heartily seconded. It was a tribute affirming More's legacy.

Writing of her benefactions in the city of Bristol, Evans stated—

[Hannah More's] interest in Christian education, and in the building of Holy Trinity Church in St. Philip & St. Jacob's Outer Parish in Bristol, to serve a particularly poor and destitute part of the city, was recognized at her death by a large subscription among her admirers…used to endow the parish, and to found the Hannah More Schools…

These were [built] in the 1840s and provided elementary education for boys, girls, and infants, drawn from 'the labouring and operative classes.'

Originally the schools had places for almost 700 children…[10]

9   *The Christian Guardian*, 438.
10 Crossley Evans, *Hannah More*, 25.

Last of all, in June 2020, one of the most fitting honours ever accorded Hannah More was bestowed: a mural, unveiled in her memory at The Hannah More School, Bristol.

On this occasion, Deputy Mayor Asher Craig said: "Hannah More was a much-loved and well-respected writer in Bristol who used her talent to champion those less fortunate than herself. As someone responsible for communities and equalities in our city, it's a privilege to have unveiled this mural today, which I hope will inspire many children and adults to give what they can to making society a better place for everyone."[11]

Hannah More would have treasured those words, with a grateful "Amen."

---

11 from the Monday June 29, 2020 article by Kofo Ajala, for *Bristol 24/7,* "New Mural Celebrates Hannah More on 275th Anniversary of Her Birth," archived at: https://www.bristol247.com/culture/art/hannah-more-mural/

Acknowledgements

This book journey began with an inquiry from my Editor, Rosanna Burton, as to my interest in writing a new narrative biography of Hannah More.

It was a timely and welcome thought—for which I'm deeply grateful.

To one and all at Christian Focus Publications, my sincere thanks for your belief in this biography, with all the care and book-craft invested in it.

My thanks also to Dr. Karen Swallow Prior for her words of encouragement at the outset of this undertaking, and the gift of kind correspondence. That makes all the difference when many days of research and reflection have yet to be completed.

Last of all, I am grateful for the templates of narrative biography reflected in the works of Barbara Tuchman and David Herbert Donald. Both knew and practiced the difficult art that historians and biographers aspire to: drawing readers into the time of the people they write about, striving to re-create their world. I have learned much from them both.

As for the metaphor of writing with "a painter's hand," that word of guidance came from Hannah More's pen. *Sit eius memoria benedicta.*[1]

---

1   a Latin phrase meaning: "may her memory be blessed."

Author's Note

Here a word, offered respectfully, for a term oft-used in books about Hannah More.

The expression "Clapham Sect," by which some refer to William Wilberforce and his colleagues in philanthropy, including More, is both a misnomer, and misleading. Its use should be discarded, especially by scholars, who seek to deal in terms of precision.

The reasons are several, and straightforward.

Those commonly counted among this group (William Wilberforce, Henry Thornton, John Thornton, Henry Venn, John Venn, Zachary Macaulay, James Stephen, John Shore, Lord Teignmouth, and Charles Grant) were all members of the Church of England, which is, quite obviously, not a sect.

And if one extends this roster, based upon collaboration, to include John Newton (a spiritual advisor for many listed above) and Hannah More—who worked so closely with Wilberforce and Henry Thornton—they too were members of the Church of England.

True, most of this group were evangelical in spiritual affinity; but here also, the wing of evangelical Anglicanism (with its long heritage) is just that, a wing, and not a sect.

By definition, a sect is "a body of persons agreed upon religious doctrines different from those of an established church...from which they have separated."[1]

None of the philanthropists listed above ever fit this description.

It is far better to use the term by which William Wilberforce referred to his colleagues in philanthropy, a *circle,* as in this wistful line from his writings on leaving Clapham for his new home, Kensington Gore, in 1808: "I give up also the living near my friends *in this circle;* yet I trust my connexion with them is so firm that the removal will not weaken it."[2]

Happily, this correction in terms is gaining currency among scholars, for example, in James Davison Hunter's Oxford University Press study, *To Change The World* (2010), which describes the nature of the "Clapham Circle."[3] May this salutary trend continue.

---

1 *The Concise Oxford Dictionary of Current English* (Oxford: 1917), 777.

2 Wilberforce, *Life of William Wilberforce,* volume 3, 387.

3 James Davison Hunter, *To Change The World* (Oxford: 2010), 73: "Wilberforce was not an isolated actor, but was surrounded and supported by a network of friends, associates, and sympathizers. Those closest to him were known as the Clapham Circle."

Christian Focus Publications

Our mission statement —

STAYING FAITHFUL

In dependence upon God we seek to impact the world through literature faithful to His infallible Word, the Bible.

Our aim is to ensure that the Lord Jesus Christ is presented as the only hope to obtain forgiveness of sin, live a useful life and look forward to heaven with Him.

Our books are published in four imprints:

CHRISTIAN FOCUS

Popular works including biographies, commentaries, basic doctrine and Christian living.

CHRISTIAN HERITAGE

Books representing some of the best material from the rich heritage of the church.

MENTOR

Books written at a level suitable for Bible College and seminary students, pastors, and other serious readers. The imprint includes commentaries, doctrinal studies, examination of current issues and church history.

CF4•K

Children's books for quality Bible teaching and for all age groups: Sunday school curriculum, puzzle and activity books; personal and family devotional titles, biographies and inspirational stories – because you are never too young to know Jesus!

Christian Focus Publications Ltd,
Geanies House, Fearn, Ross-shire,
IV20 1TW, Scotland, United Kingdom.
www.christianfocus.com
blog.christianfocus.com